Authentication and Access Control

Practical Cryptography Methods and Tools

Sirapat Boonkrong

Apress®

Authentication and Access Control: Practical Cryptography Methods and Tools

Sirapat Boonkrong
Nakhon Ratchasima, Thailand

ISBN-13 (pbk): 978-1-4842-6569-7   ISBN-13 (electronic): 978-1-4842-6570-3
https://doi.org/10.1007/978-1-4842-6570-3

Managing Director, Apress Media LLC: Welmoed Spahr
Acquisitions Editor: Susan McDermott
Development Editor: Laura Berendson
Coordinating Editor: Rita Fernando

Cover designed by eStudioCalamar

Cover image designed by Freepik (www.freepik.com)

Distributed to the book trade worldwide by Springer Science+Business Media New York, 1 New York Plaza, New York, NY 10004. Phone 1-800-SPRINGER, fax (201) 348-4505, e-mail orders-ny@springer-sbm.com, or visit www.springeronline.com. Apress Media, LLC is a California LLC and the sole member (owner) is Springer Science + Business Media Finance Inc (SSBM Finance Inc). SSBM Finance Inc is a **Delaware** corporation.

For information on translations, please e-mail booktranslations@springernature.com; for reprint, paperback, or audio rights, please e-mail bookpermissions@springernature.com.

Apress titles may be purchased in bulk for academic, corporate, or promotional use. eBook versions and licenses are also available for most titles. For more information, reference our Print and eBook Bulk Sales web page at http://www.apress.com/bulk-sales.

Any source code or other supplementary material referenced by the author in this book is available to readers on GitHub via the book's product page, located at www.apress.com/9781484265697. For more detailed information, please visit http://www.apress.com/source-code.

Printed on acid-free paper

Table of Contents

About the Author

Sirapat Boonkrong has had over fifteen years of experience in the field of information security as a student, a researcher, and now a lecturer.

After spending over ten years getting his education from high school to PhD in the United Kingdom, Sirapat began his career in 2006 as a full-time researcher at the National Electronics and Computer Technology Center, Thailand. He then moved into full-time teaching at King Mongkut's University of Technology North Bangkok, Thailand, and stayed there between 2009 and 2017.

Sirapat is currently a full-time lecturer at the School of Information Technology and DIGITECH at Suranaree University of Technology, Thailand. His main teaching and research interests are in cybersecurity, authentication technologies, and cryptographic protocol design.

About the Technical Reviewer

Kazumasa Oida has been teaching network programming, information security, and network simulation technologies at Fukuoka Institute of Technology for more than 15 years. His research interests include network performance, network traffic analysis, quality of service, cybersecurity, and complex network analysis. His current research is focused on reducing cybercrime using data analysis methods.

Acknowledgments

I am grateful for a lot of support from many people. *Authentication and Access Control: Practical Cryptography Methods and Tools* was originally just an idea and a dream. Without the wonderful support from the Apress team, this book would never become a reality. I am especially indebted to Susan McDermott, Rita Fernando, and Laura Berendson for their hard work and encouragement. I am also thankful for the helpful comments from Kazumasa Oida, the technical reviewer of the book. His comments have definitely made the book better. This book includes a lot of research done by myself and my students. Therefore, it is a good place to thank them here.

Finally, I would like to acknowledge the support from my family. I am the luckiest person in the world to be surrounded by so many loving and supportive people.

Introduction

The advent of the Internet has allowed for many services and applications, most notably in communications between users, servers, and devices. Unfortunately, this has led to many security challenges and problems. Recent examples include password leakage on large social network sites and defacement of websites. It is, therefore, necessary to study mechanisms that help reduce the risks of different types of attacks. One of those mechanisms is access control, which applies the processes of cryptography, authentication, and key establishment. Thus, this book is written with an attempt to provide a comprehensive coverage on the subject of authentication mechanisms. The book is intended for anyone wishing to understand the basic principles of cryptography and why they form an important part of authentication mechanisms. In addition, it provides readers with theories and examples of existing authentication technologies, which the author hopes will be useful and adaptable in practice. However, this book is not a manual for network or system configurations. *Authentication and Access Control: Practical Cryptography Methods and Tools* can be used in many ways. It can be used as a self-study reference. It can also be used as a supplementary textbook for computer network security and information security courses.

Each chapter of the book consists of a detailed explanation of the topic and diagrams to aid the explanation. Materials and contents in this book are gathered from various sources, including classic and recent research papers, other textbooks, as well as the author's own research.

The author hopes that this book will prove useful to readers who wish to learn more about authentication. The book is divided into eight chapters, all of which are written after an extensive review of literature and the author's own research as well as teaching experiences. What readers are expected to find in each chapter are as follows:

Chapter 1, Introduction to Cryptography, covers the basic principles of cryptography, which forms a part of authentication mechanisms. This chapter is included in this book because it is necessary to understand the basic principles of cryptography prior to getting into the details of authentication mechanisms.

Chapter 2, Public Key Infrastructure, introduces a mechanism that is considered the foundation of security for the transactions on the Internet today. It also includes how authentication is carried out prior to creating a secure communication channel.

Chapter 3, Methods and Threats of Authentication, explains three main authentication methods as well as some other existing ones. Threats to authentication mechanisms are also discussed.

Chapter 4, Password-Based Authentication. Passwords are the most popular and most commonly used authentication mechanism. It is, therefore, necessary to understand different types of passwords and theories behind password generation. This chapter also discusses the principles of secure password storing methods.

Chapter 5, Biometric Authentication, includes the discussion of biometric authentication steps together with how the efficiency of biometric-based authentication methods can be measured. This chapter also touches on the problems of biometrics, especially the threshold value. Finally, a method and an example for finding a suitable biometric threshold are illustrated.

Chapter 6, Multi-factor Authentication, explains a mechanism known as multi-factor authentication. One-factor authentication has been applied as the main authentication method for some time. It, however, does not come without any security issues. Multi-factor authentication is when more than one method or one type of authentication credential is used in the authentication process. It is increasingly used in verifying a user's identity to access information systems. This chapter provides an explanation of the principles and examples of multi-factor authentication protocols.

Chapter 7, Authentication and Key Establishment Protocols, explains the relationship between authentication and key establishment protocols. Some of the most widely used authentication protocols, including the ones that apply symmetric cryptography and the ones that apply asymmetric cryptography, are provided here. In addition, classic authentication and key establishment protocols are studied so that the same vulnerabilities will not be repeated in the future. Furthermore, basic guidelines for designing an authentication protocol are also presented in this chapter.

Chapter 8, Current and Future Trends, is the final chapter of this book. The chapter attempts to look into the future to see how the authentication process will evolve and be developed. Two of the upcoming processes are continuous authentication and cancellable authentication. This is where we look into how users are frequently authenticated during a session and how biometric authentication factors can change in the case of being compromised. In addition, current standards and authentication assurance levels are also looked at.

We have used uniform notations throughout the book and have tried to explain everything as simple as possible. We hope that what we have written in this book will be useful to readers in one way or another. We would also like to apologize in advance for any mistakes that may have gone unnoticed. Finally, it is hoped that readers will be able to gain a lot of knowledge on this particular subject matter and will be able to control access to their networks and information!

CHAPTER 1

Introduction to Cryptography

Cybersecurity has become a popular topic of interest. Most recent and widely known examples of security problems include password leakage on popular online social networks and the compromise of personal data from medical and airline sectors. Fortunately, nowadays companies, organizations, and academic institutions have put in a lot of effort to protect their assets from threats and attacks. The intent in this chapter is to provide an overview of cryptography, which is considered the foundation of all security mechanisms.

Cryptography is an academic field that has been thoroughly researched and studied. It usually contains many advanced and complicated mathematical techniques. Fortunately, authentication relies on only a handful of simple and well-known cryptographic constructions.

In this chapter, we begin by providing a definition of the word *security*. We then specifically study the concepts of symmetric cryptography, asymmetric cryptography, cryptographic hash functions, and digital signatures, all of which prove to be useful for building authentication mechanisms. More advanced techniques will be introduced in later chapters.

What Is "Security"?

The Oxford dictionary defines security as "the state of being free from danger or threat." Webster's dictionary defines security as "the quality or state of being free from danger." It is easily seen that no matter which part of the world (Europe or America) we are in, security means exactly the same thing. What if we apply the word, security, to computer networks or information systems?

© Sirapat Boonkrong 2021
S. Boonkrong, *Authentication and Access Control*, https://doi.org/10.1007/978-1-4842-6570-3_1

In terms of computer networks and information systems, we can define security as "the state of being free from attacks," "to be protected from attackers or adversaries," "a situation with no risk or no sense of threat," and "the prevention of risk or threat." On the whole, security in computer network security and information security is to use or apply any mechanisms in order to reduce risk and to avoid attacks from adversaries.

Let us analyze the previous definitions. Looking at the definitions, a question needs to be asked. "Is it really possible to be *free* from attacks or to have *no* risk?" My answer would, of course, be "no." The reason is that new technology emerges every day; hence, new threats and attacks become available every day. This means that even if we have security mechanisms in place to protect our assets from existing threats and attacks, it does not mean that the assets are safe from the new threats. Therefore, a claim to be made here is that "Security is not a goal. It is a process." If security were a goal, it would be a goal that would never be realized due to the reason stated earlier. Security is, therefore, a never-ending process if the aim is to keep up with new threats and attacks.

The CIA Model

The CIA model has nothing to do with the Central Intelligence Agency (CIA) of the US government. Both appear to be related to security, however, but in a different way. When discussing security, the CIA model usually springs to mind. The model is the standard for information security and, of course, cybersecurity of today. The model defines characteristics that cyber environment should have in order to be claimed as secure. Originally, the CIA model consists of three characteristics: confidentiality (the C), integrity (the I), and availability (the A). The CIA model can be seen in Figure 1-1.

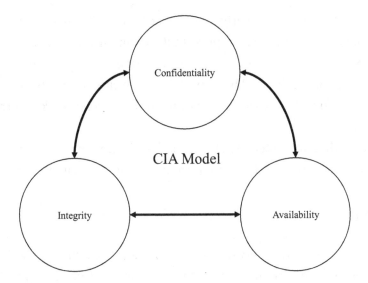

Figure 1-1. *The CIA Model*

Let us define the three characteristics depicted in the CIA model.

Confidentiality

This characteristic means keeping a secret. That is, data that are stored on any devices and data that are being transmitted in any communication channels should not be exposed to anyone, especially those who are not authorized to read them.

It is not difficult to lose confidentiality of data. In a less technical sense, an example would just be leaving a document on your table at work. Anyone, including a janitor, could come to your table and take a peek at it. In a more technical sense, an example of losing confidentiality would be an unauthorized person intercepting your data from a computer network and taking a look at them.

One mechanism that helps reduce the risk of losing confidentiality is *cryptography*.

Integrity

This characteristic means the correctness and completeness of data. That is, data that are received at a destination should be exactly the same as those that are sent from the source. Also, data that are accessed on a system should be exactly the same as when they were last stored. No changes or modifications should be allowed. When there are any changes or modifications, authorized or not, on the data, they should be detected.

There are several ways that integrity of data can be lost. The first is when the content is changed deliberately. A simple example is that a memo from Alice asking Bob to meet her is changed by a messenger from two o'clock to four o'clock. The second way to lose the integrity of data is by accident. This especially is the case for electronic data. For example, data stored on a hard disk or data transmitted on a network is corrupted due to electrical interferences.

Therefore, a method to detect any changes, modification, or even corruption of data is needed. The mechanism used for these purposes is known as a *one-way hash function*.

Availability

This characteristic means the ability to access and use the resources, whether it is computer network, system, application, or data. That is, any time an authorized person would like to have an access to any resources, they should be able to do so. However, if an unauthorized person would like to have an access, they should be denied.

To make the explanation simpler, an analogy is given here. Consider a person wanting to have access to a book at a university library. If they possess a valid library card, the librarian should allow them into the library and borrow the book. This means that the book and its content is only available to an authorized library user.

A mechanism that helps reduce the risk of an attack on availability is *authentication*, which is, of course, the focus of this book.

Principles of Cryptography

To understand the fundamentals of cryptography, it is necessary to be familiar with the following definitions:

- *Plaintext* is the original message or data, which can be read by and is meaningful to authorized people.

- *Ciphertext* is the message or data that has been encoded. It is, therefore, not legible or not meaningful to people.

- *Encryption algorithm* or *cipher* is a process of transforming plaintext to ciphertext.

- *Decryption algorithm* is a process of transforming ciphertext to plaintext.

- *Key* is the most important element in cryptography. It is used to encode (encrypt) and decode (decrypt) messages.

- *Key space* is the number of all the possible keys. For example, if an encryption algorithm uses a key that is 128 bits long, the key space will be of the size 2^{128}.

- *Cryptography* is the making of secret messages.

- *Cryptanalysis* is the breaking of secret messages. Cryptanalysis usually relies on the knowledge of the encryption algorithm and some knowledge of possible structure of the plaintext for the reconstruction of the plaintext from the ciphertext.

- *Cryptology* is the art and science of making and breaking secret codes. This means that cryptology is the combination of cryptography and cryptanalysis.

The main goal of cryptography is, of course, to encode data or messages, hence to achieve confidentiality. In designing and using a cryptographic algorithm, there needs to be some sort of principle to base the design and usage on. This is known as *Kerckhoff's Principle*.

Kerckhoff's Principle states that "a cipher must not be required to be a secret, and it must be able to fall into the hands of the enemy without inconvenience."

The idea of the principle is to have a cryptographic system where the key is the necessary component to recover the plaintext. This means that when designing and using cryptography, one must assume that its process or steps are known. The *only* secret to the cryptosystem is the key. In other words, the principle suggests that no matter what an attacker knows, as long as the key is not known, the plaintext will never be recovered.

It is very important to explain Kerckhoff's Principle early in the chapter, because it is necessary that cryptography users understand this. Many people have misunderstood that when applying cryptography to a security mechanism, it will remain secure because cryptographic algorithm is not known. This thinking is wrong since it is completely against Kerckhoff's Principle. What they should understand instead is that they cannot suggest the algorithm is not known so the mechanism or the system is secure. They have to keep in mind that the algorithm will always be known by the public, and the only thing that keeps their system safe is the secrecy of the key. To put it simply, in cryptography, the only secret is the key.

Before discussing any cryptographic algorithms, it is a good idea to look at the building blocks of these encryption techniques. The two fundamental blocks of all encryption methods are *substitution* and *transposition*. Substitution means replacing the elements of plaintext with the elements of ciphertext. The same substitution can be applied to all elements of the plaintext, or it can vary from element to element. Transposition, also referred to as permutation, means rearranging the order of appearance of the plaintext. Substitution and transposition can be carried out one after another. In more complex algorithms, they may be carried out in multiple rounds.

The substitution and transposition techniques can also be more technically referred to as confusion and diffusion, respectively.

In simple terms, *confusion* is to completely hide the relationship between the plaintext and its corresponding ciphertext. That is, confusion changes the appearance of letters in the plaintext so that the resulting ciphertext does not resemble the original message. On the other hand, *diffusion* spreads or changes positions of letters in the plaintext. Diffusion does not change the actual letters at all. All it does is to swap positions of the plaintext letters only.

The two concepts can be technically explained in more detail. As stated earlier, confusion is simply changing the appearance of letters in the plaintext so that the resulting ciphertext does not resemble the original message, and diffusion is just changing positions of letters in the plaintext. The ideas were correctly defined in the context of classical cryptography. However, in modern cryptography, especially in block ciphers, they are a little bit more sophisticated and can be explained as follows.

The origin of the ideas of confusion and diffusion came from Claude Shannon in 1949 who said

> *Assume that an attacker has some knowledge of statistical characteristics of the plaintext, such as the frequency distribution of the letters. If these statistics are reflected in the ciphertext in some way, it is possible that the attacker will be able to deduce the key or part of the key used for encryption.*

Since then *confusion* has been defined as a concept that will make the relationship between the statistics of the ciphertext and the value of the encryption key as complex as possible. This implies that even if the attacker knows the structure or statistics of the ciphertext and the way the key was used to produce it, it is still too complex to find the key.

Diffusion is a little different from confusion. In *diffusion*, the statistical structure of the plaintext is dissipated into long-range statistics of the ciphertext. This means having each plaintext digit affect the value of many ciphertext digits, or having each ciphertext digit be affected by many plaintext digits. In other words, bits from different positions in the plaintext will contribute to a single bit in the ciphertext, or vice versa. The main aim of diffusion is to make the statistical relationship between the plaintext and ciphertext as complex as possible to prevent the deduction of the key.

We have now gathered the basic principles and ideas of cryptography. Concepts of symmetric cryptography, asymmetric cryptography, cryptographic hash functions, and digital signatures will be explained. All of them actually form a building block for generating authentication protocols as well as ensuring the security of such protocols.

Symmetric Cryptography

Symmetric cryptography is when a sender and a receiver share the same key. That key is used for both encryption and decryption processes. In other words, in symmetric cryptography, one key is used for encryption, and the exact same key is used for decryption. The basic concept of symmetric cryptography is shown in Figure 1-2.

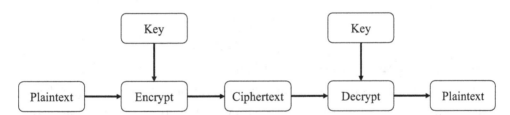

Figure 1-2. *Basic Concept of Symmetric Cryptography*

Figure 1-2 sums up the encryption and decryption processes of symmetric cryptography quite nicely. A plaintext message is fed into an encryption algorithm, which also takes a key as another input. The output of this process is a ciphertext message. To obtain the plaintext, the ciphertext is fed into a decryption algorithm. Provided that the key used to decrypt the message is the same as the one used to encrypt, the output plaintext will be the same as the input plaintext.

When the plaintext P is encrypted with the symmetric key K, it will result in the ciphertext C, which can be expressed as: $C = E(P, K)$ or $C = \{P\}_K$. Similarly, when the ciphertext C is decrypted with the symmetric key K, the plaintext P will be obtained, provided that the key used is the correct key. This can be expressed as: $P = E(C, K)$ or $P = \{C\}_K$.

There are two main categories of symmetric cryptography. They are stream ciphers and block ciphers.

Stream Ciphers

Stream ciphers have a function that stretches a given key into a long stream of bits. This long stream of bits is known as a *keystream*. This keystream is then used as an encryption and decryption key. In the encryption and decryption processes, the keystream is XORed with the plaintext and ciphertext, respectively. Because the encryption process is the XOR operation, stream ciphers apply the concept of confusion only. Examples of stream ciphers are A5/1 for GSM telephones and RC4 for wireless security mechanisms (WEP and WPA1).

As mentioned, the main feature of any stream cipher is the generation of a keystream, which will be used for encryption and decryption. Let us convert this description into mathematical formulae to make it simpler to understand. The core function of stream ciphers is the one generating a new keystream.

$$StreamCipher(K) = S,$$

where K is the key and S is the new keystream.

Once the keystream has been generated, an encryption process can begin. The encryption is done be XORing ($\oplus$) the keystream with a plaintext message, bit by bit. A ciphertext message is produced as a result. The process is summarized as follows:

$C = P \oplus S$ which can be expanded as

$$C_0 = P_0 \oplus S_0, C_1 = P_1 \oplus S_1, C_2 = P_2 \oplus S_2, \ldots,$$

where $C = C_0 C_1 C_2 \ldots$ is the ciphertext,
$P = P_0 P_1 P_2 \ldots$ is the plaintext, and
$S = S_0 S_2 S_2 \ldots$ is the keystream.

To decrypt the ciphertext correctly, the same keystream must be used. That means the decrypting entity must hold the same key, K, and the same *StreamCipher()* function, so that the same keystream, S, can be generated. The decryption process is just carrying out the XOR ($\oplus$) operation between the ciphertext and the keystream, as follows:

$P = C \oplus S$ which can be expanded as

$$P_0 = C_0 \oplus S_0, P_1 = C_1 \oplus S_1, P_2 = C_2 \oplus S_2, \ldots,$$

where $P = P_0P_1P_2\ldots$ is the plaintext
$C = C_0C_1C_2\ldots$ is the ciphertext, and
$S = S_0S_2S_2\ldots$ is the keystream.

Stream ciphers will not be discussed in much detail, due to the fact that for a few years now, no new stream ciphers have been invented. Nowadays, block ciphers are more widely used and are said to provide higher level of security.

Block Ciphers

A *block cipher* divides a plaintext message into fixed size blocks of n bits and generates fixed size blocks of ciphertext of n bits. The ciphertext is produced by having blocks of plaintext iterated in rounds of specified functions. The inputs of each round are the output of the previous round and the key. These functions in each round are known as the *round functions*.

At this point, there are a few things that need to be explained which concern with the thinking behind block ciphers. Firstly, since the size of a plaintext block is n bits, the number of different plaintext blocks is, therefore, 2^n. The important idea is that when the plaintext is transformed into ciphertext, their relationship must appear random so that cryptanalysis is difficult to carry out. Another essential idea of block ciphers is that each plaintext block must produce exactly one ciphertext block. The transformation is known as *reversible* or *nonsingular*.

Let us consider this for a moment. Suppose a 4-bit plaintext block is used, there can be $2^4 = 16$ different patterns of plaintext and ciphertext. It can be seen that if the size of the block is small, it will not be different from a classical substitution. However, if we make n large, it will not be practical from an implementation and performance point of view.

Horst Feistel in 1973 took this problem into consideration and proposed that a method that alternates substitutions and permutations should be used in the construction of block ciphers. Many cryptographers have taken the idea and designed many modern block ciphers since. The Advanced Encryption Standard or AES is one of many that has adopted such idea.

AES

Advanced Encryption Standard, or AES, was invented in the 1990s to be used in place of the older and insecure Data Encryption Standard (DES). It is based on Rijndael algorithm. It was later published as a standard in 2001. AES has become one of the more secure, more popular, and widely used symmetric encryption algorithms today. The algorithm has been applied in various security protocols such as IPSec, SSH, and WPA2. AES comes in three variants based on different key sizes – 128, 192, and 256 bits. Hence, they are called AES-128, AES-192, and AES-256, respectively.

The structure of the AES algorithm is quite simple. The inputs into the algorithm consist of a 128-bit (or 16-byte) block of plaintext and an encryption (or decryption) key of any of the three sizes stated in the standard. It then produces an output of ciphertext which is also 128 bits in size. The construction works as follows: First, the plaintext input is first transformed by being XORed with the encryption key. The resultant value is then processed by the round functions, where each round incorporates a round key K_i into its computation. Each K_i is generated by the key expansion function, which takes the original key K_0 as its input. The number of rounds N_r to be processed by AES depends on the size of the key used in the algorithm. That is, ten rounds are required for a 128-bit key, 12 rounds are required for a 192-bit key, and 14 rounds are required for a 256-bit key. Finally, a 128-bit ciphertext is produced as a result. The schematic of the AES structure is illustrated in Figure 1-3.

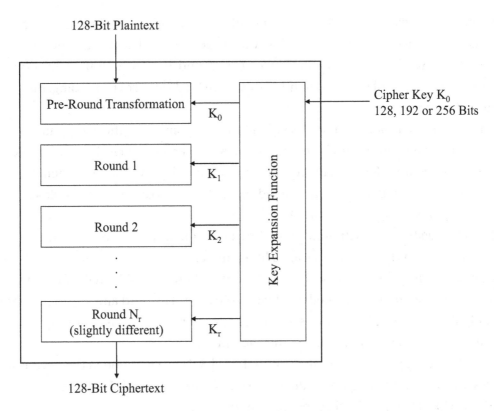

Figure 1-3. *Schematic of AES Structure*

Each round of the AES algorithm is comprised of four subprocesses or round functions known as the SubBytes() function, the ShiftRows() function, the MixColumns() function, and the AddRoundKey() function.

In the SubBytes() function, each of the 16 bytes in the block is substituted by looking up the fixed substitution table (S-Box) provided by the AES standard. This process results in the changes in all the values in the block.

The ShiftRows() function shifts rows of the state to the left by different offsets. That is, there is no shift in the first row. The second row is circularly shifted one byte to the left. The third and fourth rows are circularly shifted two and three bytes to the left, respectively.

The MixColumns() function mixes the data or changes the values of the data within each column of the data block. The four bytes in each column are calculated using simple matrix multiplication, whose formulae are predefined in the AES standard. It should be noted that this function is not performed in the final round.

In the AddRoundKey() function, XOR operations are carried out. This function XORs the values in a data block with the round key K_i of each round. That is, each byte in the block is XORed with the corresponding byte of the round key. The output of this function is then fed as an input of the next round. If this is the final round of processing, the output is the ciphertext.

The decryption process of the AES algorithm is very similar to the encryption process, but done in reverse. In other words, the AES decryption algorithm still works in the same structure. However, the round functions are slightly different, albeit the number of subprocesses is the same, including the InvSubBytes(), InvShiftRows(), AddRoundKey(), and InvMixColumns() functions.

The AddRoundKey() function works in the exact same way as the one in the encryption method. The other three are a little different.

InvShiftRows() does circular right shift. That is, there is no shift in the first row. The second row is circularly shifted one byte to the right. The third and fourth rows are circularly shifted two and three bytes to the right, respectively. This is obviously the reverse of the ShiftRows() function in the encryption process.

InvSubBytes() works in a similar way to the SubBytes() function in the encryption process. However, for decryption, a different substitution table or S-Box is used. This table is also fixed and provided by the AES standard.

The other round function used in the AES decryption process is the InvMixColumns() function. The InvMixColumns() process is also just the multiplication of matrices, albeit with different numbers from the MixColumns() process. The formulae used by the InvMixColumns() function are predefined by the AES standard.

Modes of Operation

As explained earlier, it seems straightforward to carry out encryption and decryption processes using block cipher, as long as our input fits into one block, 128 bits or 16 bytes in the case of AES algorithm. The problem is that most inputs in real life are longer than one block. Therefore, a method is needed to help us deal with this difficulty. This is where *modes of operation* come in. One of the main jobs of modes of operation is to help encrypt and decrypt anything that is larger than one block. There are many existing modes of operation that can be used, but in this book, only *cipher block chaining* or *CBC* mode is introduced, because it is the foundation of many variants of modes of operation that are used today.

The cipher block chaining or CBC mode of operation divides a message into blocks of the size required by the block cipher. For example, for AES encryption, the size of each block is 128 bits. A random IV (initialization vector) is generated and used to XOR with the first message block. The result is then encrypted with a key using a block cipher to obtain a ciphertext block. This ciphertext block is then used to XOR with the second message block. The result is then encrypted with the same key to produce the second ciphertext block. This ciphertext block is then used to XOR with the third message block, and the same process continues until the final message block. At the end, all the ciphertext blocks are concatenated to obtain the final ciphertext.

The encryption in the CBC mode operation can be summarized in mathematical form here:

$$c_i = E\left(m_i \oplus c_{i-1}, K\right); for\ i = 2, 3, 4, \ldots$$

But *for i* = 1

$$c_i = E\left(IV \oplus m_1, K\right)$$

where $E(m, K)$ is the block cipher encryption with key K on message m and $\oplus$ is the XOR operation.

Once the message has been encrypted, it is ready to be sent. However, sending the ciphertext alone is not adequate since the recipient would not be able to decrypt it. The reason for this is that the recipient would also need to know what the initialization vector or IV is. This means that when sending the ciphertext, it is necessary to attach the IV with the ciphertext.

When the ciphertext, together with the IV, is received, the decryption process can be carried out. The decryption process in the CBC mode is a reverse operation of the encryption. In other words, the final ciphertext block is the first to be decrypted. The result of this decryption is then XORed with the previous ciphertext block to obtain the corresponding plaintext block. The next ciphertext block (from the last) is decrypted next. The result is XORed with the previous ciphertext block to obtain the corresponding plaintext block. The process continues to the very first ciphertext block, which is decrypted and XORed with the IV to get the first plaintext block. At the end, all the plaintext blocks are concatenated to obtain the original message. Note that only if the key used for decryption is the same as that used for encryption will the correct message be obtained.

The decryption in the CBC mode operation can be summarized in mathematical form as follows:

$$m_i = D(c_i, K) \oplus c_{i-1}; \text{ for } i = 2, 3, 4, \ldots$$

But *for i* = 1

$$m_1 = D(c_1, K) \oplus IV$$

where $D(c, K)$ is the block cipher decryption with key K on ciphertext c and $\oplus$ is the XOR operation.

This section has introduced the concept of symmetric cryptography in that in order to carry out the encryption and decryption processes, the same secret key must be used. It is also pointed out that the basic principles of confusion and diffusion are applied in the modern symmetric cryptography methods to ensure that it is complex and strong. To encrypt and decrypt messages that are bigger than a block, a mode of operation is required. CBC mode of operation has been explained here.

Asymmetric Cryptography

Asymmetric cryptography is another type of cryptography. It is sometimes known as *two-key cryptography*, *non-secret cryptography* or, more commonly, *public key cryptography*. In asymmetric cryptography, one key is used for encryption, and a different key is used for decryption. The security of asymmetric cryptography is based on a special mathematical structure known as a *trap door one-way function*. This is a function that is easy to compute in one direction, but very difficult to compute in the other direction. Using a trap door one-way function as a property of asymmetric cryptography implies that an attacker will not be able to use any public information to recover the secret.

In public key cryptography, every user holds two keys: a *public key* and a *private key*. As the names suggest, public keys are available to public and anyone can have access to them, but private keys are to be kept secret by the owner and can be known only by the owner.

Suppose that Bob possesses a public key and a private key. Anyone who wants to send a message to Bob will encrypt the message with Bob's public key. However, only Bob can decrypt the message with his private key. Apart from encryption and decryption, public key cryptography also allows Bob to *digitally sign* messages using a private key, and other users can verify Bob's signature by using Bob's public key. Digital signatures will be explained later on in the chapter.

In any asymmetric cryptography, each user possesses two keys. One is for encryption, called a public key. The other key, which is different but related, is used for decryption, called a private key. They have one very important characteristic in that even though an attacker knows the public key and the encryption algorithm, it is still computationally infeasible to determine the private key. In other words, an attacker must not be able to compute the private key even if they know the public key and/or the encryption/decryption algorithm.

In public key cryptography, when sending a message to a user, we encrypt the message with that receiver's public key. When the user receives the encrypted message, they decrypt it with their own private key. The overview of public key cryptography is shown in Figure 1-4.

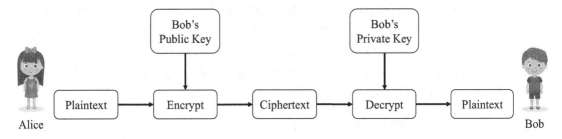

Figure 1-4. *Basic Concept of Asymmetric Cryptography*

From Figure 1-4, when Alice sends a message to Bob, she encrypts it with Bob's public key. When Bob receives the ciphertext, he decrypts it with his private key. Let us take a look at the four general steps of asymmetric cryptography:

1. Each user generates a pair of keys to be used for the encryption and decryption of messages.

2. Each user places one of the two keys in public. This is the public key. The other key is kept private. This is the private key.

3. If Alice wishes to send a confidential message to Bob, Alice encrypts the message using Bob's public key.

4. When Bob receives the message, he decrypts it using his own private key.

When the plaintext P is encrypted with the public key $+K_i$ of user i, it will result in the ciphertext C, which can be expressed as: $C = \{P\}_{+K_i}$. Similarly, when the ciphertext C is decrypted with the private key $-K_i$ of user i, the plaintext P will be obtained, provided that the key used is the correct key. This can be expressed as: $P = \{C\}_{-K_i}$.

We now should have a grasp of the concept of asymmetric cryptography in general. Popular algorithms include RSA, ElGamal, and Elliptic Curve Cryptography or ECC. However, we will only take a look at the most commonly used one in RSA.

RSA

RSA is a public key cryptosystem invented by three gurus in the field of security: Rivest, Shamir, and Adleman. RSA is one of the most popular public key cryptosystems today, because it is used in many Internet-driven transactions. This, therefore, is the reason why we need to understand how this algorithm works.

RSA follows the four general steps of public key cryptography, namely, key generation, key distribution, encryption, and decryption. We begin with the RSA key generation process, which can be explained as follows:

1. Choose two large prime numbers p and q.

2. Compute the product $N = pq$.

3. Choose e relatively prime to $(p - 1)(q - 1)$.

4. Find the multiplicative inverse of $e \bmod (p - 1)(q - 1)$, and denote it as d, where $d = e^{-1} \bmod (p - 1)(q - 1)$.

At the end of Step 4, we should have all the necessary components in $N = pq$, e and d, to construct the RSA keys. N is known as the *modulus*. e is known as the *encryption exponent*. d is known as the *decryption exponent*. The RSA keys consist of one public key in (N, e) and one private key in d.

RSA encryption is accomplished by the following equation:

$$C = M^e \bmod N$$

where C is the ciphertext,

M is the message,

e is the encryption exponent, and

N is the modulus.

That is, the message M is raised to the power of e. It is, then, divided by N. The remainder is the ciphertext, C.

RSA decryption is as easy as the encryption process. It is accomplished by the following equation:

$$M = C^d \bmod N$$

where M is the message,

C is the ciphertext,

d is the decryption exponent, and

N is the modulus.

That is, the ciphertext C is raised to the power of d. It is, then, divided by N. The remainder is the message, M.

We have now seen how the RSA key generation, RSA encryption, and RSA decryption work. For the RSA algorithm to function properly and securely, there are a few requirements that need to be achieved. They can be explained as follows:

1. It should be computationally easy for any entity to generate a public and private key pair.

2. It should be computationally easy for any sender, knowing the public key and the message, to generate the corresponding ciphertext.

3. It should be computationally easy for the receiver of the ciphertext to decrypt it using their private key to recover the plaintext.

4. It should be computationally infeasible for any adversary, knowing the public key, to determine the corresponding private key.

5. It should be computationally infeasible for any adversary, knowing the public key and the ciphertext, to recover the corresponding plaintext.

From the stated requirements, there are two operative words that need explanation. The first is "computationally easy," and the second is "computationally infeasible." The two terms are very important in the context of security and can be defined as follows.

A *computationally easy* problem is defined as a problem that can be solved in polynomial time with respect to the input length. In other words, if the length of the input is n bits, then the time to compute the function or to solve the problem does not exceed n^a, where a is a fixed constant.

On the other hand, a *computationally hard* problem is defined as a problem whose effort to solve grows faster than polynomial time with respect to the input size. In other words, if the length of the input is n bits, the time to compute the function or to solve the problem is proportional to 2^n.

This implies that it must be simple and fast for any entity to generate the RSA keys and to compute the encryption and decryption processes, provided that the required components are available. However, it must be very difficult or impossible for any entity to determine the private key and to find the plaintext without the necessary private key.

This section has introduced the concept of asymmetric cryptography in that a public key of the recipient is used to encrypt a message and their private key is needed for the decryption process. Because both symmetric and asymmetric cryptography have been explained, let's try to get them to work together.

Hybrid Cryptosystem

The primary advantage of symmetric cryptography over public key cryptography is the efficiency. On the other hand, the primary advantage of public key cryptography over symmetric cryptography is in the key distribution process. This is due to the fact that no shared secret key is required in asymmetric cryptography.

You may wonder what this "no shared secret key is required" means. In public key cryptosystems, of course, keys have to be shared, but those are public keys. They do not need to be secret. Therefore, it is easier and more convenient to distribute public keys in asymmetric cryptography. In symmetric cryptography, however, keys have to be kept secret between two entities. This makes secret key distribution a problem.

It seems that both types of cryptography have an advantage over one another. The question is that how do we get the best out of both worlds? The answer to that is *hybrid cryptosystem*. In a hybrid cryptosystem, public key cryptography is used to encrypt a symmetric key. That means this shared secret can be securely distributed between two entities, that is, symmetric key distribution will become more secure. Symmetric cryptography is then used for encryption and decryption during the actual message transmissions. An overview of a hybrid cryptosystem is as follows:

$$Alice \rightarrow Bob : \{K\}_{+K_{Bob}}$$

$$Bob \rightarrow Alice : \{M_1\}_K$$

$$Alice \rightarrow Bob : \{M_2\}_K$$

This message transmission illustrates that Alice sends a secret symmetric key, K, to Bob by encrypting it with Bob's public key. This method would make K secure. Bob then decrypts the ciphertext with his private key to obtain K. Bob and Alice can now start using K with symmetric cryptography to encrypt and decrypt subsequent messages, M_i.

It can be seen that asymmetric cryptography is used to assist in distributing the symmetric key only. Once both entities have obtained the key, symmetric cryptography is used to encrypt messages. The reason for this is because when transmitting messages, symmetric cryptography is faster and more efficient.

Distributing the secret symmetric key this way is safe, because Bob is the only one who can carry out the decryption. Once the symmetric key is obtained, all subsequent messages are encrypted and decrypted with this key.

Cryptographic Hash Functions

Cryptographic hash functions or hash functions produce what we call *cryptographic check values* or *hash values*. A hash value or a *hash* can be thought of as a fingerprint of a message. A hash is computed by inputting a message or data into a hash function, and the output is a smaller block of data that represents the original message. Usually it is very difficult to find two or more messages with the same hash. This is why a hash is a kind of a fingerprint of the data. Just to reemphasize, one purpose of a hash value is for detecting data modifications.

There are two categories of cryptographic hash functions: *modification detection code (MDC)*, which is a "cryptographic fingerprint" of a message, and *message authentication code (MAC)*, which includes a secret key in the computation and, therefore, enables a verification of authenticity of a message and even the intention of message modifications.

Before going any further, it is very important to understand unique properties of cryptographic hash functions. They do have specific properties of their own as follows:

1. Compression – A hash function always reduces the size of the original data. Given a large input, a hash value is always smaller than the original message. That is, for any size of input x, the output length of $y = H(x)$ is small, where $H()$ is a hash function. For example, if x is of the size 256 bytes, a hash function $H()$ will reduce the length of the message to, say, 128 bits only. In truth, it does not matter what the input size is, the output length of the hash function is always the same, provided that the same hash function is used. Even if the size of the input is zero, the output will be the same as that of other input sizes.

2. Efficiency – It is stated that it must be easy to compute $H(x)$ for any input x. That means the computational cost must not be expensive to compute any hash values. In modern hash functions, only computationally cheap operations, such as shifts, additions, and logical operations, are used.

3. One Way – A hash function is a one-way function. That means it is easy to compute $y = H(x)$ for any message x. However, it should be very difficult or impossible to find the message x from the hash

value y. It will become obvious later that due to the way hash values are computed and the way the inputs are compressed, it is very difficult to revert the hash values back to their original value.

4. Weak Collision Resistance – This is the first property of collision resistance. This property states that if we know the message x and its hash value $H(x)$, it is not possible to find another message y such that its hash value $H(y)$ is equal to $H(x)$. In other words, in an attacker's point of view, what they know are the hash value $H(x)$ and its original input x. What they want to do is to find another input y whose hash value $H(y)$ is the same as $H(x)$. However, this property of cryptographic hash functions explicitly states that the attacker must not be able to accomplish this.

5. Strong Collision Resistance – This is the second property of collision resistance. This property states that not knowing any messages or hash values in advance, it is not possible to find two different messages x and y such that the hash values of both messages are the same where $H(x)$ is equal to $H(y)$. In the point of view of an attacker, this is different from the previous property. Here, the attacker does not know or have the target hash value. What they have to do is to find two different inputs x and y that will produce the exact same hash values, that is, $H(x) = H(y)$. However, this property of cryptographic hash functions explicitly states that the attacker must not be able to accomplish this.

For the purposes of security, two aspects will be looked at more closely: collision resistance and one-wayness. These properties will be explained in order to gain an understanding of why it is useful and necessary to have a hash function that satisfies them.

The first to be discussed is *collision resistance*. A collision occurs when two distinct inputs produce the same output. Therefore, formally, a hash function $H()$ is collision resistant if it is infeasible to find two values, x and y, such that $x \neq y$, but $H(x) = H(y)$.

We would like to point out that earlier we said that it is "infeasible to find" a collision, but we did not say that no collisions exist. In truth, collisions exist for any hash function. Let us look at it this way. The input space contains all possible strings and numbers of all possible lengths, but the output space contains only strings and numbers of a specified fixed length. This implies that the input space is infinite, while the output space is finite. That means there must be input strings or numbers that map to the same output or hash value. Indeed, the term "infeasible to find" is used in the definition, because although collisions exist, it is still very difficult to find one and it takes a very long time to do so. For example, for a hash function with a 256-bit output, we would have to compute the hash function $2^{256}+1$ times in its worst case, and about 2^{128} times on average before finding a collision with a probability of 0.3.

Why is collision resistance useful? If a hash function is collision resistant, then it allows us to use the hash value to detect any corruptions and changes that occur to a message or a file. In other words, when Bob sends a message M to Alice, he computes the hash value of the message $H(M)$ and attaches it to the message before transmitting it to Alice. When Alice receives the message, she computes the hash of the received message and compares it with the received $H(M)$. If the hashes are the same, she can then conclude that the received message has not been tampered with. The integrity of the message M remains intact.

The second property to be looked at is *one-wayness*. Some may even call this property as information *hiding*. The one-wayness property tells us that if the output or a hash value of the input x or $H(x)$ is known, there is no feasible way to find out what the original input x is.

Why is one-wayness useful? If a hash function is a one-way function, then it allows us to use it to conceal the message. For example, if Bob wants to store a password in a database, he can use a hash function to compute a hash value of the password or $H(password)$ before storing it. This way, although an adversary sees $H(password)$, it will be very difficult or infeasible for them to find the original password from the hash value. In other words, the real value of the password is hidden from the adversary due to the one-wayness property.

On the whole and in the context of cryptography, if $H()$ is a cryptographic hash function that is both collision resistant and one-way, it is claimed that $H()$ has the necessary security properties and is suited to be used in cryptographic protocols.

The properties of cryptographic hash functions have been discussed. Let us take a look at some hash functions that are commonly used today. The first falls into the modification detection code or MDC category. The second is in the message authentication code or MAC category. The hash functions that will be overviewed are called SHA-256 and CBC-MAC, respectively. Other hash functions that are less popular include MD5, SHA-1, and the newly developed SHA-3 algorithms.

SHA-256

SHA-256 is a cryptographic hash function that can take in any arbitrary length of inputs and produces a fixed-length output of 256 bits. Like any other cryptographic hash functions, SHA-256 makes use of a method known as the *Merkle-Damgard transform* which divides the input M into fixed-length blocks M_1, M_2, ..., M_i (512 bits in this case), pads the last block, and appends the actual length of the message to the end of the block.

The cryptographic hash function SHA-256 is then applied on each of the block M_i. That is, the hash function SHA-256 takes as input the result of the application of SHA-256 on the previous block. For the first block, to which there is no previous block output, an initialization vector (IV) is used. Note that the value of the IV is fixed and is already specified in the standard. The output from the last block is the result of the computation of the SHA-256 on the input. The structure of the SHA-256 hash function is illustrated in Figure 1-5.

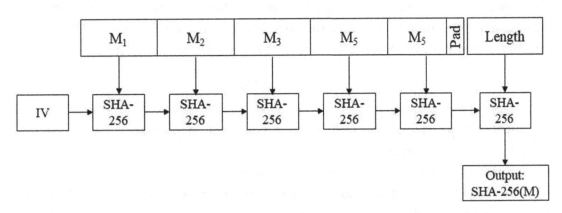

Figure 1-5. *Merkle-Damgard Transform in the SHA-256 Hash Function*

Therefore, as an outline, the operations of the SHA-256 hash function can be expressed as follows:

$$h_1 = H\left(IV, M_1\right)$$

$$h_2 = H\left(h_1, M_2\right)$$

$$h_3 = H\left(h_2, M_3\right)$$

$$h_i = H\left(h_{i-1}, M_i\right)$$

where h_i is the output from the hash function $H()$ on the ith block,

M_i is the ith block of the message M, and

$H()$ is a cryptographic hash function, SHA-256 in this case.

Generally, SHA-256 uses the structure of the Merkle-Damgard transform to take in a 512-bit data block and 256-bit value from the previous block (256-bit IV for the first block) and produces a 256-bit output, which is then fed into the next block. If there are no subsequent blocks, the 256-bit output is the actual resultant hash value of the input, also known as a 256-bit digest.

CBC-MAC

The cipher block chaining MAC or CBC-MAC is a cryptographic hash function in the message authentication code or MAC category. For any hash function in the MAC category, a symmetric key K is required for the computation of a hash value. That is:

$$MAC = H_K\left(M\right)$$

where $H()$ is a cryptographic hash function, CBC-MAC in this case,

M is an arbitrary-length message, and

K is a secret key shared between sender and recipient.

The name CBC will definitely look familiar. This is because it is the name of the mode of operation that was discussed in the block cipher section earlier. The name is used here because a block cipher encryption together with the CBC mode of operation is applied to produce a hash value or a CBC-MAC of a message.

For the sake of simplicity of discussion, we assume that confidentiality is not required, but integrity is. In order to generate a message authentication code or a MAC, the data is encrypted in the cipher block chaining mode of operation. The process is the exact same process as the one described earlier in the Block Ciphers section. For the integrity purposes, only the final ciphertext block is used as the CBC-MAC or a hash. This can be described as follows. Suppose there are i blocks of message.

$$C_1 = E\left(M_1 \oplus \text{IV},\text{K}\right),$$

$$C_2 = E\left(M_2 \oplus C_1,K\right),$$

$$C_i = E\left(M_i \oplus C_{i-1},K\right) = MAC$$

Where C_i is the ciphertext of message block i,

M_i is the block i of the message M,

$\oplus$ is the XOR operation, and

$E(x, K)$ is the block cipher encryption on x using the key K.

Remember that the purpose of having a MAC is so that the receiver of the message can check for the completeness or correctness of the data. Therefore, after the MAC of a message has been calculated, it is attached to the message, together with the IV used in the calculation. That is, the sender sends the IV, the message, and the MAC to the receiver as one packet.

After receiving the packet, the receiver repeats the MAC calculation with the IV and message parts to obtain MAC'. The receiver compares the received MAC and the newly calculated MAC'. If they are the same, the received data is correct, and hence, the integrity is intact. However, if the MAC and MAC' differ, it means that the received data has been corrupted or altered in some way, or the sender does not have the shared key K, which makes it different from the original data. Thus, the data can be discarded.

Note that the detail of the computation of the SHA-256 hash function and CBC-MAC is intentionally omitted since it is only required that the purposes, properties, and structures of the hash functions are understood in order to move forward to the rest of the book.

Digital Signatures

Public key cryptosystems, as already seen, are able to encrypt and decrypt data. When encrypting, a public key is used. When decrypting, a private key is used. In addition, public key cryptosystems have another ability, which is to generate *digital signatures*. This section will explain the concept of digital signatures, how they are generated and verified.

In security, there is a mechanism known as authentication. *Authentication* is a process used to confirm a person's identity. In computer networking and data transmissions, sometimes it is necessary to verify the origin of the data or the identity of the sender. Digital signature is the mechanism to do this.

Two properties are usually desired from digital signatures. First, only you can make or generate your signature, but anyone who sees it can verify that it is valid. Second, it is required that the digital signature is tied to a particular document or message, so that it cannot be used to endorse a different document or message. How can we generate and verify digital signatures?

The first thing to be said about digital signatures is that they are generated by using a private key. In other words, when a person would like to attach their digital signature to a message, they would create the signature by "encrypting" the message with their private key. The idea of using a private key to generate digital signatures makes it similar to handwritten signatures in that it is very difficult to find two persons with the exact same private key. This is how each digital signature is different from one another, which implies the fact that only you can make your signature.

We have mentioned that digital signatures can be generated from the sender's private key together with the message being sent. Therefore, anyone, who has access to the signer's public key, can verify the signature. We can explain the process with a simple example. If Alice wants to send a message with her signature to Bob, she signs it with her private key. When Bob receives the message and Alice's signature, Bob will have to verify the signature with Alice's public key. This satisfies the requirement that anyone who sees the signature can verify it, provided that they know the signer's public key.

For digital signatures, it is possible for an entity to sign it directly "on" a message, but there is a problem with this. The problem with signing directly on the message is that most of the time the size of the message is large, and doing mathematical operations on a large piece of data is not efficient. Therefore, there is a need for another mechanism that can make the signing process become more efficient. This mechanism is known as *hash functions*, which has already been discussed in the earlier section. Let us now take a look at the process of generating and verifying digital signatures.

Suppose Alice wants to send a signed message to Bob. She carries out the following steps:

1. Alice applies a hash function, $H()$, to the message, M, to obtain: $H(M)$, which is the hash value or hashed message of the message, M.

2. Alice signs the hashed message with her private key

    to get: $H(M)_{-K_{Alice}}$.

3. Alice can now send a signed hashed message together with a

    message, which may be or may not be encrypted: $M, H(M)_{-K_{Alice}}$

    or $\{M\}_{+K_{Bob}}, H(M)_{-K_{Alice}}$.

Step 3 is the message and signature sending step. We can see that there are two choices for the sender. The first choice, $M, H(M)_{-K_{Alice}}$, is used when there is no need for message confidentiality. That is, the message, M, is not encrypted. The second choice, $\{M\}_{+K_{Bob}}, H(M)_{-K_{Alice}}$, is used when message confidentiality is necessary. That is, the message, M, is encrypted with the receiver's public key, in this case, Bob's.

Suppose Bob receives $\{M\}_{+K_{Bob}}, H(M)_{-K_{Alice}}$ and would like to verify Alice's signature. He takes the following steps:

1. Bob decrypts $\{M\}_{+K_{Bob}}$ with his private key to obtain M.

2. Bob applies the same hash function (as Alice) to M (from the previous step) to get $H(M)$.

3. Bob "decrypts" $H(M)_{-K_{Alice}}$ using Alice's public key to obtain $H(M)$.

4. Bob compares the hash values from Step 2 and Step 3.

5. If they are equal, the signature verification is a success. However, if they are not, either someone has been trying to impersonate Alice or the message M has been altered in some way. Hence, the signature verification is unsuccessful.

It can be seen in Step 4 that by using as well as comparing the hash values during the signature verification process, we have a mechanism for checking message integrity as a by-product as well. In other words, by applying digital signature to message transmission, not only do we know the origin of the message, we also have a mechanism for checking data integrity, which is a security characteristic that we want.

We have now learned the overviews of digital signature generation and verification. Let us now look at the actual methods, RSA signature generation and RSA signature verification, used to accomplish those two processes.

RSA Digital Signature Generation and Verification

For RSA signature generation, it is as easy as the following steps:

1. Produce a hash value of the message.

2. Raise it to the power of *d mod N*, where *d* is the sender's private key and *N* is the modulus.

3. Attach the result as signature to the message.

The digital signature obtained can be written in mathematical form as follows:

$$S = H(M)^d \ mod \ N$$

where *S* is the digital signature of the message *M*.

For the RSA signature verification process, the following steps are carried out:

1. Produce a hash value of the received message.

2. Raise the signature part of the received message to the power of *e mod N*, where *e* and *N* are the components of the public key of the message sender or the signer.

3. Compare the two hash values. If they are the same, then the verification is a success. If not, then the verification is unsuccessful.

By looking at the following equation, one can see how the signature verifier obtains the hash value in the second step of the preceding process. The second step states that the signature part is raised to power of *e mod N*, which is

$$S^e \ mod \ N = H(M)^d \ mod \ N$$

$$= H(M)^{de} \ mod \ N$$

Let us remind ourselves that from Step 4 of the RSA key generation process, *de mod N* = 1. Therefore, carrying on from the previous and applying the stated formula, we obtain

$$H(M)^{de} \bmod N = H(M)^{1} \bmod N = H(M)$$

Having obtained *H(M)*, the message receiver can then compare this with the hash value obtained from the first step, and the signature verification can be continued. That is, if the two hash values match, the signature verification is said to be successful. However, if they do not match, the signature verification fails and the whole message can be discarded.

Non-repudiation

This section explains why digital signatures are really needed. Both asymmetric and symmetric cryptography can provide confidentiality through encryption processes. However, there is one characteristic that asymmetric cryptography can provide, but symmetric cryptography cannot. This is *non-repudiation*.

Before giving the definition of non-repudiation, there is one thing to remind ourselves. Public key cryptosystems, as already explained, allow users to digitally sign messages. Users can "stamp their signature" on messages. A digital signature is generated by making use of the user's private key. For example, if Alice would like to put her signature on a message, she would apply her private key to a function when signing it. This information is necessary for explaining non-repudiation.

So, what is non-repudiation and how is it related to digital signatures? Non-repudiation is when it is not possible for the origin or the sender of the data or the message to deny that the data is originated from them. Public key cryptosystems achieve this characteristic by using digital signatures. If or when Alice sends a message to Bob with her signature attached to it, there is no way Alice can deny that she has sent that message. Bob can also prove that Alice is the one who has sent the message (with the signature verification process).

Why is it not possible for Alice to deny that the message comes from her? The reason is because the message has got Alice's signature on it. Alice's signature is generated from Alice's private key, as explained earlier. When it is Alice's private key, it means that Alice is the only person possessing the key. Therefore, the message must have come from her.

It is thus obvious that to achieve non-repudiation or to prevent anyone from denying that they have sent the data, a digital signature is required. This is the reason why digital signatures are important for the security of message transmission as well as cryptographic protocols.

Summary

This chapter lays the foundations for the later chapters by providing an introduction to cryptography. This consists of the concepts of the important elements which form building blocks for authentication methods and cryptographic protocols. These elements include symmetric cryptography, asymmetric cryptography, cryptographic hash functions, and digital signatures. It will be seen in later chapters how they can bring about the security of authentication mechanisms.

Bibliography

Boonkrong, S. (2014). *The Art of Protecting Networks and Information.* Bangkok, Thailand: King Mongkut's University of Technology North Bangkok Press.

Dworkin, M. (2004). *Recommendation for Block Cipher Modes of Operation: The CCM Mode for Authentication and Confidentiality.* Computer Security Division, Information Technology Laboratory, National Institution of Standards and Technology.

Menezes, A. J., Vanstone, S. A., & Van Oorschot, P. C. (2011). *Handbook of Applied Cryptography.* Boca Raton, Florida, USA: CRC Press, Inc.

NIST. (2001). *Advanced Encryption Standard (FIPS PUB 197).* Information Technology Laboratory, National Institution of Standards and Technology.

NIST. (2008). *Secure Hash Standards (FIPS PUB 180-4).* Information Technology Laboratory, National Institution of Standards and Technology.

Rivest, R. L., Shamir, A., & Adleman, L. M. (1978, February). A Method for Obtaining Digital Signatures and Public-key Cryptosystems. *Communications of the ACM, 21*(2), 120–126.

CHAPTER 2

Public Key Infrastructure

It is not possible to discuss authentication without at least touching the concept of public key infrastructure or PKI. This is because today's complex ecommerce or any Internet transactions require rigorous and thorough security mechanisms. Public key cryptography is one such mechanism that can support the required security measures and solve security problems.

Public key infrastructure, as the name suggests, works based on asymmetric cryptography whose benefits include confidentiality, integrity, and non-repudiation. We can think of public key cryptosystems as a support for security mechanisms. In order to have successful security mechanisms, it is important to have a solid infrastructure. A public key infrastructure or PKI is a foundation on which other security applications or systems are built.

Let us provide a summary of what the problem is for the communication between two entities on the Internet. Suppose that Alice and Bob are both connected to the Internet and would like to communicate with one another. The first question is: How does Alice know that the other entity is really Bob? Similarly, how can Bob be sure that he is really communicating with Alice? This is the issue of trust, which in fact has been a big problem over network communication up until these days.

The second issue to be considered is that even though Alice and Bob find a way to verify each other's identity, the transmission of messages between them will still not be secure. This is especially the case in our scenario when the communication between Alice and Bob takes place over the Internet, which is considered a public or an untrusted network. Within the insecurity of communications, there are several aspects that cannot be omitted. They include the confidentiality and integrity of the transmitted messages. Moreover, the authenticity (or the origin) of the message is sometimes required to be verified, which leads to the non-repudiation characteristic. We can now see that the security issues that are present while communicating on the Internet begin with the problem of trust, which is combined with confidentiality, integrity, and non-repudiation

© Sirapat Boonkrong 2021
S. Boonkrong, *Authentication and Access Control*, https://doi.org/10.1007/978-1-4842-6570-3_2

issues. Public key infrastructure has, therefore, been designed and implemented as an attempt to resolve them. This is why it is important to dedicate this chapter to the description and explanation of how public key infrastructure works.

PKI's Uses and Benefits

Before we get into the explanation of how public key infrastructure functions and what components it consists of, let's discuss examples of its uses and benefits so that its utilities can be appreciated. First of all, it needs to be mentioned that PKI does not have a particular business function. Rather, it provides a foundation for many security services. The main function of PKI is the distribution and use of public keys and public key cryptography for security purposes. Examples of the places that PKI is used as the foundation of security services include secure socket layers (SSL) and hypertext transfer protocol (HTTPS), both of which help secure transactions and message transmission between web browsers and web servers. In addition, the secure electronic transaction or SET protocol which is how credit card payments are facilitated can only function securely with the help of PKI. PKI, or at least some of its components, has also been applied in the design of many authentication protocols today. Some of these protocols are explained in the later chapters of this book.

Some key benefits that PKI and public key cryptography offer to business transactions are as follows:

- Reduces transactional processing expenses

- Reduces risks

- Enhances efficiency and performance of systems and networks

- Reduces complexity of security systems

These benefits are realized because without PKI, all applications on computer networks and the Internet would have to implement their own security mechanisms, which, of course, would put a lot of overhead on transactions and the applications themselves.

We now have seen some of the uses of PKI and its benefits. It is necessary to understand the framework of PKI and how various components fit together.

PKI Framework

As previously mentioned, the main function of PKI is to support the use of asymmetric cryptography, which means that the generation and distribution of public keys need to take place. The process of public key distribution is done by the use of one principal component of PKI known as a digital certificate which is basically an electronic document that binds an entity to its public key. Other components that allow PKI to function include a certificate authority (CA), a registration authority (RA), and directory services. These three ingredients actually lead to the implementation of digital certificates, which in turn can be used to identify different entities on the network.

We briefly explained in the beginning of the chapter that trust is the major issue that exists on the Internet. A trust hierarchy is established as a principle of PKI. On the Internet or any public networks, there will be entities that do not previously know each other. Hence, there is no adequate trust between them to perform any required transactions. It is the job of the PKI with the help of a CA that some trust can be established between those entities.

PKI has got many logical components, but for the purpose of authentication and secure communication, we will focus only on the main ones. They include end entities or subscribers, certificate authorities, hardware security modules (HSM), public key or digital certificates, registration authorities, and certificate revocation lists.

End entities or *subscribers* are any users or entities that require a digital certificate to identify themselves. These entities must at least have a capability to generate a public and private key pair for themselves. They must have a means of securely storing the private key, too.

Certificate authority or *CA* is defined by the Internet Engineering Task Force or IETF as "an authority trusted by one or more users to create and assign public key certificates." In other words, a CA functions as follows: to establish trust, each entity on the Internet must individually request for a digital certificate from a CA. Upon receiving a certificate request, the CA performs entity authentication to ensure that this particular entity is suited for owning and eventually using a digital certificate. The entity authentication done by the CA is usually based on the rules established in its certificate practices statement or the CPS. Once the entity authentication is complete, the CA generates and issues the requestor a digital certificate, which is signed, and in fact can only be signed, by the CA. The CA's signature and digital certificate vouch for the identity of this particular individual. The certificate can now be used in an authentication process to establish trust with other principals on the Internet.

One thing to be noted is that the public key of the CA's must be distributed to all individuals that trust the CA, so that the digital certificates that are issued and signed by this CA can be verified. The CA's signature generation and verification processes follow the exact same method as the one explained in Chapter 1. We refer the reader back to that chapter for the description of these processes.

There will be a time when digital certificates become invalid. This happens due to various reasons. The certificates may have expired. Some may have been compromised by either the private key of the certificate owner has leaked, or even worse the private key of the CA is known to attackers. Either way, these digital certificates will be revoked and deemed invalid. When this occurs, they will be added to a directory called the *certificate revocation list* or the *CRL*. This directory or database is attached to the CA. Entities can look up the CRL to ensure that any individual's digital certificate is still valid; hence, it does not exist in the CRL.

Hardware security module or *HSM* is a very important module in PKI. The trust in the PKI depends on the signature of the CA. This means that it is essential to keep the CA's private key as secure as possible. It is suggested that a CA should only store its private key in specialized computer equipment known as hardware security module or HSM. A hardware security module, by definition, is a piece of hardware and associated software that are inside a PC or a server and are able to provide cryptographic functions. Its only job is to ensure that the CA's private key is kept secure and inaccessible to any unauthorized parties.

Another important component is a *digital certificate* or a *public key certificate*. A digital certificate provides the binding of an end entity and its public key. A certificate usually contains enough information for others to validate and verify the identity of the owner of that particular certificate. A digital certificate should contain at least the serial number of the certificate itself, the name of an entity, identifying information about the entity, expiration date of the certificate and, of course, the entity's public key. Other information that can be included could be the CA's name and types of algorithm used to generate and verify the certificate. However, the most important element of any digital certificate is the digital signature of the CA who issued the certificate. The information and format of the digital certificate must follow a standard known as the X.509 standard, which is specified and detailed in the RFC 5280 document. Figure 2-1 shows an example of what a digital certificate looks like.

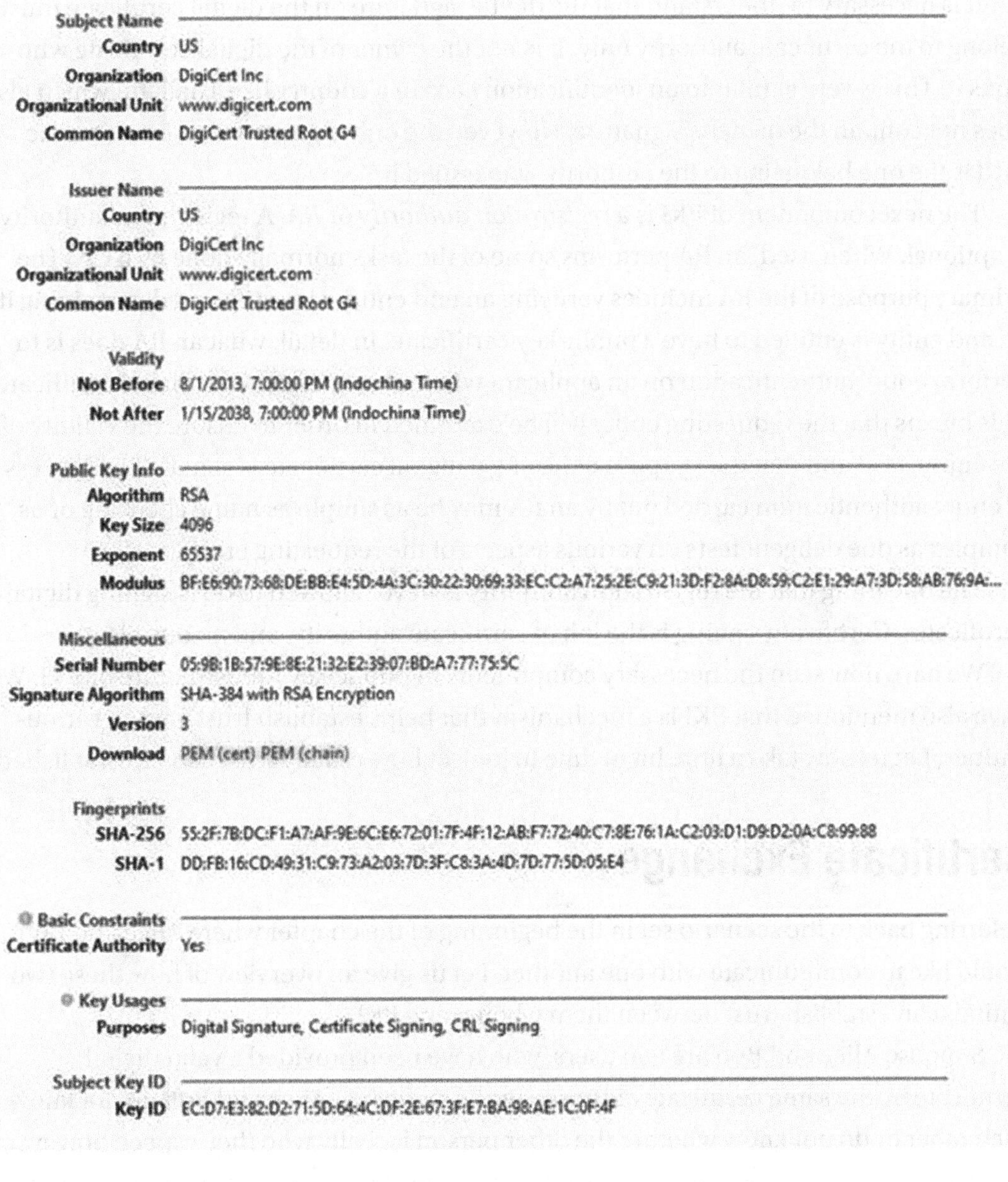

Subject Name	
Country	US
Organization	DigiCert Inc
Organizational Unit	www.digicert.com
Common Name	DigiCert Trusted Root G4
Issuer Name	
Country	US
Organization	DigiCert Inc
Organizational Unit	www.digicert.com
Common Name	DigiCert Trusted Root G4
Validity	
Not Before	8/1/2013, 7:00:00 PM (Indochina Time)
Not After	1/15/2038, 7:00:00 PM (Indochina Time)
Public Key Info	
Algorithm	RSA
Key Size	4096
Exponent	65537
Modulus	BF:E6:90:73:68:DE:BB:E4:5D:4A:3C:30:22:30:69:33:EC:C2:A7:25:2E:C9:21:3D:F2:8A:D8:59:C2:E1:29:A7:3D:58:AB:76:9A:...
Miscellaneous	
Serial Number	05:9B:1B:57:9E:8E:21:32:E2:39:07:BD:A7:77:75:5C
Signature Algorithm	SHA-384 with RSA Encryption
Version	3
Download	PEM (cert) PEM (chain)
Fingerprints	
SHA-256	55:2F:7B:DC:F1:A7:AF:9E:6C:E6:72:01:7F:4F:12:AB:F7:72:40:C7:8E:76:1A:C2:03:D1:D9:D2:0A:C8:99:88
SHA-1	DD:FB:16:CD:49:31:C9:73:A2:03:7D:3F:C8:3A:4D:7D:77:5D:05:E4
⊕ Basic Constraints	
Certificate Authority	Yes
⊕ Key Usages	
Purposes	Digital Signature, Certificate Signing, CRL Signing
Subject Key ID	
Key ID	EC:D7:E3:82:D2:71:5D:64:4C:DF:2E:67:3F:E7:BA:98:AE:1C:0F:4F

Figure 2-1. *An Example of a Digital Certificate*

It can be seen in Figure 2-1 that the information includes the owner's basic information, the digital certificate issuer or the CA, the validity period of the certificate, the public key information of the owner of the certificate, and the algorithm to be used to verify the CA's signature.

It is necessary to understand that the digital signature on the digital certificate must belong to the certificate authority only. It is not the owner of the digital certificate who signs it. This is very similar to an identification card in a country like Thailand which also does not contain the owner's signature. However, the only signature that exists on the card is the one belonging to the authority who issued it.

The next component of PKI is a *registration authority* or *RA*. A registration authority is optional. When used, an RA performs some of the tasks normally done by a CA. The primary purpose of the RA includes verifying an end entity's identity and determining if an end entity is entitled to have a public key certificate. In detail, what an RA does is to perform entity authentication on an applicant who has requested for a digital certificate. This means that the requesting entity will be examined in order to ensure the validity of the entity itself and that the purpose of having a digital certificate is sound. The process of entity authentication carried out by an RA may be as simple as name checking or as complex as due deligent tests on various aspects of the requesting entity.

The one thing that the registration authority is never allowed to do is signing digital certificates. Certificate signing is the job of certificate authority, and no one else.

We have now seen the necessary components in public key infrastructure or PKI. We have also mentioned that PKI is a mechanism that helps establish trust among various entities. Let us now take a little bit of time to look at how exactly trust can be established.

Certificate Exchange

Referring back to the scenario set in the beginning of the chapter where Alice and Bob would like to communicate with one another. Let us give an overview of how these two entities can establish trust between them when using PKI.

Suppose Alice and Bob are two users, who have been provided a valid digital certificate by the same certificate authority or the same CA. Alice and Bob do not know each other or do not know whether the other person is really who they expect, however. When Alice and Bob would like to communicate, they first have to establish some sort of trust between each other. The process begins by Alice sending her digital certificate to Bob. Bob, having received it, will then verify the CA's signature on the certificate using the CA's public key, which Bob already possesses (because Bob has also obtained his certificate from this CA). If the verification is a success, Bob knows that Alice's certificate is valid. Other processes that Bob carries out to ensure the validity of the certificate include checking the expiration date on the certificate as well as checking the certificate validity with the certificate revocation list at the CA.

If all are fine, the certificate is said to be valid. Bob then sends his own certificate to Alice, so that she can verify it using the same process. If the verification of the CA's signature on Bob's certificate is a success and all other validity checking processes are successfully done, Alice knows that this particular certificate is valid. This implies that at the end of the process, both Alice and Bob can at least be certain that the certificate received from the other party is valid. Hence, some trust is said to have been established between them. This process is known as *certificate exchange* and can be simply expressed as

$$Alice \rightarrow Bob : Cer_{Alice}$$

Bob verifies the signature and checks the validity of the certificate.

$$Bob \rightarrow Alice : Cer_{Bob}$$

Alice verifies the signature and checks the validity of the certificate.

Here Cer_i is the digital certificate that belongs to an entity i.

It is evident that the certificate exchange process is easy for end entities under the same CA to authenticate or validate one another. However, it is possible that end entities under one CA may need to authenticate end entities under a different CA. This is where *cross certification* comes in.

Before discussing what cross certification is and how it is carried out, it is useful to spend some time on a concept of trust models in PKI. Existing trust models include hierarchical, distributed, and peer to peer. The selection of a trust model depends on the business objectives and the trust relationships already existing in the environment. Having said that, the most used trust model in public key infrastructure is the hierarchical trust model.

The *hierarchical* trust model is the most typical implementation of PKI. The hierarchical trust model allows end entities' certificates to be signed by a single CA, with that CA having another CA as its parent CA. For example, there may be one root CA at a national level that signs the certificates of financial institutions. Then each financial institution itself would be or could be a CA that signs the certificates of the account holders.

There are two types of hierarchical trust models. They are known as a tiered hierarchy and a flat hierarchy. In a tiered hierarchy with multiple CAs, compartmentalization of risk can be established, but each CA requires so much administrative effort. On the other hand, a flat hierarchy with a single CA is much easier to administer. However, a failure of that single CA will corrupt the entire trust model. Even though there are two types of hierarchical trust models, it has to be said that the tiered hierarchy is a lot more popular. A typical example of the tiered hierarchy is depicted in Figure 2-2.

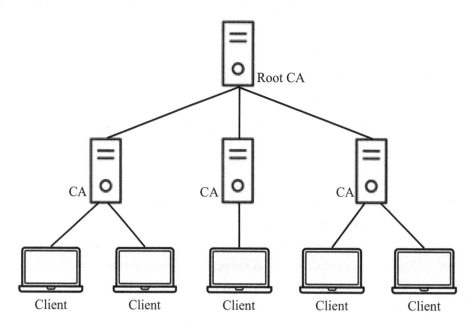

Figure 2-2. *A Tiered Hierarchical Trust Model*

In the tiered hierarchical trust model in Figure 2-2, there is a trust point. From the previous example, a trust point for the financial institutions is the national or root CA. A trust point for account holders is their institution's CA. In other words, there will always be one CA in a higher level of the trust hierarchy that is trusted by different certificate authorities in a lower level. This is why and how cross certification works.

Let us go back to our previous scenario where Alice and Bob have obtained their digital certificates from different certificate authorities. With the availability of the tiered hierarchical trust model, it will be possible for Alice to verify and validate Bob's certificate, and vice versa, through a process called cross certification.

Cross certification is when a CA cross certifies another CA by performing various due diligence tests. In this case, Alice's CA and Bob's CA will have to cross certify one another to ensure that each CA is really an authorized CA. After the certificate authorities cross certify one another, the clients, Alice and Bob in this example, will also trust the other

CA and any certificates signed by it. Therefore, Alice and Bob can now gain each other's trust by verifying and validating the certificate even though they were issued by different certificate authorities.

The cross certification process can allow PKI deployment to be both extensible and scalable.

PKI Process

We have already seen the components of public key infrastructure and how trust can be established via certification exchange as well as cross certification. Let us get into a little more detail of what other processes are involved in PKI.

Application

To obtain a digital certificate, an individual or an organization must apply for it. The application process is a simple form fill-in process, which requires the certificate requestor to provide such information as name, address, contact detail and reason for having a digital certificate and how long to have for. Some CA may ask for the public key during the application process. Some may ask for it later.

Entity Authentication

Once the application form is sent to the authority which could either be a certificate authority (CA) or a registration authority (RA), *entity authentication* is done. How entity authentication is carried out depends on the business risk model. The authentication may be one of extreme due diligence if high security is needed (e.g., a passport agency). On the other hand, the authentication may be one of very simple process if the business is not very security concerned (e.g., film or video on-demand business). Sometimes it is necessary for some businesses to replicate an existing manual process that requires some form of identification. For example, to apply for a passport, the agency should replicate the same process they use today.

Entity authentication is an important process, because if a sufficient level of validation does not occur during the original authentication of an entity, any subsequent reliance on the credentials and certificates issued to that identity could be suspicious.

Digital Certificate Generation

The next process is *certificate generation*. This process consists of many subprocesses, which include public key acquisition, end entity's identity verification, certificate formatting, and certificate signing.

The first subprocess is *public key acquisition*. This is the process where a CA requests for a public key from an end entity that applies for the certificate. The CA may allow the public key to be sent electronically over the Internet. Alternatively, the CA could use more sophisticated means such as mandating out-of-band manual methods (e.g., using bonded couriers or delivery services). The next is *end entity's identity verification*. Just as in the entity authentication process, the amount of information needed to carry out verification depends on the business risk model. The CA may simply take the entity's word that they are who they are, or the CA could institute more stringent measures, such as a detailed due diligence process. The most important factor in the process is to ensure that an entity's identity is correctly verified.

Next is the matter of generating a digital certificate. This begins with *certificate formatting*, which is the process where all the required data to be placed in the certificate is collected and formatted. The format of digital certificate usually follows the X.509 standard, as already mentioned earlier. Some of the necessary information to have in the certificate includes the entity's name or ID, the entity's public key, the cryptographic algorithm used for signature verification, and the expiry date of the certificate. Once all the information is in place, the *certificate signing* takes place. Here, the CA generates its digital signature and puts it on the certificate. That is, the certificate is signed by using the CA's private key. The certificate can now be either published or distributed.

On the whole, if Alice and Bob would like to obtain a digital certificate, they will have to go through the following steps, which are also depicted in Figure 2-3:

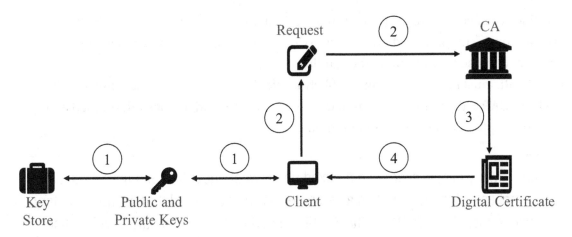

Figure 2-3. *Digital Certificate Acquisition Process*

1. Alice and Bob each generates a public and private key pair and stores them with the private key being kept secure.

2. Alice and Bob each provides his and her public key, name, and descriptive information to an RA through an application process.

3. The RA validates Alice and Bob's credentials and forwards the certificate requests to the CA.

4. The CA generates a certificate for Alice and Bob by formatting public key and other information and signs the certificate with the CA's private key.

5. The CA issues the signed certificates that belong to Alice and Bob to the correct owner.

Note that we have earlier stated that the registration authority is optional. The preceding process is followed if an RA exists. However, if an RA does not exist, all the steps will be carried out by the CA itself.

Digital Certificate Revocation

One final process that needs to be explained in PKI is *certificate revocation*. Certificate revocation can occur due to many reasons. The first is when a digital certificate expires according to the expiration date stated in the certificate. Other reasons are when digital certificates have to be made prematurely expired. Example situations could be the CA's private key is compromised, the user is no longer a customer, or there is a change in information used to determine the validity.

A CRL must be published and publicly available. An example of such directory is LDAP. LDAP is the industry's current directory of choice and has been developed as an X.500 compliant protocol for the Internet.

Note   Many people seem to get mixed up between the X.500 and the X.509. Let us emphasize that the X.500 is a computer network standard that defines directory services, including LDAP, and the X.509 is a portion of that standard which defines the structure of digital certificates and PKI.

The timely publication of the CRL is critical in Internet and e-commerce environments because security depends on it. This is especially true during the latency period between when a CA revokes a certificate and its subsequent publication. At present, there is a protocol that helps resolve this latency problem. The protocol is called the *Online Certificate Status Protocol* or *OCSP*. It is a mechanism that actually requests, in real time, a status check for a particular certificate from the originating CA. This reduces or even eliminates the need for the CA to publish a CRL.

Summary

This chapter discusses the importance and functionalities of public key infrastructure or PKI. PKI is based on asymmetric cryptography. The job of PKI is to provide the foundation for security applications or systems. The main components of PKI include end entities, certificate authorities, registration authorities, digital certificates, and certificate revocation list. The principal function of a certificate authority and PKI in general is to generate digital certificates that bind end entities with their public keys. The certificates can be used to establish trust among end entities. Apart from generating certificates, revocation is something that is part of PKI as well.

Bibliography

Boeyen, S., Santesson, S., Polk, T., Housley, R., Farrell, S., & Cooper, D. (2008). *Internet X.509 Public Key Infrastructure Certificate and Certificate Revocation List (CRL) Profile.* RFC Editor.

Boonkrong, S. (2014). *The Art of Protecting Networks and Information.* Bangkok, Thailand: King Mongkut's University of Technology North Bangkok Press.

Buchmann, J. A., Karatsiolis, E., & Wiesmaier, A. (2013). *Introduction to Public Key Infrastructures.* Springer Publishing Company, Incorporated.

Menezes, A. J., Vanstone, S. A., & Van Oorschot, P. C. (2011). *Handbook of Applied Cryptography* (1 ed.). Boca Raton, Florida, USA: CRC Press, Inc.

Rivest, R. L., Shamir, A., & Adleman, L. M. (1978, February). A Method for Obtaining Digital Signatures and Public-key Cryptosystems. *Communications of the ACM, 21*(2), 120–126.

CHAPTER 3

Methods and Threats of Authentication

In an ideal world, we would like to use the best technologies to countermeasure the risks to confidentiality, integrity, and availability. It is learned in the previous chapters that confidentiality is achieved by the use of encryption and the integrity of data can be inspected by the use of cryptographic hash functions. This chapter will look at another aspect of information and communication security, which is access control mechanism. Access control deals with the availability characteristic of security in the CIA model and refers to issues concerning access to system and network resources. There are actually four main parts to the access control mechanism. They are identification, authentication, authorization, and accounting.

In general, a typical approach to the management of information security is to analyze risks and to control or mitigate them through available security mechanisms. In this regard, access control, especially user identification and authentication, plays a vital role by ensuring the assurance of the user's rights before they are granted access to computer and network resources.

This chapter provides the background knowledge of what authentication mechanism is and what authentication methods are available, before discussing possible threats that could provide dangers to such mechanisms.

What Is Authentication?

Suppose a computer and communication system consisting of hardware, software, processes, data, and network belongs to an organization. From the inside and outside of the organization, only selected individuals or objects (including applications and

© Sirapat Boonkrong 2021
S. Boonkrong, *Authentication and Access Control*, https://doi.org/10.1007/978-1-4842-6570-3_3

services) are allowed to enter and use the system. The question is: how do we know which individuals or objects have the permission to do so? This is where an access control mechanism, especially authentication, becomes necessary.

As mentioned, there are four processes to an access control mechanism – identification, authentication, authorization, and accounting. First of all, *identification* is just identifying who each user is. This is, for example, done by issuing a username or a user ID. Secondly, *authentication* is a process used for determining whether or not users are allowed access. In addition, authentication is a process used for confirming the identity of a user. That is, once a username is entered, the user must prove that this username really belongs to them. The next thing that usually comes after authentication is authorization. *Authorization* is a process that deals with restrictions and limitations on access. Authorization tells what each user is and is not allowed to do or access. In other words, authorization gives users their access rights to resources. The fourth part of access control is accounting. *Accounting* keeps records of who has entered the system, what that person has done, and when. To put it simply, accounting is a process of keeping a log of the system.

We have now learned the overview of what access control is. Let us focus more on authentication.

As mentioned, authentication is a process of confirming or validating an individual's identity. The fact that the individual or user claims that they are the owner of the identity does not necessarily mean that it is true. Therefore, for the user to be granted the permission or the rights to have an access and use the resources, they must provide an evidence to prove their identity to the system. This is what authentication is.

In an authentication process, an individual is required to provide a credential in order to prove their identity. Different systems may require different types of credentials. Some may even require more than one credential from the individual. In today's computer and communication systems, an individual is usually asked to present a credential in the form of a password. However, credentials also come in other forms, such as a PIN number, an authentication token, or a representation of a body part.

Typically, there are two components involved in the process of entity authentication. They are known as a supplicant and an authenticator. They are depicted in Figure 3-1 and can be described as follows:

Note   When the term "entity authentication" is mentioned, an entity can be a person, a process, an application, a client, or even a server.

---

1. Supplicant – This is an entity that will provide their identity and prove that this identity is valid. As a result, this entity will either be authenticated or not be authenticated.

2. Authenticator – This is a party that checks the credential or credentials of the supplicant and states whether or not the supplicant's identity proving process is successful. An authenticator can be a person, a process, or a server.

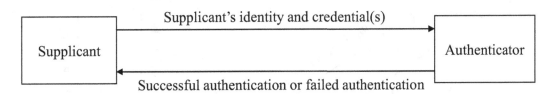

Figure 3-1. *Two-Party Authentication Process*

However, there are times when a third component is required in the authentication process. This third component is usually known as a trusted third party or TTP, whose job is to analyze the received identity and credential. The trusted third party also makes the decision to whether or not the authentication process is a success, which means that the trusted third party becomes the authenticator of the process. The non-supplicant party can be called a responder as a result. A typical authentication process involving three parties is illustrated in Figure 3-2.

It can be seen that the authenticator acts as the trusted third party because it is the one who makes the decision whether to allow or deny access. The responder in this scenario could be a system or an application that does not have the ability to verify a supplicant's identity by itself.

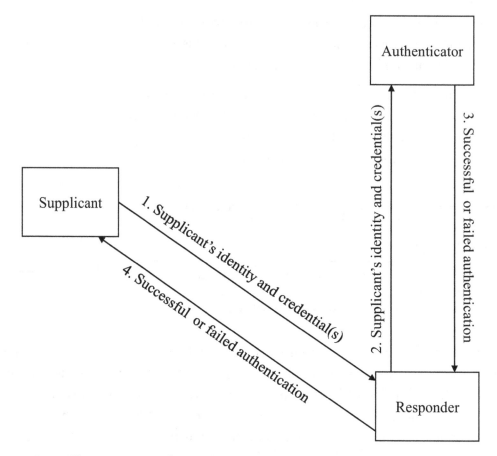

Figure 3-2. *Three-Party Authentication Process*

This section provides an overview of what authentication is. The next sections will explain different authentication methods, which include the something-you-know method, something-you-have method, and something-you-are method.

Factors of Authentication

Authentication is the process of confirming one's identity. In order to carry out the process of confirming the identity, the systems or resources requiring authentication usually ask for evidence from the entity attempting to do the authentication. This evidence is known as *factors of authentication*. Some may also call them *credentials*. In other words, when a user claims to be someone, they need to provide further information to prove that they are really who they say they are. That information is a factor or factors of authentication.

For example, a user goes to a cash point in order to withdraw some cash. When the card is inserted into the machine, it is used as a claim of the user's identity. The next step is for the user to prove that they are really the owner of the card. This is done by the cash point asking something that can only be provided by the actual owner of the card. It could be a four- to six-digit PIN code or a fingerprint. These are examples of factors of authentication.

The next sections will give descriptions of commonly used factors of authentication. They are something you know, something you have, and something you are.

Something You Know

Something you know is a method which a supplicant uses what they remember to prove their identity. In other words, the user would use what is stored in their memory to prove that they are really who they claim to be. A good example for this authentication method is a password or a PIN code for a cash point.

In a simple view, something-you-know authentication process works in two parts as follows: The first is the registration phase. The second is the authentication phase. During the registration, a supplicant or a user chooses a password of their choice. The password is then stored in a password database, which marks the end of the registration. Note that there may be some processing done to the password before storing. However, for the sake of simplicity, this process will be ignored and will be explained in detail in Chapter 4.

In the authentication stage, the supplicant enters their password. The comparison is then made between the entered password and the previously stored password. If they match, an access to the system or resources is granted. Otherwise, the access is denied. This process is depicted in Figure 3-3.

Registration

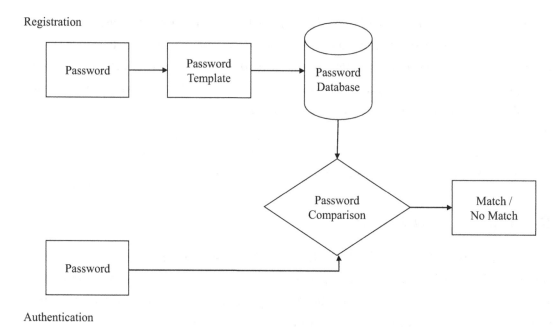

Authentication

Figure 3-3. *Typical Something-You-Know Authentication Process*

Some have asked whether or not a username or an email address is a something-you-know factor of authentication since they have to be memorized and entered into a system when logging in. The answer is no. Usernames and email addresses are not considered as a factor of authentication. They are simply used to claim an identity of the user or supplicant, which is known as identification. A password or a PIN code is the element used to prove the ownership of the identity. Hence, it is a something-you-know factor of authentication.

Something You Have

The second factor of authentication requires that a supplicant has a physical item in their possession. This includes smart cards and authentication tokens. An *authentication token* is a small device, usually in the form of a key ring, with a screen to display a set of numbers. The numbers on the token's screen is used as a passcode for the authentication process. An authentication token can be either synchronous or asynchronous. A synchronous token is synchronized with an authenticator or an authentication server. They use the time to generate a number that will be entered during the user login phase. That is, the token has a function $f()$ that takes the current time *t* as an input and computes a password PWD_t for that particular moment. In simple terms, this can be expressed as $PWD_t = f(t)$. When a user would like to log into a system, they enter a username together with the number displayed on the token.

For the verification process, the authentication server carries out the same process. That is, the authentication server also uses the function $f()$, which takes the current time *t* as its input, to compute the password PWD_t. The computed and received passwords are compared. If they match, the supplicant is allowed to enter the system, or is successfully authenticated. The authentication process of a typical synchronous authentication token is illustrated in Figure 3-4.

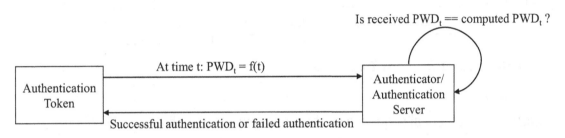

Figure 3-4. *Synchronous Token Authentication Process at Any Time t*

Note   The number or password computed by the token and authentication server changes according to the current time. For an RSA SecurID Token, which is an example of an authentication token, the number on the token changes every minute and is also synchronized with the authentication server.

Asynchronous authentication token is the second type of token which works in a slightly different way from the synchronous one. With this type, the token and server do not have to be time-synchronized. When a user would like to log in, an authentication server will send the user a random sequence of digits, which will then be entered into the token. The authentication token computes a passcode from the entered numerical sequence as a response. To complete the login process, the user enters the passcode into the system to gain access.

In other words, when logging into a system, the challenge *x* generated by the authentication server is used as an input into a function $f()$, usually a hash function, on the token. The password $PWD_x = f(x)$ is then computed and transmitted to the authentication server by the token. On the authenticator side, the verification process is carried out by also computing the $PWD_x = f(x)$, which is then compared with the received password. If they match, the authentication is a success, else the process fails. The authentication process of a typical asynchronous authentication token is illustrated in Figure 3-5.

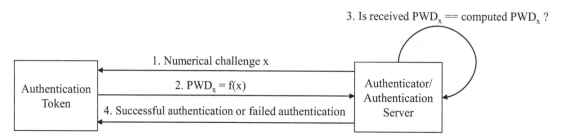

Figure 3-5. *Asynchronous Token Authentication Process*

Note   The numerical sequence or challenge generated by the authentication server changes every time a supplicant attempts to log in. Hence, the password changes every time, too.

The main advantage of using an authentication token, either synchronous or asynchronous, is that the user's password changes every time they log in. This is also known as *time-based one-time password* or *TOTP* for the synchronous token and *hash-based one-time password* or *HOTP* for the asynchronous token. Both of them reduce the risk of passwords being guessed by attackers.

Something You Are

The third authentication factor deals with the characteristics of the supplicant. This is a process of using body measurements, known as *biometrics*. Simply put, the something-you-are factor of authentication requires that the authenticator authenticates the supplicant by using biometric information. Commonly used biometrics for authentication purposes include fingerprint, palm print, hand geometry, face, iris and retina. However, only fingerprint, retina and iris are considered truly unique. With today's technology, other types of biometrics include signature dynamics and keyboard typing pattern.

This method of authentication can be thought of as a traditional identification and authentication method. For example, when a person enters a bank, they are asked to show a photo ID. The person is then identified and authenticated based on their biometric parameters. That is, the bank matches the face of the person with the face on the ID card. This is a form of facial recognition and can be analogous with today's biometric authentication method.

The process of biometric authentication works in two main parts. The first is the registration or enrollment. The second is authentication. In the registration phase, biometric data is captured by a biometric sensing device, such as a fingerprint scanner for fingerprint data or a camera for facial data. The captured data is then processed in order to extract and transform it into a biometric template. The obtained biometric template is stored in a database where an authentication process can be made later.

The authentication process begins when the biometric data of the supplicant is captured and processed for the extraction and transformation to obtain the person's biometric information. It is then compared with the biometric template which is stored in the database. If they match, the authentication process is a success. Otherwise, the authentication process fails. This process is summarized in Figure 3-6.

On the whole, biometric authentication works by comparing the user's actual characteristic with the stored data in order to determine if the user is really they are claiming to be. Biometric authentication comes with an issue, which is the fact that it is possible for human characteristics to change over time. This is due to aging, illness or injury. Therefore, *fallback* or *failsafe* authentication mechanisms should be created just in case.

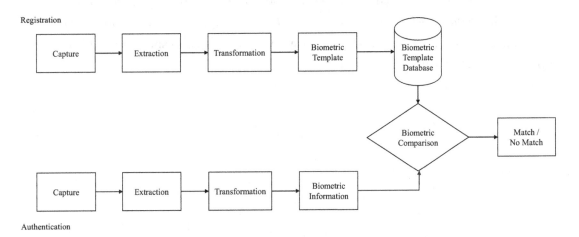

Figure 3-6. *Typical Biometric Authentication Process*

Other Factors of Authentication

The three factors of authentication mentioned earlier are considered the most commonly used credentials in any computing systems. This section will explore and explain other existing, albeit less popular, authentication factors that can also be used to prove the identity of the supplicant.

Something You Process

This type of authentication factor is based on the ability of a supplicant to process things. The something-you-process factor works with human cognitive level of authentication. In other words, instead of asking the supplicant to enter their password, the system asks them to perform a mathematical or logical task. Typically, these tasks involve some secrets known to the user as well as some variable values provided by the system. The output of the process done by the user will form a new code or a new pass that will be used in this particular authentication session between the user and the system. This authentication method provides a different outcome each time the supplicant processes the given task. It means that the value used to authenticate the supplicant by the authenticator differs from session to session.

Figure 3-7 shows a simple example of an authentication mechanism based on the something you process. During the formula registration phase, the user must memorize the positions in the given grid, the mathematical operations or their choice, and the constant number, if any. These will form their personal mathematical formula. For example, the mathematical formula from the grid formed during the registration phase could be $aa * 1 + bb + 3$, where aa and bb are examples of grid positions in the intersections of row a with column a and row b with column b, respectively. This is something that the user has to memorize.

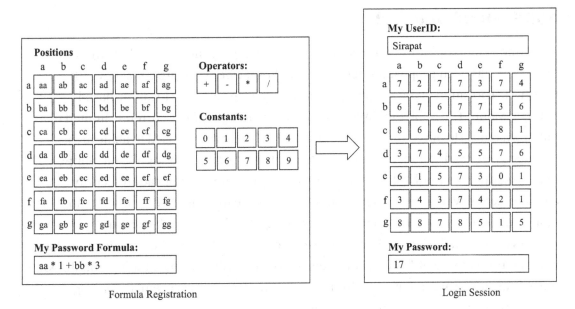

Formula Registration   Login Session

Figure 3-7. *An Example of Something-You-Process Authentication*

During the login session, the user is presented with a grid with a random value in each cell. In order to log in, they have to compute the outcome of the formula chosen in the registration stage.

Carrying on with the same example in Figure 3-7, the value in the cell *aa* is 7. The value in the cell *bb* is 7. Therefore, the result of the mathematical formula $aa * 1 + bb + 3$ is $7 * 1 + 7 + 3 = 17$, which is entered as the passcode for this particular login session.

Note   The numbers in the cells of the grid change each time a new login session begins. This means that the result of the calculation, based on the memorized formula, should form a one-time passcode that allows the supplicant to login successfully.

Although the one-time passcode, as noted previously, produced by the user's computational process is a positive point, this something-you-process authentication is time consuming and cognitively demanding. This is due to the process of recalling the mathematical formula and the process of computing the outcome during the login session. This is one of the reasons why this type of authentication factor is not as commonly used as the ones mentioned earlier.

Somewhere You Are

The somewhere-you-are factor of authentication, although not as well-known as the others, has been proposed since the 1990s. Somewhere you are concerns with the physical location of the supplicant. Some may even call it the location-based authentication. The implementation of the somewhere you are is currently limited in online systems. However, there are several methods that can be used to achieve this.

Firstly, an IP address can be used to detect the location of the supplicant. Suppose that the supplicant would like to use a service that requires a geolocation security check. When they register to use the service, they state that they live in the Kingdom of Thailand. That means if someone attempts to log in to this particular account from an IP address located in the United States, the service will either notify the supplicant that an attempt from outside of Thailand has been made or it will terminate the session thinking that it is an adversary trying to log in. The use of an IP address is useful in making an effort to protect the account from an adversary.

Some financial institutions use this particular method to detect payment frauds. For instance, if the last known location of a user was in the Kingdom of Thailand, however, a few minutes later, the same account is logged in or the credit card associated to this account is used in China, this could indicate an unusual activity.

Another method of using the somewhere-you-are factor is mobile based and also used by financial institutions. This method suggests that the geolocation of the user's mobile device is proximate to that computer being used for the current session or transactions. Based on the result, the banking system can make a decision whether to accept or reject the transactions. This process of the authentication using the somewhere-you-are factor is shown in Figure 3-8.

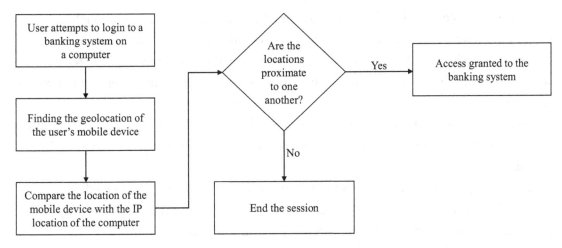

Figure 3-8. *Example of Applying Somewhere-You-Are Factor of Authentication*

The preceding authentication procedure has the following advantage: Suppose a user walks away from their computer without logging out, leaving the current session open. In a normal situation, any other user can utilize this opened session to try to impersonate this user. The somewhere-you-are factor can reduce the risk by authenticating the user's mobile device's geolocation. The session can remain active if the locations of the mobile device and the computer are identical. However, if there is enough error on the location, the session can automatically be closed. Thus, no other users should be able to come in and use the user's session.

Somebody You Know

The somebody-you-know factor of authentication works based on the human social relationship. The somebody-you-know authentication method was designed for an emergency situation where an authentication token is not available to the user. When the token is not available, there must be another means for the user to utilize in order to log into a computer system. This is where the relationship between users comes in. The process works as follows.

In the enrollment stage, the relationship between two users, say Alice and Bob, is recorded by the server as an asker and a helper. When Alice, the asker, who has lost the ability to use her authentication token, wants to log into the system, she contacts Bob, the helper. The channel of contact can be either over a telephone or face to face in order to make it easy for Bob to authenticate Alice, either by voice recognition over the phone or face recognition during face-to-face contact, respectively.

Once Bob is certain that the asker is really Alice, he uses his own client machine to carry out his authentication with the server, who also verifies the asker–helper relationship of Alice and Bob. If the relationship verification is successful, Bob receives a vouchcode from the server, who marks that there is an ongoing helping session between Alice and Bob.

Bob, the helper, then gives the vouchcode to Alice, the asker. This can be done orally in the case of telephone communication or as a written value in the case of face-to-face contact.

At this stage, Alice enters her username, password, and the newly received vouchcode to the server. The server then verifies Alice's password and vouchcode and makes the decision to either accept or reject the authentication attempt.

If the authentication succeeds, the server provides the asker, Alice, with a temporary password. Subsequently, Alice can carry out an authentication process with the server using her password together with this temporary password, which will usually be valid for one or two days.

The vouching and authentication process based on the relationship between the asker and helper is summarized in Figure 3-9.

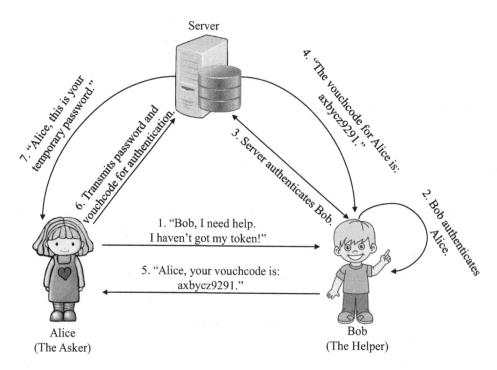

Figure 3-9. *Somebody-You-Know Authentication Process*

It is important to note that this authentication process only works if and only if the relationship between the asker and helper is valid and successfully verified by the server. This implies that it is necessary for a user to know someone if they would like to carry out an authentication process without the availability of their authentication token. There is one disadvantage to this somebody-you-know method. That is, the helper must have an access to the Internet. Otherwise, they will not be able to request and obtain the vouchcode for the asker. However, it is the process that can assist the asker in an emergency situation as explained.

Threats of Authentication

We have seen that the goal of authentication is to validate and confirm the identity of a supplicant. It is normal for computer systems to ask the supplicant or user to carry out authentication. At the same time, there will be an adversary who tries to penetrate the system and compromise the authentication mechanism. This section, therefore, looks at different approaches that an attacker can use to attempt to break the authentication mechanism of computer systems. However, let us first try to understand the differences between the three words that are related to the content of this section. They are vulnerability, threat, and attack.

Firstly, a *vulnerability* is a weakness in a system that makes a threat occur. It refers to the inability to resist hostile challenges. Secondly, a threat is defined as a potential danger that may occur. In other words, a *threat* is any danger that has a likelihood of occurring to an asset. It does not matter whether it actually occurs or not. As long as there is a chance of occurring, it can be referred to as a threat. Thirdly, an *attack* is a malicious action that exploits a vulnerability, damages, or gains unauthorized access to a computing resource. An attack's aim is almost always to cause harms or damages to an information system.

Some authentication methods, especially the ones that rely solely on usernames and passwords, are considered broken. In fact, the Open Web Application Security Project or OWASP has ranked *broken authentication* as number 2 in the list of most seen application vulnerabilities. It is, therefore, important to understand the threats that are common to authentication mechanisms.

Default Passwords

A *default password* is a predefined and preconfigured password for a piece of software or a device. Default passwords are commonly used for network equipment such as routers, switches, wireless access points, as well as Internet of Things (IoT) devices. Typical examples of a default password include *admin, password, attack,* and *1234*. Default passwords represent one of the major issues to authentication mechanisms and are very often overlooked.

In many cases, system engineers and developers are so busy working on the implementation of functionality of the systems that they forget about the default passwords. If the default passwords remain unchanged, it can cause a serious problem in that an adversary can easily find a default password for any devices or software on the Internet. Once the password is obtained, the attacker can then log into the device or system and often has the privilege of an administrator. The problem becomes more severe in the case of the IoT environment where many devices' make and brand can be readily seen by anyone. Hence, a default password can also be comfortably found.

Fortunately, there are ways to counteract the security of default passwords. Firstly, the vendor of software and hardware can employ more secure and unique default passwords. Secondly, the software and hardware vendor can design their devices or systems in such a way that the users are forced to change the password when the default password is used for the first time. Thirdly, on users' responsibility, the users or device owners must change the default password to a stronger password when they first enter the system or the device.

Eavesdropping

Eavesdropping or *sniffing* is basically an act of listening to private communications of others without their permission. Therefore, eavesdropping is an easy method to obtain a supplicant's password as well as other credentials from the traffic on a computer network.

Many applications, devices, and systems transmit information, including passwords and other credentials over the network in an unencrypted format. Typical examples include FTP and HTTP. In their default configurations, these protocols do not encrypt any messages and packets. That means if an adversary wants to eavesdrop or sniff packets off the network, using such application as Wireshark, they will be able to easily obtain passwords in the plaintext format.

Man-in-the-Middle Attacks

Man-in-the-middle or *MitM* attacks occur when an adversary comes in between two hosts, whether they are a supplicant and an authenticator or a customer and a website, and all messages and communications go through them. By being in between two entities, the attacker can receive and send messages to both parties. That means the attacker can impersonate both entities, making one believe that the attacker is the other. Moreover, not only receiving and transmitting messages from the involving entities, the attacker can also alter and even delete portions of those messages. Thus, an attack on authentication can be carried out as follows.

Provided that the attacker is in between the supplicant and the authenticator usually by acting as a legitimate wireless access point, they can intercept authentication messages, which may include the username and password of the supplicant. The intercepted information can then be relayed by the attacker to the authenticator, making the authenticator believe that the attacker is the supplicant.

In order to reduce the risk of this type of attack, strong encryption is recommended. Another method that can help prevent the attack is the application of a virtual private network or VPN. Both of these methods ensure that the attacker cannot decipher the messages being transmitted during the authentication session.

Password Guessing

Since the beginning of information technology, entity authentication is usually done with a username and a password. Therefore, password guessing is when an adversary tries to guess the username and password and then authenticate as the legitimate user. Obtaining usernames is not difficult for an attacker. This is because a username is frequently just an email address of that user or the attacker might know the naming convention used by that particular organization. Sometimes the attacker even has an access to the directory containing all the usernames of an organization. This is especially the case for an internal attacker. For the password guessing attack, the attacker simply guesses one or more passwords that are likely to be the one used by the user.

The first method that an adversary can use to guess a password is a *brute-force attack*, which is also known as an exhaustive search. This is an attack where the attacker tries to generate all possible combinations of a password and attempts to authenticate to the system using the username with different combinations of password. The amount of time taken to carry out this attack depends on the size of the password. In simple terms,

In order to protect users' passwords and credentials, encryption techniques such as AES-128 and AES-256 can be applied. This way, even if the information is sniffed by an attacker, they will still not be able to read it in a meaningful way, making it more secure.

Replay Attacks

A *replay attack* is another popular way to attack authentication mechanisms. To carry out this attack, it is required that an attacker has an access to the network between two communicating principals. This type of attack can still work even though the attacker does not have an access to the plaintext format of users' credentials.

The replay attack is done by the attacker copying an entity's password or credential and using it to carry out authentication with the other entity. The purpose is to impersonate the user whose password or credential is copied. Put it simply, the attacker copies the message or credentials and then sends this same message to an authenticator, hoping that they will be successfully verified.

Timestamping is when the sender of the message records and includes the time that the message is constructed and transmitted. When the message is received, the recipient can check whether the time on the message is current or has already past. It is, therefore, a mechanism that can be used to prevent this type of attack.

In a typical challenge-and-response mechanism, an authenticator generates a random string called a nonce (or number used once) and presents it as a challenge to the supplicant. The supplicant will then manipulate the challenge in some predefined way such as encrypting it or hashing it before sending the result back to the authenticator as the response. Next, the authenticator verifies the received response. The strength of the challenge-and-response mechanism depends on the randomness of the challenge. It should be noted that the challenge has to be freshly generated each time the authentication session takes place. A simple view of the challenge and response is as follows:

$$Supplicant \rightarrow Authenticator : Request\ to\ Authenticate$$

$$Authenticator \rightarrow Supplicant : Nonce_{Authenticator}$$

$$Supplicant \rightarrow Authenticator : H(Nonce_{Authenticator}, Password_{Supplicant})$$

if the size of the password is 8 characters, which is 64 bits, the total number of password combinations will be 2^{64}. With today's technology, the number of different guesses per second by an ordinary computer is approximately 100,000,000 guesses. That means it would take a normal computer around 184,467,440,737 seconds or 5,850 years.

It is clear that password brute-force attack is very time consuming due to the large number of password combinations. Therefore, to decrease the time required to guess the password, a dictionary attack can be carried out. A *dictionary attack* is a method an attacker uses to breach a password-protected authentication mechanism by attempting each word in a dictionary as a password. It is possible for this attack to be successful because many users tend to use word in a dictionary as their password. However, the dictionary attack becomes more complicated when users choose longer and stronger passwords. As a result, a new variety of the dictionary attack, known as password dictionary attack, has been formed.

A *password dictionary* attack is still considered a brute-force attack and also a dictionary attack. This time an attacker tries to guess a user's password by using a dictionary of commonly used passwords. Over a period of time, an attacker or a community of attackers has collected a lot of data containing passwords that are thought to have been chosen by users. The data in the database can then be used as password guesses when attempting to compromise the authentication system. In addition, these commonly used passwords can lead to an attack called password spraying attack.

A *password spraying attack* is a type of attack that relies on a few popular passwords that are used by users. These passwords are used to attempt to access a large number of accounts. In other words, a password spraying attack is when an attacker takes a large number of accounts or usernames and tries to authenticate them with one or a very small number of passwords. It is done with the hope that they will be successfully authenticated by the authenticator, hence being able to impersonate the legitimate user.

All the password guessing attacks can be prevented by asking users to select a strong password and to stop password reuse in different password-protected systems. More detail on passwords and password-based authentication will be provided in the next chapter.

Credential Stuffing

Credential stuffing is actually another form of password guessing attack. This type of password attack has become more widespread in recent years. *Credential stuffing* is an attack that takes advantage of the users' failure to select different passwords for different accounts. In other words, credential stuffing works because users reuse their password for various accounts, and statistically more than 73% of passwords are reused.

The way the attacker carries out credential stuffing is as follows: First, the attacker tries to acquire a password or credential of a user by breaching a system or from a leaked-password directory that may be available on the Internet. A compromised password is then used in an attempt to log into various other accounts or systems of the same user.

There are several suggestions made by OWASP for preventing credential stuffing attack. They include the use of different passwords for different accounts, the use of a CAPTCHA, and the use of multi-factor authentication (MFA) which will be explained in detail in Chapter 6.

Social Engineering

Social engineering is considered a very powerful approach to attacking user authentication. Social engineering techniques usually involve the use of personal and interpersonal skills, but very often without the need of information technology. When carrying out social engineering, what an adversary does is to try to trick a user into believing that they are required to provide some specific information or even perform a specific action. In the context of information security, social engineering is normally carried out with an aim of having the user disclose their confidential information.

For example, a social engineer might act as a system administrator, ring a user, and inform them that their user account needs an immediate fix. The user, being worried and scared as well as believing that this is a genuine request, provides the attacker with their username and password. The attacker can now log into the user's account and accomplish their goal of impersonating the user.

Nowadays, social engineering comes in three different shapes and forms. They are in-person social engineering, phone social engineering, and digital social engineering.

In-Person Social Engineering

In-person social engineering is carried out in order to gain access and gather confidential information. A common example is when an adversary pretends to be a technician to gain access to an organization or even employees' computers. In some cases, a person is hired as a rogue employee so that they can gain access to the competitor's information and premises. Several other notable examples of the in-person social engineering techniques include neurolinguistic programming (NLP), six degrees of separation, and bar hopping.

Neurolinguistic programming or *NLP* is performed by an attacker in order to get another person to like them. Once the attacker gets physically close to the target, they will try to match the voice, tone, vocabulary, and body language so that the target subconsciously becomes more comfortable. This way, the social engineer is able to control the conversation, which allows them to direct the conversation and gain what they are after – information.

Six degrees of separation is when a social engineer selects a target and uses social media to gain their trust. In other words, the attacker first identifies a victim, which could be an executive of a target company. The attacker then tries to reach out the victim's friends and family on social media. They will eventually request an introduction to the victim via the friends or family as a mutual friend. Once the victim is comfortable with the attacker, the attacker can begin the process of going after the information they want.

Bar hopping is basically when a social engineer buys a victim a few drinks in a pub or at a bar with an aim of getting the victim drunk, so that information can be extracted from them more easily. This is done with the fact that people tend to talk more when they are drunk.

Phone Social Engineering

The phone social engineering is said to be the most common method of social engineering. The preceding administrator phone call is just one example of this technique. The phone social engineering technique is typically used to apply anger and panic and to carry out a vishing attack.

The *anger* tactic begins by an attacker tracking the movement of the executive-level employees. Suppose an executive is about to leave for another city or country; the attacker will make a call to the executive's office and fake their frustration that they cannot access some very important files. The attacker will at some point pretend to be very angry and demand access to those files immediately. The ultimate objective is for the office employees to give in and the attacker able to access those files.

In the *panic* tactic, an attacker makes a phone call to a user saying that their account has been compromised. The attacker convinces that user that the attacker is a person from the technical support unit and is able to help. However, in order to fix the problem, the attacker informs the user that a username and password are required. In many cases, the social engineer pretends to walk the user through the process, making them believe that this is a complex issue and the attacker is helpful as well as authentic. The problem is that the user has already given the adversary their confidential information.

Vishing occurs when a social engineer, pretending to be a bank, rings a target with a prerecorded message. Typically, the message informs the target of an unusual activity of their bank account. The automated message then instructs the target to make a phone call to a specified number. When the call is made, the victim is asked to enter the credit card number, bank account number, and other confidential information such as date of birth and expiration date of the credit card. This way, the attacker can end up with the information necessary to access the account and make fraudulent use of the credit card.

Digital Social Engineering

Digital is another social engineering technique that is gaining popularity these days. Many tactics have been employed by an attacker, including pretexting, device leave behind, broad-based phishing, and spear phishing.

Pretexting is when an attacker sends an email with a trustworthy-looking domain. The email is made to look like it is from an executive-level employee or a known contact. For example, Figure 3-10 shows an email that is sent from a fake domain `sut.co.th`, which looks very similar to the legitimate one of `sut.ac.th`. It is also sent with a real name of a known contact, `Sirapat Boonkrong`.

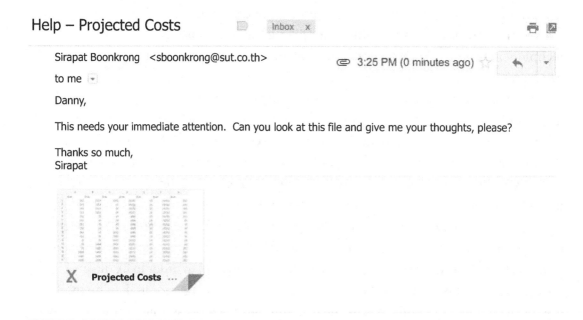

Figure 3-10. *Example of Pretexting*

Once an attention is received from the recipient, the attachment might be clicked and the malware is installed on the target's computer, which can allow an attacker to monitor or gain access to the machine.

The *device leave behind* tactic is another example of digital social engineering. This is when an attacker intentionally leaves behind a USB flash drive, an external hard disk, or any type of storage device around an office. The adversary often writes a tempting label on such device, such as salary records or secret documents. Anyone who falls for this trap and uses the device can be infected by malicious software once the device is plugged into their computer. Again, if the machine is infected, the adversary will be able to access it. Hence, confidential information can be obtained by the attacker.

The next tactic in the digital social engineering is *phishing*. A phishing attack uses email, social media, or instant messaging application to trick victims into providing confidential information or visiting malicious websites. Statistically, a phishing attack can successfully compromise around 1 in 20 people.

A typical phishing attack aims at compromising a generic group of users, which sometimes can be called broad-based phishing. The *broad-based phishing* technique begins with an attacker trying to acquire a list of email addresses. The attacker designs an email that looks relevant to a broad group of users, such as from Google. The phish email is then distributed. The adversary waits and sees whether any users fall for their trick. If so, some secret credentials will be collected by the attacker and will be used to access the users' accounts. Figure 3-11 illustrates an example of a broad-based phishing email.

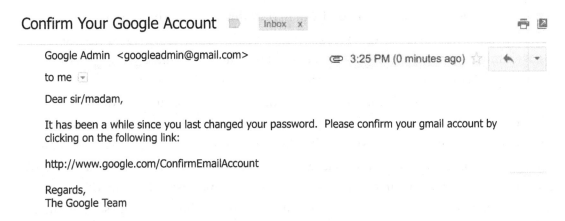

Figure 3-11. *Example of a Broad-Based Phishing Email*

Another form of phishing is known as spear phishing. *Spear phishing* usually requires more time and research for designing a more specific email for a more specific group of target users. The email may be from a university or a bank so that the email looks more personal, which plays on emotions such as fear and curiosity. The aim of spear phishing is the same as the broad-based phishing, which is to gain confidential information, especially users' login credentials. The way spear phishing is carried out is that an adversary picks their targets and starts designing an email which looks legitimate. The victim, who believes that the email is really from a trusted source, provides secret credentials. The attacker can then use them to access sensitive data. An example of a spear phishing email is shown in Figure 3-12.

Figure 3-12. *Example of a Spear Phishing Email*

It should be noted and understood that in phishing attacks, when a phishing email appears to be from or to be targeting the executive-level employees in an organization or a government agency, the phishing attack becomes a *whaling attack*. Of course, the aim of the attack is to steal sensitive information or to gain access to a computer system.

Since it is easier to hack humans than machines, there needs to be a way to prevent social engineering. A better way to reduce the risk of being attacked by social engineering is to educate users so that they become more aware of the risk. Another way is for users to be more cautious. That is, when an email is received, the users should look more carefully at the domain of the sender's email. In some cases, if unsure of the email or the actions asked to be carried out, the users can always check with the source, such as their university or their bank. Moreover, in the case of in-person social engineering, users should be careful not to give out any confidential information to strangers.

In order to make the different types of threat and their countermeasures more intuitive and accessible, they are summarized in Table 3-1 as follows.

Table 3-1. *Potential Threats to Authentication and Countermeasures*

Potential Threats to Authentication	Possible Countermeasures
1. Default Passwords	- Use unique default passwords - Force users to change the default passwords
2. Eavesdropping	- Use strong encryption
3. Replay Attacks	- Apply a challenge-and-response mechanism
4. Man-in-the-Middle Attacks	- Use strong encryption - Use a virtual private network (VPN)
5. Password Guessing	- Create strong passwords - Stop password reuse
6. Credential Stuffing	- Use different passwords for different accounts - Apply multi-factor authentication
7. Social Engineering	- Increase user awareness

Summary

This chapter introduces different methods and factors of authentication, including something you know, something you have, and something you are as well as other existing factors. Authentication, as claimed, is said to be the first line of defense before an adversary enters a system or a network. It is not without any risks, however. The chapter, therefore, presents threats that are common to authentication mechanisms. In addition, suggestions to countermeasures that can help reduce the risks from those threats are also explained.

Bibliography

Al-Fairuz, M. A. (2011). *An Investigation into the Usability and Acceptability of Multi-channel Authentication to Online Banking Users in Oman.* Ph.D. Thesis, University of Glasgow, School of Computing Science, Glasgow.

Boonkrong, S. (2012, December). Security of Passwords. *Journal of Information Technology, 8*(2), 112–117.

Boonkrong, S. (2014). *The Art of Protecting Networks and Information.* Bangkok, Thailand: King Mongkut's University of Technology North Bangkok Press.

Jesudoss, A., & Subramaniam, N. P. (2014). A Survey on Authentication Attacks and Countermeasures in a Distributed Environment. *Indian Journal of Computer Science and Engineering, 5*(2), 71–77.

Perez, L. P. (2015). *Seamless and Strong Authentication on Mobile Devices Based on User Activity.* Ph.D. Thesis, Universidade Da Beira Interior Engenharia, Portugal.

Todorov, D. (2007). Mechanics of User Identification and Authentication: Fundamentals of Identity Management. New York, USA: Auerbach Publications, Taylor & Francis Group.

Vongsingthong, S., & Boonkrong, S. (2015, July). A Survey on Smartphone Authentication. *Walailak Journal of Science and Technology, 12*(1), 1–19.

CHAPTER 4

Password-Based Authentication

Among today's factors and methods of authentication, the something-you-know factor, more specifically password, is the most commonly used. It remains the main method for proving user's identity for email accounts, Internet banking accounts, and other online services. This is understandable given the fact that every user is only required to remember their password, instead of having to carry an authentication token or an additional smart card.

Apart from its convenience, another reason that the something-you-know factor is favored by many systems and services is because of its simplicity. The most basic setup is where a supplicant would like to authenticate themselves to the authenticator. Assuming that they both share the knowledge of the password (normally, the supplicant sends it to the authenticator during the registration process), the exchanges of messages in a basic password-based authentication mechanism are as follows:

$$Supplicant \rightarrow Authenticator : Supplican's ID, Password_{Supplicant}$$

$$Authenticator \rightarrow Supplicant : Authentication\ Succeeded\ or\ Failed$$

This is, as mentioned, the most basic setting of the password-based authentication protocol. Other more secure variations have been proposed and will be explained in this chapter. Having said that, because of its simplicity, it has become a mechanism of choice of many systems, services, and protocols.

Due to its popularity in being the main authentication method, it is important to understand how to securely choose and store passwords in such a way that it can prevent attackers from cracking the users' passwords. This chapter discusses many aspects of password security, starting from a way to generate a secure password to ways to securely

© Sirapat Boonkrong 2021
S. Boonkrong, *Authentication and Access Control*, https://doi.org/10.1007/978-1-4842-6570-3_4

store a password. Moreover, other existing variations of passwords will be illustrated. It will be explained that the most commonly used method for storing passwords today, that is, MD5 or SHA-1 hashing, may not be the best solution. Thus, better solutions in salting passwords and dynamic salting and placement are introduced.

Passwords

Password, as already suggested, is the most popular authentication method in computing today. That is why we feel that there is a need to discuss passwords in detail.

Before going any further, let us briefly establish here what an ideal password should be. On the whole, it has been suggested that an ideal password should be something that a user can remember, something that a computer can verify, and something that nobody else can guess. This sounds easy, but is difficult to achieve. The problem with passwords nowadays is that people tend to choose "bad" passwords. These are the passwords that are easy to "crack." What is the solution to this? One solution is to use randomly generated cryptographic keys. This would make the work of cracking a password equivalent to the work of a brute force or exhaustive key search. Does using randomly generated cryptographic keys for passwords sound plausible? Let us compare keys and passwords.

Keys vs. Passwords

Suppose an attacker Trudy is confronted with a 64-bit cryptographic key. That means there are possible 2^{64} keys in total; thus, on average, Trudy must try 2^{63} keys before finding the correct one.

This time, suppose Trudy is confronted with an eight-character password. Each character is 8 bits long, which means there are 256 possible choices for each character. Therefore, the total number of possible passwords is $256^8 = 2^{64}$ passwords. The number appears to be equivalent to the exhaustive key search problem. But, is it really?

One issue with passwords is that users do not select passwords at random. The reason is because they have to remember it. For example, users are more likely to choose an eight-character password as *password*, rather than something random like *s9@KOpwA*. The implication of this is that clever attackers would make far fewer than 2^{63} guesses before getting the correct password. In other words, the actual number of passwords is far fewer than the number of keys of the same size. The majority of randomly generated passwords is not taken into account since they are not used anyway. It could, therefore, be claimed that the nonrandomness of passwords reduces the amount of work carried out by attackers to crack a password and is also at the root of many of the most serious problems with passwords.

Choosing a Password

It has been mentioned that weak or bad passwords create problems with security. Examples of bad passwords include "Alice", "Doraemon", "09111979", and "JohnSmith". The first password sample, "Alice", is just a name of a user. This would be a very easy guess. The second password, "Doraemon", would also be easy to guess if anyone knows that the user is a fan of Doraemon, a popular Japanese cat robot. The third is just the user's date of birth, and the fourth contains a first name and a surname of the user. It is clear that all of these examples are weak passwords, because they are not difficult for attackers or anyone to guess.

Authentication can be thought of as the first line of defense of a network or a system. That means security can be said to rest on passwords as a main authentication method. Therefore, passwords should be difficult to crack and easy for users to remember. Examples of a better password include "sHJiLJM50Emim", "876261400154", "D0raem0n", and "IaratTKb". Let us analyze each one in turn to see whether it fits our criteria for good passwords: easy to remember and difficult to guess.

The first password, "sHJiLJM50Emim", appears to be random, which makes it very difficult to guess. However, it is not easy to remember. The second password, "876261400154", consists of 13 digits. This seems difficult to guess, but also difficult to remember. It has been documented that well-trained military personnel are only able to memorize up to 12 digits. That means for regular users, it is near impossible to memorize that many random digits. The third password, "D0raem0n", looks a good password due to the mixture of letters and numbers. However, this may not be the case, because if anyone knows that the user is a fan of Doraemon, they could try to make a guess. The fourth example, "IaratTKb", is difficult to guess. It is also very easy to remember, even though the password appears to be random. This fourth example of password is made by a password creation method known as a passphrase.

A *passphrase* is a series of characters derived from a set of words or a sentence. One way to generate a passphrase is that a user thinks of their favorite sentence, then takes the first letter of each word, and puts them together. For example, a user's favorite sentence might be "I adore reading all the Three Kingdoms books." Taking the first letter of each word, the passphrase formed from this sentence would be "IaratTKb". Users do not actually have to take the first letter of each word. Any letter can be used, but taking the first letters would be the easiest to remember.

Passphrases are said to be the source of the better passwords that should be used. The following widely published and well-known password experiment confirms this claim. The experiment divides people into three groups. Group A selects passwords consisting of at least six characters, with at least one non-letter. Group B selects passwords based on passphrases. Group C selects passwords consisting of eight randomly selected characters. The aim of the experiment is for the experimenters to crack those chosen passwords, and the results are as follows: In Group A, about 30% of passwords are easy to crack, and users find their passwords easy to remember. In Group B, about 10% of the passwords are cracked, and users find their passwords easy to remember. In Group C, about 10% of the passwords are cracked, but users find their passwords difficult to remember. From the password experiment, it is clear to see that passphrases provide the best option for passwords. This is because they are difficult to crack, yet easy to remember.

Quality of a Password

In theory, however, it is possible to measure the quality of a password using what is known as *password quality indicator* or *PQI*. Before going into the detail of PQI, it is necessary to reemphasize that when an adversary attacks a password, they simply try different combinations until a match to the correct password is found. The strategy that can be applied by an attacker is to try commonly used passwords before trying to brute force all combinations of password candidates. In other words, a likely path followed by a password attacker could be in the order of

- Trying regular dictionary words

- Trying passwords in password dictionary

- Trying one or two variations of characters in the regular dictionary words

- Trying all possible combinations of lower case letters, upper case letters, and digits based on words in the regular dictionary

- Brute forcing all possible combinations of password candidates

On the whole, the quality of a password depends on how long it takes to find the correct match of that particular password. The longer it takes, the better the quality of the password is. Therefore, it is claimed that the quality of a password can be measured by *how different it is from a dictionary word, how long it is*, and *how big the password character set is.*

One method for measuring the difference between two strings is to use Levenshtein's editing distance. This method practically counts the number of single character manipulations – insertion, deletion, or modification – needed to make the two strings the same. For example, the distance between "bat" and "cat" is 1, and the distance between "net" and "bat" is 2. This means that how different a password is from words from the dictionary can be measured by checking Levenshtein's editing distance.

The second factor of the quality of a password is how long it is. The length of a password is basically the number of characters contained in the password. It is believed that the length of a password is the key in deciding how long it takes to crack it.

Thirdly, it is necessary to understand that a password is made of different characters from different character groups or character sets. It is well documented that printable characters can be divided into four groups, which are

- Group 1 contains 26 lower case letters:

  abcdefghijklmnopqrstuvwxyz

- Group 2 contains 26 upper case letters:

  ABCDEFGHIJKLMNOPQRSTUVWXYZ

- Group 3 contains 10-digit characters:

  0123456789

- Group 4 contains 31 special characters:

  ~!@ $ # %^& * ( ) _ - + = {} | [ ] \ : " < > ? ; ' , . /

Therefore, in order to measure the character sets used in a password, the *password complexity index* or *PCI* has been proposed. In detail, the values of 26 is assigned to Group 1, 26 is assigned to Group 2, 10 is assigned to Group 3, and 31 is assigned to Group 4. This means that if a password contains a character from Group 1, the value of 26 is added to this password's PCI. If a password also contains a character from Group 4, 31 will be added to its PCI, and so on. However, the value of each Group is only added once. In other words, if the characters of a password are only drawn from Group 3, such as

"12345", its PCI value will only be 10. In addition, if a password contains only characters from the same group, it is said that the password has the *Standard Password Format*. A password is said to be in the standard format if it has the PCI value of 10. For example, "12345", "987654", and "234982734" are in the standard format. However, "ab12345", 987654xy", and "12+34aB" are not.

Using the preceding information, the effective length of a password can be calculated as follows: Suppose a password has the PCI value c and length m. The number of all possible password combinations of the same format is c^m. This implies, for example, that it is possible to find the length (L) of all possible passwords in the standard format, which has the PCI value of 10. That is, the equation $c^m = 10^L$ is obtained. L can, therefore, be calculated by the equation $L = m * log_{10}c$. Here, L is known as an effective length of a password. For example, the effective lengths of the passwords "abcdefghi" and "A\$b8" are 12.34 and 7.88, respectively.

What this tells us is that the password quality indicator or PQI can be defined as a pair of (D, L), where D is the Levenshtein editing distance of the password to the dictionary words and L is the effective password length. It has been found that when $D \geq 3$ and $L \geq 14$, a password is considered a good password. As we know, $D \geq 3$ means the password is at least three characters different from the dictionary words, and $L \geq 14$ means that there are at least 10^{14} possible combinations of passwords to be tried to crack.

Apart from the preceding method, which can be used to measure the quality of a password, the probability of a password being cracked can also be analyzed as follows: Let L be the length of time a password is valid, G be the number of password guesses possible in one second, A be the number of possible characters in each password position, M be the password length, and P be the password space, which is calculated by $P = M^A$. The probability or the likelihood N that a password can be cracked is, thus, calculated by $N = (L * G)/P$.

For example, let us assume that a password is valid (L) for the length of 30 days or 2,592,000 seconds and the number of password guesses (G) that can be made in 1 second is 100,000,000 guesses, using an ordinary computer. Thirdly, the number of possible characters in each password position (A) is 93, which comes from the 4 possible character groups stated previously. Fourthly, the password length is 8. This means that $P = 8^{93}$. Therefore, the probability of the likelihood (N) that the password will be cracked is $N = (2,592,000 * 100,000,000)/8^{93} = 2.67 * 10^{-70}$.

This section explains issues with the way users choose their passwords and recommends a simple method for selecting a better password. Once a password is chosen, the quality of the password can also be examined using a couple of methods, as explained. After a password has been selected, the next step is to securely store it. Next section provides explanation and analyses of different password storing methods.

Storing Passwords

In the past few years, a number of high-profile companies have seen their passwords leaked to the online public even though a lot of efforts have been put into protecting them. Unfortunately, disclosure of password databases is one of the main aims of hackers' community. Therefore, it is important to understand how passwords can be stored and what each storing method means for the security of passwords. Let us go through and analyze each method in turn.

Plaintext Passwords

The most basic way that a password can be stored is in plaintext. This means that in a password file or a password database, usernames and passwords are stored in a human-readable form. That is, if a password is *testpassword*, it is also stored in a database as *testpassword*. When a user enters their username and password, the system checks them against the database to see if they match.

This is the worst possible method for storing passwords, in security context. Most reputable systems and websites do not store passwords in their plaintext form. This is because if the password database is obtained or accessed by an attacker, everybody's passwords are immediately known and compromised.

Encrypted Passwords

In order to reduce the risk of passwords being exposed as plaintext, some systems and websites have adopted encryption as their solution. Encryption, as a reminder, uses a secret key to transform a plaintext password into a random string of text or ciphertext. This means that if an adversary were to get hold of a password database, they would not be able to see what the real passwords are. Only passwords in ciphertext format would be seen. The adversary would need to have the secret key to decrypt them. This does not sound so bad, does it? An example of how passwords are stored in encrypted format is illustrated in Table 4-1.

Table 4-1. *Examples of Encrypted Passwords*

Password	Encrypted Password
Admin	C18A9E9AA6ABA7C3D188F944FC78E99E
password	E00460FD7EB0917D9BA8C9F35A65FFBC
superman	0BBCD954C56B60CC494925BEE1D3C758
D0raem0n	BEF5EDC17F05DE6B3C9E9FCBCBB2FA21
MtFbwY	FA624063C11E1E2DB37646AF727EB066

There are several issues with this method. The first is the type of cryptography to be used. Would symmetric cryptography or asymmetric cryptography be more suitable? If symmetric cryptography were to be used, how many keys would be required? Would one key be used for all entries, or would a different key be used for each entry? If one key were used to encrypt all passwords and an attacker were able to get hold of the key, all records would be compromised. If one key were used for each entry and there were thousands of records, key storage would create another problem. This is, therefore, a key management problem. On the other hand, if asymmetric cryptography were to be used, efficiency of computation would be something to consider.

Another problem with this method is that the secret key, both symmetric and private key, is often overlooked and stored on the same machine or server that stores passwords. What happens if the server gets hacked? The hacker would not have to do much work to obtain the secret key, which would allow them to decrypt all the passwords. This implies that this method is not as secure as it seems.

Hashed Passwords

Hashing is similar to encryption in the sense that it transforms a password into a random string of letters and numbers. However, as already explained, hashing ensures at least two things. Firstly, it is infeasible to do the reverse of a hash. It is not possible to take the hashed password and run the hashing algorithm backward in order to get the original password. Secondly, it is very improbable that two different passwords will produce the same output of random string of letters and numbers.

Hashing is, or at least used to be, the most widely used method for storing passwords both on a local network and on the Internet. A hash function works by taking a password as its input and scrambling it to produce a seemingly random result. Two popular hash functions used for storing passwords are MD5 and SHA-1. Examples of what passwords look like after being hashed are shown in Table 4-2.

Table 4-2. *Examples of Hashed Passwords*

Password	MD5	SHA-1
admin	21232f297a57a5a743894a0e4a801fc3	d033e22ae348aeb5660fc2140aec35850c4da997
password	5f4dcc3b5aa765d61d8327deb882cf99	5baa61e4c9b93f3f0682250b6cf8331b7ee68fd8
superman	84d961568a65073a3bcf0eb216b2a576	18c28604dd31094a8d69dae60f1bcd347f1afc5a
D0raem0n	3cd70ea8040d94980c4644d6a3e29b3f	058ded9bbbadf334515454d8030bbff8c50b0f89
MtFbwY	b4e7d9a5aed04ac29736a311433dfde6	73160bfef9d2b95f4fce443d4283a13105279bb8

Hash functions are often used in password systems because instead of storing passwords in clear text, only the hash values of the passwords are stored. Since it is almost impossible to reverse the hash, the hashing method seems to be a secure way of keeping passwords.

When a user logs into a system, the hash value of the entered password is computed and compared with the hash in the password database. If they match, the password is correct. If not, the user will have to give another attempt. Moreover, since it is said that the hashes are unique, it is very likely that the user will only be able to log in with the correct password.

Unfortunately, over the past several years, a number of Internet companies found that their password databases had been cracked even though their users' passwords had been hashed. The reason that this had occurred is because there is a downside to this method, which is a type of attack known as the rainbow table attack.

To go into a little bit more detail, the problem with simple hash functions is that it is possible for hackers to precompute hash values of a vast number of passwords and store them in a database. This database of precomputed hash values is known as a *rainbow table*. If a password database leaks, with the help of rainbow tables (which is essentially a list of billions of different hashes and their matching strings of text), hackers can just

79

look up the hashes in the rainbow table. In order to see how this works, just try typing 5f4dcc3b5aa765d61d8327deb882cf99 into Google. It will quickly be seen that it is the MD5 hash for "password".

If hashes are not found in the rainbow table, it means that they are the hashes for long and complex passwords that have not been precomputed yet. This is one reason why picking a long and complex password is a good idea, since hackers will not have had it already precomputed. In addition, it is a good place to mention a relatively new cryptographic hash function known as *Argon2*, which is actually a recommended function to be used for password storing. One special feature that Argon2 has is that it is possible to specify memory cost, time cost and hash length so that the hash function works in a less predicatable way, which in turn makes it harder to crack.

Salted Passwords

A way to ease the concerns of the rainbow table is with a component called *salt*. Salting a hash means adding a random string of letters and numbers, called a salt, to the beginning or end of a password before hashing it. In other words, instead of just hashing a password, $H(password)$, $H(salt \| password)$, or $H(password \| salt)$, where $\|$ means concatenation, is computed.

Suppose a password, "password", is chosen by a user. A random salt value such as "fh90$$PA28" is then generated by the system. Therefore, instead of just computing the hash value of "password", $H(password)$, $H(passwordfh90\$\$PA28)$ is calculated to obtain the hash value 29e20a65f0d0336463b0391174ac74b3 for MD5 or the hash value b6ac9606d892f5af75ec9ceb39435a1e5f567dcf for SHA-1. Or if the system opts to put the salt value in front of the password, the hash value $H(fh90\$\$PA28password)$ is computed to obtain 191673df9b0770e1a32cfd71ae00052e for MD5 and 0debe946b686492301fe4ada680161e885ee8c34 for SHA- 1.

In order to illustrate the security of the salting method, the obtained hash values could be entered into Google, which acts as a rainbow table. One will see that no results are returned, which indicates that no corresponding text has been found. It can be seen that even though the original password is a weak password in "password", the salt value can assist in reducing the risk of it being cracked via the rainbow table. Thus, it can be claimed that by using the salting method, password storage becomes more secure than the normal hashing method. However, the placement of the salt value has only been either as a prefix or a suffix of a password. This has raised one important question. That is, does the position of the salt value affect the strength of password storing?

Dynamic Salt Generation and Placement

It can be seen and confirmed with a simple example in the previous section that using a salt value as a prefix or a suffix of a password increases the security of password storage. However, there has been a study that demonstrates that with repeated experiments, it is possible for an attacker to find a fixed point of the salt placement. Once the position of the salt was found, the security would be drastically reduced by, again, the use of the rainbow table.

Rainbow table has become the main culprit of attacks on passwords. One particular reason is how quickly hashes can be computed. For hashing with the MD5 algorithm, it was found that to construct a rainbow table for alphanumeric passwords that were one to seven characters long, it would take approximately five days. Moreover, it would only take around three and a half days to carry out cryptanalysis on all possible hashed passwords in the rainbow table.

Fortunately, there is one way that can be used to reduce the risk of being attacked by the rainbow table. That is, to dynamically generate salt values and place them at appropriate positions so that the passwords become more tolerant to an attack.

It has been studied and revealed that the three factors that can affect the strength of the password storage are the quality of the password, the generation of the suitable salt value, and the way the salt value is placed into the password.

Password Quality Adjustment

First of all, it is important to inspect the quality of the password registered by the user, before actually storing it. This is done to ensure that it becomes more difficult for an adversary to try to compromise it. During the password inspection process, the password quality index, explained in the "Quality of a Password" section, can be applied. The password quality index requires that a strong password should contain at least eight characters, three of which should be special characters, with some numbers to also be present.

If the quality of the password being inspected is lower than required, it will be adjusted accordingly. This is essentially the dynamic salt generation process. That is, for each password being inspected, a different salt value will be generated. Which salt value is generated depends on the quality and components of each password.

For example, if the original password lacks special characters, some special characters will be added. If the password lacks number, random numbers will be generated and added to the password. This will also ensure that the length and quality of the password is at least of what is required.

Suitable Salt Sizes

Speaking of the required length or size, it is necessary to produce a salt value of the suitable size for each password. It needs to be reemphasized that the quality of a password can be measured by the time taken to crack it. A harder-to-crack password should consist of at least eight characters that contain three or more special characters. A better password should contain numbers as well.

With the specified criteria, together with the study of rainbow table generation and computation of hash values, it is possible to analyze and determine a suitable size of a salt value. From previous studies, it has been found that if the input is nine characters long or larger, then it is very difficult to generate a complete rainbow table or the database with all possible plaintext and hash value pairs. Moreover, the time taken to hash any inputs that are 10 to 32 characters long would take approximately the same amount of time. Anything longer than 32 characters would take noticeably longer. Consequently, it has been claimed that the suitable sizes of a salt value is between 80 and 256 bits or 10 and 32 characters.

The suitable sizes of a salt are now known. Thus, a salt value can be generated for each password. The question is how to integrate the salt value with the original password in such a way that the resultant string is strong enough to prevent attacks.

Salt Placement

Before specifying where the salt value is to be placed in the password, a placement pattern needs to be generated. It is to be understood and realized that the placement pattern should be dynamic since it depends on the starting password and the chosen salt value. That means a different password and different salt value will have a different placement pattern. The placement pattern can be determined as follows.

First, the starting password is used as an input to a hash function, such as MD5, to obtain its hash value. Second, the password and its hash value are converted into binary. The next step is to XOR ($\oplus$) the binary values of the starting password and its own hash value. Only the least significant bit (rightmost bit) of each byte is to be XORed, however. The obtained value will then be used as the rule for the placement of the salt value. In order to make the pattern finding more intuitive, we provide a simple example as follows.

Suppose the starting password is *password*. The password is input into MD5, an example of a hash function, to obtain the hash value of 5f4dcc3b5aa765d61d8327deb882cf99. For the pattern generation purpose, we will only take the first *n* bytes of the hash value, where *n* is the number of bytes of the password. In this example, *password* is eight bytes long, so only the first eight bytes of the hash value is used, which is 5f4dcc3b5aa765d6. The password and the hash value are converted into binary as shown in Table 4-3.

Table 4-3. *Password and Its Hash Value*

Password	01110000 01100001 01110011 01110011 01110111 01101111 01110010 01100100
Hash value	01011111 01001101 11001100 00111011 01011010 10100111 01100101 11010110

Continue with the example, the binary values in Table 4-3 are XORed with one another. As stated, only the least significant bit of each resulting byte will be used as the placement pattern. Using the preceding example, the value 1010101010 is obtained from $0 \oplus 1$, $1 \oplus 1$, $1 \oplus 0$, $1 \oplus 1$, $1 \oplus 0$, $1 \oplus 1$, $0 \oplus 1$, and $0 \oplus 0$, respectively. This is the salt placement pattern for this particular password example.

As mentioned, the obtained value represents how the salt value is to be placed within the password. As far as the position of the salt value is concerned, it has to be noted that putting the salt in front of, in between, and at the back of the password will be avoided altogether. This is because having the salt in any of these positions is considered and proved insecure. Based on an analysis of a study, the following rule is used to determine how the salt value is going to be integrated into the password:

> *If the bit value of the pattern is 0, no salt is to be placed into the password at that position. If there are two consecutive 0 bits in the placement pattern, two salt characters are to be placed into the password at the position. If the bit value of the pattern is 1, one character of salt is placed into the password at that position. If bit values of the pattern run out and there are still unused salt characters, append the rest of the salt characters to the end of the password.*

How Does It All Work?

We have seen that in order to dynamically generate a salt value, the password quality has to be examined. After a suitable salt value has been generated, a placement pattern is determined prior to placing the salt into the password. These steps can be summarized in Figure 4-1.

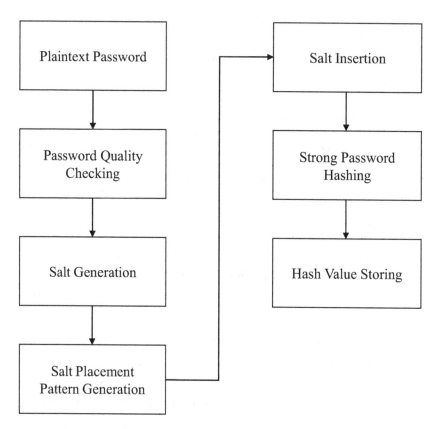

Figure 4-1. *Salt Generation and Placement Algorithm*

We believe that it is best to explain how every step works together here so that the actual dynamic salt generation and placement algorithm can be intuitively followed.

Suppose a user enters a password to be registered on a system in plaintext format. The quality of the entered password is evaluated against the required criteria. A salt value is then generated in such a way that its size is appropriate for this particular password. Note that, with this method, each password will be provided with a different salt value. The objective of this step is to ensure that when combining the password with the salt value, a stronger password will be obtained before hashing or storing it.

Once an appropriate salt value is acquired, a salt placement pattern will be computed. This is done by XORing the least significant bit of each byte of the original password with the least significant bit of each byte of its hash value. The next step is to insert the salt value into the password. This is done in accordance with the salt placement pattern, obtained earlier, and the salt placement rule, stated in the previous section.

What will be achieved at the end of this process is what is believed to be a stronger password. It will then be input to a one-way hash function. The resultant hash value is the value stored in the system's password database.

A Working Example

Now that we have seen the concept and steps necessary for dynamically generating and placing a salt value into a password in order to create a stronger password and more secure method of password storage, a working example is provided in this section. This is done in order to ensure that all the steps are understood and carried out correctly.

Suppose the starting password is *password*. As suggested by the algorithm, the password quality is examined. It turns out that the original password does not contain any special character or number, which means that it does not meet the strong password criteria. Next, a salt value is generated in such a way that when combining with the password, a stronger password is achieved. In this case, let us say that the salt value *%@&03U+* is chosen.

The salt placement pattern can now be computed. This is done by XORing the least significant bit of each byte of password with the least significant bit of each byte of the first *n* bytes of its hash value, eight bytes in this case, to obtain 10101010, which is the salt placement pattern. Let us now insert the salt into the password. It should be reminded that at the moment, we have the original password, *password*; the salt value, *%@&03U+*; and the salt placement pattern, *10101010*.

The salt insertion process begins by looking at the first character of the password, *password*, and the first bit of the placement pattern, whisch is 1. According to the salt placement rule, when the placement pattern is 1, a salt value is to be added at this position. Therefore, the first character of the salt value is taken and placed behind the first character of the password to obtain *p%assword*. We then look at the second character of the password and the second bit of the placement pattern.

The second bit of the placement pattern is 0. According to the salt placement rule, when the placement pattern is 0, no salt is added at this position. We next look at the third character of the password and the third bit of the placement pattern.

The third bit of the placement pattern is 1. That means to be in accordance with the rule, one salt character is to be added at this position. We, therefore, obtain *p%as@sword*.

The next character and the next bit of the placement pattern are next to be considered. The current bit of the placement pattern now has the value of 0, which means nothing will be inserted at this position.

We are now at the fifth character of the password and the fifth bit of the salt placement pattern. The placement pattern bit has the value of 1. This means one character of the salt value will be placed behind the fifth character of the password, which now becomes *p%as@sw&ord*.

The next value of the placement pattern bit is 0, which means that no salt will be inserted at the current password position. The seventh bit of the placement pattern is 1. Therefore, one salt character will be inserted into the current password position. Thus, *p%as@sw&or0d* is obtained.

At this stage, the final character of the starting password and the final bit of the salt placement pattern are reached. Here, the final placement pattern bit has the value of 0, which means nothing is to be added. However, the salt placement pattern has now run out of bits, but there are still three salt characters left. The placement rule states that if this is the case, the remaining salt characters will be appended to the end of the current password. We, therefore, have *p%as@sw&or0d3U+* as our result.

From what has been explained, it can be seen that the salt value and the original password have been integrated with one another to result in a password that meets the strong password criteria. The resultant password, *p%as@sw&or0d3U+*, can now be hashed and stored in the password database.

The process of salt generation and placement for this particular example is summarized in Figure 4-2.

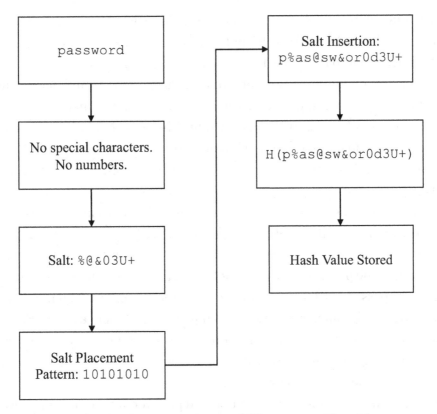

Figure 4-2. *Example of Salt Generation and Placement Algorithm*

Is It Secure?

Now comes an important question. Does the dynamic salt generation and placement method, explained earlier, provide better security than the existing methods? In order to answer this question, a simple analysis can be given as follows.

Although a rainbow table is readily accessible, a hash value is visible, and a salt value is known to an attacker, the way that the salt value is inserted into the password is still unknown. Furthermore, each password is associated with a different salt value, based on its quality. The way the salt is inserted into each password is also different. Thus, compromising the password with the use of rainbow table has become much more difficult.

In addition, it is believed that even though the attacker gets hold of the source code, the salt placement pattern will still be unknown. This is because the pattern is determined by the original plaintext password. This implies that the only way the attacker can find out the salt placement pattern is by knowing the original password, which is not stored anywhere. Thus, it is not possible for the attacker to figure out what the salt placement pattern is. Hence, the password should still be secure.

Further analysis on the security of the dynamic salt generation and placement has also been studied by comparing the attack tolerance between this method and the other existing password storage methods, including the no-salt or hash-only method, multiple-hash-iteration method, fixed salt method (the same salt and position are used for all passwords), and dynamic salt method (different salts concatenated to different passwords).

The analysis was done on 50 different passwords – 25 were weak and the other 25 were stronger. Examples of the weaker passwords were *123456*, *password*, and *qwerty*. On the other hand, the stronger passwords included *Jul1eLovesK3v1n*, *ILov3MyPi@no*, and *Doct0rH0use*. The password cracking tool called hashcat was used to try to compromise the passwords. It turned out that using the dynamic salt generation and placement method, explained previously, was the most secure since no attack was successfully carried out on any of the passwords, weak or strong. Comparing this with other password storage methods, the attack success rates were between 24 and 92%, depending on what the original password was.

On the whole, the dynamic salt generation and placement scheme for password storage is another method that should be in consideration when security is to be achieved in storing passwords.

Grid-Based Passwords

Passwords do not only come in text, number, and special character formats. Due to the issues that traditional passwords have faced over the years, another variety of passwords has gained its popularity. This is known as a *grid-based password*, which simply means using components within a matrix as passwords. One common example is graphical passwords.

Graphical passwords basically use pictures within a given grid. Graphical password mechanisms have been designed as an alternative to traditional passwords. This is based on the fact that humans can remember pictures better than text. In the context of security, if the number of pictures used as passwords is sufficiently large, the password space can become larger than that of textual passwords. This can lead to a better resistance to brute-force attacks.

Principally, a graphical password is an authentication mechanism that works by having users select a correct set of images, sometimes in a specific order, or by asking users to reproduce something that they have created earlier.

From this definition, and since graphical passwords are just an example of grid-based passwords, grid-based passwords can be divided into two categories. They are *recognition-based* and *recall-based* systems.

Recognition-Based Systems

Recognition-based systems are also known as *cognometric* systems or *searchmetric* systems. They require that users memorize a set of images, text, or numbers during password creation or registration and then they must be able to identify their selected elements among others during the login stage.

The very first system in this category was produced in the year 2000 and is called the Deja Vu system, which works by asking the user to select a number of random images generated by the program. The user will then be asked to identify their preselected images in order to be authenticated. An example of the Deja Vu graphical password scheme can be seen in Figure 4-3.

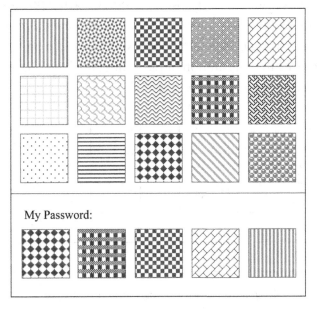

Figure 4-3. *Deja Vu System*

Let us get into the detail of Deja Vu. In the test system (originally done by the creator), a panel of 25 images was displayed, while the user must identify 5 images that matched their preselected ones. In theory, the password space or the number of all possible passwords for this 25-image panel can be calculated as $\binom{N}{M}$ for N images in a panel and M images to be selected by the user. For example, in the Deja Vu test system, the password space is $\binom{25}{5} = 53,130 \approx 2^{16}$, which was claimed by the creators to be resistant to dictionary attacks. One other advantage of this scheme is the resistance to social engineering attacks. This is because the images are generated randomly by the program, which makes it difficult for users to share with or even describe the images to others. However, there are a couple of obvious potential problems. The first is that the choices of the images could be predictable since users may select the images that include their favorite colors. The second is, of course, the risk of shoulder surfing where an attacker can observe and memorize the images selected by the users. As a result, many researchers have stepped away from this traditional recognition-based system to a position recognition-based system instead.

Position recognition-based systems have a similar setting to the traditional recognition-based systems in that users are still provided with a grid. However, with this type of recognition-based systems, users have to memorize the position of their chosen cells rather than the elements they have selected. One of the most famous examples of this type of system is PassLogic, which requires users to select a pattern in the grid of random numbers during the registration or password choosing phase. A typical process of creating a password is shown in Figure 4-4.

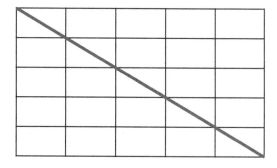

Registered or First Time Password: 20289

Figure 4-4. *A Typical Registration Stage of a Position Recognition-Based System*

Figure 4-4 shows that when a user is presented with a grid filled with random numbers, they select a number of cells of any pattern. In this case, a diagonal pattern is chosen, as displayed on the right-hand side of the figure. Therefore, for the registration purpose, the user's password is created from the numbers lined in the selected pattern, which is 20289, in this particular example.

When the same user tries to log in, they are also presented with a grid of the same size, but with a different random number in each cell. As their login credential, the user simply enters the numbers following their unique cell positions or pattern in relation to the grid. Following on from the same example, the pattern will be the diagonal pattern, from the top left-hand corner to the bottom right-hand corner. This is illustrated in Figure 4-5.

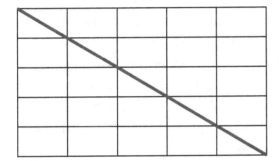

9	3	6	8	0
5	4	2	1	7
0	2	6	8	9
1	5	7	2	3
0	3	4	5	8

Login or Second Time Password: 94628

Figure 4-5. *A Typical Login Stage of a Position Recognition-Based System*

It can be seen that when logging in, the same user enters the numbers that lie in accordance with the registered pattern. In this particular example, the diagonal pattern is used. Therefore, the login password is 94628.

On the whole, the position recognition-based authentication system asks users to create a secret pattern by choosing a number of positions in a given grid of any size. When logging in, the users can create a password by simply following the same pattern or path. As long as the pattern remains unknown to other people, the authentication system is said to still be secure.

The position recognition-based system, as seen from its unique process, provides users with one major advantage, which can be explained as follows. Each time a grid is presented to the users, the numbers in the grid are changed. This means that whenever the users log in, their password changes every time. Hence, a one-time password or

OTP is generated using this authentication method, which makes it less likely that an adversary will be able to guess the actual password. Even though the position recognition-based authentication system appears to offer a certain level of security, it is appealing to study this type of mechanism in more detail, especially in the context of security.

Security Analysis

With a grid-based authentication method, specifically the position recognition-based system, it is thought that its security depends on the size of the grid. In other words, a larger grid would provide more combinations of possible patterns or passwords. Therefore, it is less prone to a brute-force attack.

Let us examine the security of the position recognition-based system in more detail. The security is analyzed in two folds. The first is the examination of the number of possible cell selection combinations (at least eight cells), together with the number of possible numerical passwords from the selected eight cells. Numerical passwords are considered to make it consistent with the previous PassLogic example. This part of the analysis is called *theoretical strength* analysis. The second is the investigation of how users would actually choose their secret pattern in a given grid of various sizes. This part of the analysis is called the *practical strength* analysis.

From the preceding explanation, the strength or security of a grid is said to be depended on the number of possible combinations of numbers or positions. Therefore, the strength of a grid $Grid_{Strength}$ can be computed from the following equation:

$$Grid_{Strength} = \frac{n!}{r!(n-r)!} + 10^r \qquad (4.1)$$

where n is the total number of cells in a grid,

r is the number of cells that users choose (at least eight), and

10^r is the number of possible numerical combinations from the selected r cells.

Note that the numerical value within each cell is between 0 and 9, so there are ten possible numbers.

In order to illustrate the security of a grid, let us assume grid sizes of 30 cells, 60 cells, 90 cells, 120 cells, 150 cells, and 180 cells. Let us first analyze the theoretical strength of the grid of those sizes, with an assumption that the number of cells that a user selects is eight (as eight is the recommended length of a traditional password). Using Equation 4.1, it is possible to quantitatively show the theoretical strength of a grid of each size as follows.

Table 4-4 shows that the strength or security of a grid increases as the grid gets larger. This represents the fact that larger grids can withstand a brute-force attack than smaller ones, *in theory*.

Table 4-4. *Theoretical Strength of Each Grid to Withstand Brute Force*

Grid Size (Number of Cells)	Strength (Number of Possible Combinations)
30	$5,852,925 + 10^8$
60	$2,558,620,845 + 10^8$
90	$77,515,521,435 + 10^8$
120	$840,261,910,995 + 10^8$
150	$5,257,211,409,450 + 10^8$
180	$23,342,337,775,350 + 10^8$

As stated earlier, the practical strength also needs to be explained. A study of how users select cells as their password in each grid size was conducted. Figures 4-6 to 4-11 display how the cells were selected by approximately two hundred volunteers that participated in the study. Each figure shows a heat map that represents the frequency of cell selection. The darker color (red) represents the cells that were selected by a higher percentage of users, whereas the lighter color (green) represents the cells that were selected by very few or none. The numbers represent the percentage of users who selected that particular cell.

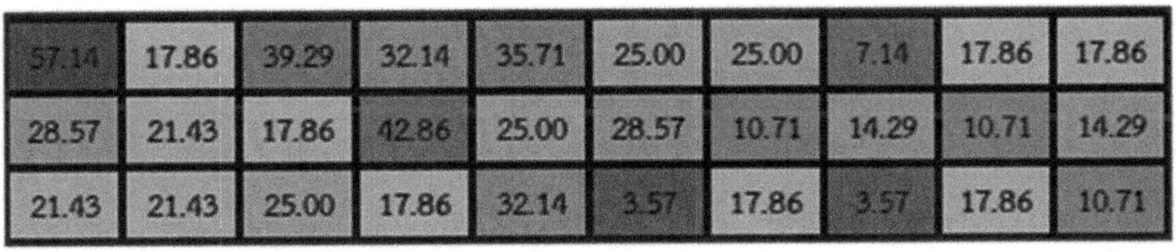

57.14	17.86	39.29	32.14	35.71	25.00	25.00	7.14	17.86	17.86
28.57	21.43	17.86	42.86	25.00	28.57	10.71	14.29	10.71	14.29
21.43	21.43	25.00	17.86	32.14	3.57	17.86	3.57	17.86	10.71

Figure 4-6. *Cell Selection in a 30-Cell Grid*

48.28	31.03	10.34	3.45	6.90	3.45	0.00	3.45	6.90	6.90
31.03	37.93	24.14	13.79	6.90	6.90	13.79	3.45	6.90	3.45
17.24	34.48	34.48	13.79	6.90	10.34	10.34	3.45	6.90	3.45
10.34	20.69	10.34	24.14	0.00	3.45	10.34	17.24	10.34	0.00
17.24	13.79	10.34	13.79	24.14	3.45	13.79	6.90	6.90	6.90
10.34	17.24	6.90	13.79	10.34	24.14	3.45	6.90	3.45	10.34

Figure 4-7. *Cell Selection in a 60-Cell Grid*

25.00	19.64	21.43	10.71	8.93	8.93	8.93	8.93	7.14	10.71
10.71	26.79	8.93	3.57	7.14	7.14	1.79	0.00	5.36	3.57
14.29	7.14	26.79	8.93	5.36	5.36	3.57	3.57	1.79	5.36
12.50	12.50	3.57	17.86	8.93	7.14	5.36	8.93	0.00	7.14
14.29	8.93	7.14	0.00	19.64	10.71	0.00	3.57	0.00	3.57
5.36	3.57	10.71	5.36	3.57	25.00	3.57	3.57	3.57	5.36
7.14	5.36	12.50	5.36	8.93	3.57	17.86	3.57	1.79	7.14
5.36	7.14	5.36	5.36	10.71	7.14	3.57	16.07	3.57	5.36
8.93	7.14	5.36	1.79	5.36	3.57	3.57	3.57	16.07	3.57

Figure 4-8. *Cell Selection in a 90-Cell Grid*

41.94	19.35	6.45	3.23	6.45	0.00	0.00	0.00	6.45	3.23
12.90	29.03	25.81	0.00	6.45	9.68	3.23	6.45	3.23	0.00
6.45	16.13	25.81	16.13	6.45	3.23	9.68	0.00	0.00	0.00
6.45	9.68	6.45	25.81	12.90	6.45	6.45	0.00	0.00	6.45
9.68	19.35	9.68	9.68	19.35	16.13	0.00	0.00	3.23	3.23
6.45	16.13	16.13	9.68	16.13	32.26	16.13	9.68	3.23	0.00
6.45	3.23	12.90	3.23	9.68	6.45	22.58	9.68	3.23	0.00
3.23	19.35	0.00	3.23	3.23	6.45	6.45	16.13	12.90	3.23
9.68	9.68	9.68	3.23	9.68	3.23	3.23	3.23	6.45	9.68
9.68	9.68	0.00	12.90	0.00	3.23	0.00	3.23	3.23	6.45
0.00	9.68	12.90	3.23	3.23	0.00	6.45	3.23	3.23	0.00
0.00	12.90	6.45	3.23	0.00	0.00	0.00	6.45	0.00	6.45

Figure 4-9. *Cell Selection in a 120-Cell Grid*

34.48	24.14	27.59	17.24	3.45	13.79	0.00	0.00	6.90	17.24
24.14	24.14	20.69	6.90	3.45	3.45	3.45	0.00	3.45	3.45
10.34	17.24	13.79	10.34	0.00	6.90	0.00	3.45	3.45	0.00
13.79	6.90	24.14	13.79	3.45	10.34	3.45	0.00	6.90	6.90
6.90	13.79	13.79	13.79	20.69	3.45	3.45	3.45	0.00	0.00
13.79	6.90	17.24	10.34	13.79	6.90	0.00	3.45	0.00	3.45
17.24	0.00	17.24	6.90	6.90	13.79	10.34	0.00	3.45	0.00
6.90	10.34	3.45	3.45	3.45	0.00	10.34	10.34	0.00	3.45
13.79	10.34	0.00	0.00	10.34	3.45	3.45	6.90	0.00	3.45
6.90	13.79	6.90	10.34	3.45	0.00	0.00	0.00	3.45	6.90
0.00	6.90	10.34	6.90	3.45	0.00	0.00	0.00	3.45	0.00
3.45	6.90	13.79	6.90	0.00	3.45	0.00	0.00	0.00	0.00
0.00	10.34	10.34	0.00	0.00	0.00	0.00	0.00	0.00	0.00
6.90	0.00	10.34	3.45	0.00	0.00	0.00	0.00	0.00	0.00
3.45	3.45	6.90	0.00	3.45	3.45	0.00	0.00	0.00	0.00
0.00	3.45	6.90	3.45	0.00	0.00	3.45	3.45	0.00	0.00
6.90	6.90	6.90	3.45	0.00	0.00	0.00	0.00	6.90	3.45
13.79	6.90	10.34	0.00	0.00	3.45	3.45	3.45	3.45	6.90

Figure 4-10. *Cell Selection in a 150-Cell Grid*

28.57	14.29	4.76	14.29	0.00	4.76	4.76	4.76	4.76	4.76
19.05	28.57	4.76	4.76	0.00	0.00	0.00	0.00	4.76	0.00
14.29	19.05	23.81	23.81	4.76	4.76	4.76	0.00	9.52	9.52
9.52	14.29	0.00	28.57	4.76	4.76	4.76	0.00	4.76	0.00
14.29	9.52	19.05	9.52	19.05	9.52	0.00	0.00	4.76	0.00
9.52	9.52	9.52	14.29	9.52	28.57	4.76	4.76	0.00	0.00
9.52	9.52	14.29	19.05	9.52	4.76	14.29	4.76	0.00	0.00
14.29	14.29	9.52	14.29	4.76	0.00	0.00	14.29	4.76	0.00
9.52	0.00	19.05	9.52	14.29	0.00	0.00	0.00	9.52	0.00
9.52	0.00	14.29	9.52	0.00	9.52	0.00	0.00	0.00	9.52
23.81	14.29	9.52	4.76	0.00	0.00	0.00	0.00	0.00	0.00
14.29	9.52	4.76	14.29	4.76	0.00	0.00	0.00	0.00	4.76
14.29	9.52	9.52	14.29	0.00	0.00	0.00	0.00	0.00	0.00
14.29	0.00	0.00	4.76	0.00	4.76	4.76	4.76	0.00	0.00
9.52	0.00	0.00	9.52	4.76	0.00	0.00	4.76	0.00	0.00

Figure 4-11. *Cell Selection in a 180-Cell Grid*

From the heat maps of cell selection, it can be observed that the participants tended to choose the cells toward the left-hand side of the grid, especially in the top left area. The right-hand side, especially in the bottom right area of the grid, was significantly less popular. Many of them remained unchosen. In more detail, the figures show that 26 cells were not picked by any of the users in the 120-cell grid. Exactly 57 cells and 63 cells were not of anyone's choice in the 150-cell grid and 180-cell grid, respectively. These account for 21.67%, 38.00%, and 35.00% of all the available cell positions in the 120-cell, 150-cell, and 180-cell grids, respectively.

The way that the users selected the cells, as seen in the figures, directly affects the strength or security of the grids. In other words, when there are many unselected cells, the combination space or the number of all possible cell selection combinations, based only on the number of the chosen cells, becomes smaller. Hence, it is now relatively easier for an adversary to attempt a brute-force attack on the grid-based authentication mechanism.

In order to confirm what is explained previously, Table 4-5 shows the physical strength of the 60-cell, 90-cell, 120-cell, 150-cell, and 180-cell grids. It can be seen that the combination space or the number of possible cell selection combinations has decreased when being compared with the theoretical strength in Table 4-4.

Table 4-5. *Physical Strength of Each Grid to Withstand Brute Force*

Grid Size (Number of Cells)	Strength (Number of Possible Combinations)	Percentage of Strength Reduction
60	$1, 652, 411, 475 + 10^8$	35.42
90	$48, 124, 511, 370 + 10^8$	37.92
120	$111, 315, 063, 717 + 10^8$	86.75
150	$101, 841, 441, 273 + 10^8$	98.06
180	$681, 927, 413, 310 + 10^8$	97.08

It should now be obvious from Figures 4-6 to 4-11 that the larger the grid size, the higher the number the unchosen cells will be. This, in turns, means that the strength to withstand a brute-force attack has also been reduced. Table 4-5 shows that with the sizes of 150 and 180 cells, the strength has been reduced by almost 100%, physically, with the strength of the 120-cell grid being decreased by almost 90%. This implies that there would be nearly twice less work for an attacker who would attempt to carry out a brute-force attack on those grids than it claimed theoretically.

Recall-Based Systems

A recall-based grid password system is sometimes known as a *drawmetric* system. This is because it requires users to draw, recall, and reproduce a secret drawing. In this type of system, users usually draw their secret diagram on a grid.

The first recall-based system is called *Draw a Secret* or *DAS* which was designed and created in 1999. It works by asking a user to draw on a 2D grid using either a stylus or, more commonly, a mouse. The drawing done by the user can consist of one continuous line or any number of lines within the provided cells in the grid. This drawing is then used as the graphical password template for this particular user.

When attempting to authenticate themselves, the user simply "recalls" and re-draws their picture to match the template. An example of the Draw-a-Secret graphical password scheme can be seen in Figure 4-12.

Please draw your secret image in the grid.

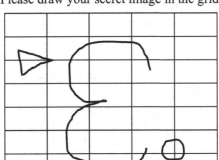

Figure 4-12. *Draw-a-Secret System*

Let us get into the detail of the Draw-a-Secret system. First of all, the usability issue has not really been studied much. However, a study found that users tended to draw simple images with only one to three strokes or lines. The authentication success rate was also found to be only between 57 and 80%. Another aspect of Draw a Secret that cannot be overlooked is, of course, the number of possible passwords. This is also known as the size of the theoretical password space. It is said that the theoretical password space is related to the coarseness of the given 2D grid and the maximum password length. The creator of the Draw-a-Secret scheme stated that for a 5 x 5 grid and maximum length 12, the theoretical password space has a cardinality of 2^{58}.

It can be seen that this particular graphical password scheme provides a theoretical password space comparable to text passwords. However, there is a high possibility that users would make their graphical passwords predictable with only one, two, or three simple lines.

The Draw-a-Secret or DAS graphical password scheme has formed a basis for many other similar schemes. The first to make an improvement on DAS was the BDAS scheme, which added a background image to DAS in order to encourage users to draw more complex passwords. Another interesting recall-based system is called *Passdoodle*, which again was created based on the DAS scheme. However, not only Passdoodle allows users to create freehand drawing passwords, but it also uses a more complex password matching method, which takes into account the number of lines, line colors, and even the drawing speed.

One of the most well-known recall-based graphical password scheme is known as the *Pass-Go* scheme, which was proposed in 2008. The scheme was inspired by an old Chinese board game in which players place tokens on the intersection points of the grid. In the Pass-Go scheme, when registering, users select intersections on the grid as a way to enter their passwords. When the users want to authenticate themselves, all they have to do is to select the correct intersection points. A typical Pass-Go authentication scheme can be seen in Figure 4-13.

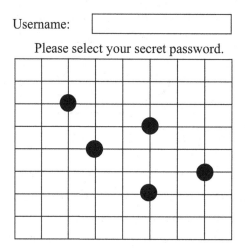

Figure 4-13. *Pass-Go Scheme*

For the security aspect, it is claimed that this particular graphical password scheme offers a very large theoretical password space that is similar to that of a 256-bit password for the most basic Pass-Go scheme. Different colors also add to the complexity of its security. However, the Pass-Go scheme is still susceptible to a shoulder surfing attack.

In the case of usability, the Pass-Go method gives a better result than the original Draw-a-Secret scheme. In other words, the Pass-Go method was tested with over 160 users. The success rate of authentication was approximately 78%, which on average was considerably higher than what the original Draw-a-Secret method has achieved.

Android Pattern Lock

Another graphical password which falls under the recall-based system and is familiar to many users today is the Android pattern lock or the pattern screen lock method on a smart phone. This type of graphical password was introduced by Google in 2008 with the launch of its Android mobile operating system as an alternative to the screen lock password. The pattern lock method is still widely used on Android smart phones until these days.

This pattern lock method provides users with nine dots in a 3 x 3 grid formation. The users draw lines to connect any number of dots to create a pattern, usually between four and nine dots. The pattern is then used as the password for unlocking the smart phone. An example of the Android lock pattern interface is shown in Figure 4-14.

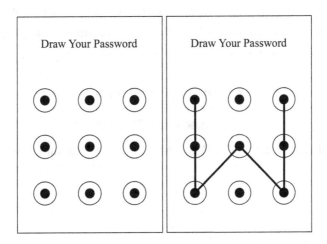

Figure 4-14. *Android Lock Pattern*

It is important to provide an analysis of this type of authentication. The first to be shown is the pattern space or the number of possible combinations of the lock patterns. As mentioned, the Android pattern lock consists of nine dots in a 3 x 3 grid formation. The rules for the pattern to be valid are as follows. The minimum number of dots of the chosen pattern is four and the maximum is nine. There can be no jumps from one dot to another. However, if a dot has already been selected, a jump over that particular dot is allowed. From the number of dots and the rules, the number of possible pattern combinations based on the number of selected dots is shown in Table 4-6.

The problem with the Android pattern lock is not different from that of traditional password. In other words, research has shown that they are also easy to guess. The following is what a research found from an analysis of around four thousand lock patterns. The researcher found that 44% of the patterns were started at the top left dot and 77% of all the patterns were started at one of the four corners. The average number of dots used in a lock pattern was five, which means there are only 7,152 combinations for an attacker to work with. The researcher also discovered that a significant portion of the studied patterns only contained four dots, which would leave the number of possible combinations of 1,624. This is massively fewer than the strength of the four-character passwords, which has 2^{32} or over four billion possible combinations. Moreover, the ways the patterns were drawn were mostly from left to right and top to bottom, which contributes to the easiness of guessing. Therefore, it can be conclusively said that the Android pattern lock is actually worse than the traditional password of the same length in terms of theoretical strength or number of possible combinations. This is especially true when taking into account of how users tend to choose simple lock patterns.

Table 4-6. *Theoretical Strength of Android Pattern Lock*

Length (Number of Dots)	Theoretical Strength (Number of Possible Combinations)
4	1,624
5	7,152
6	26,016
7	72,912
8	140,704
9	140,704
Total	389,112

In addition, a form of attack on the Android pattern lock that cannot be overlooked is the shoulder surfing attack. One research even suggested that it was possible to film from a distance and video process what was recorded in order to learn what the lock pattern of that user was. The result of the research showed that it was possible to crack that pattern lock in five attempts 95% of the time, provided that the video quality was decent enough.

One reason, as mentioned previously, that the Android pattern lock is not difficult to crack is the fact that users tend to choose simple and common patterns. This is equivalent to users choosing such weak passwords as *123456*, *password*, or *letmein*. Many of the lock patterns that are frequently chosen by users are fashioned after an alphabet letter. In many cases, they are even the first letter or an initial of the name of the user, their spouse, or their child. The implication is that the number of guesses could be drastically reduced if an attacker knew the name of the user or anyone close to them. A few examples of commonly used lock patterns that mimic a letter of the English alphabet are shown in Figure 4-15.

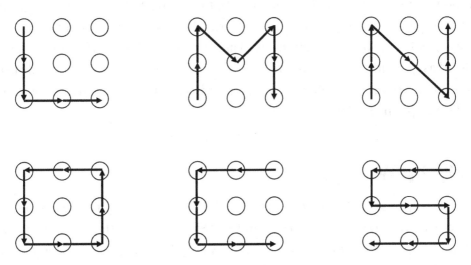

Figure 4-15. *Examples of Weak Android Lock Patterns*

In order to make the Android pattern lock more secure, it is recommended that users choose more complex patterns. This would make it harder for an adversary to trace the precise sequences and patterns. However, similar to the traditional text passwords, more complex patterns could also mean that users cannot remember what the patterns are. Examples of the Android lock patterns that can be categorized as more complex are shown in Figure 4-16.

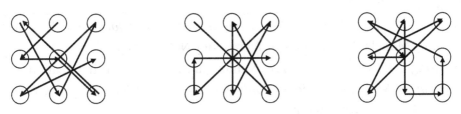

Figure 4-16. *Examples of More Complex Android Lock Patterns*

Summary

Passwords, the something-you-know method, are considered the most popular way for carrying out authentication. This chapter, therefore, explains how stronger passwords can be generated and how to store them more securely. Although currently there is one password storage technique which makes use of randomly generated salt values to assist in making the password storing procedure more secure, this chapter still provides an improved process. The dynamic salt generation and placement is consequently explained and illustrated.

In addition to the traditional text passwords, this chapter describes and discusses an alternative known as the grid-based passwords. These consist of two main techniques, which are the recognition based and recall based. Both of them can also be considered as graphical passwords and have been the basis of several commonly used authentication systems, including the popular Android pattern locks that are on all the Android smart phones today.

Bibliography

Andriotis, P., Tryfonas, T., Oikonomou, G., & Yildiz, C. (2013). A Pilot Study on the Security of Pattern Screen-LockMethods and Soft Side Channel Attacks. *Proceedings of the Sixth ACM Conference on Security and Privacy in Wireless and Mobile Networks*. Budapest, Hungary: ACM.

Belk, M., Pamboris, A., Fidas, C., Katsini, C., Avouris, N., & Samaras, G. (2017). Sweet-Spotting Security and Usability for Intelligent Graphical Authentication Mechanisms. *Proceedings of the International Conference on Web Intelligence* (pp. 252–259). Leipzig, Germany: ACM.

Biddle, R., Chiasson, S., & Van Ooorschot, P. C. (2012, August). Graphical Passwords: Learning from the First Twelve Years. *ACM Computing Surveys, 44*(4), 19–41.

Boonkrong, S. (2012, December). Security of Passwords. *Journal of Information Technology, 8*(2), 112–117.

Boonkrong, S. (2014). *The Art of Protecting Networks and Information*. Bangkok, Thailand: King Mongkut's University of Technology North Bangkok Press.

Boonkrong, S. (2019). An Analysis of Numerical Grid-Based Authentication. *Proceedings of the Ninth International Conference on Information Communication and Management*. Prague, Czech Republic: ACM.

Boonkrong, S., & Somboonpattanakit, C. (2016, February). Dynamic Salt Generation and Placement for Secure Password Storing. *IAENG Journal of Computer Science, 43*(1), 26–37.

Loge, M. D. (2015). *Tell Me Who You Are and I Will Tell You Your Unlock Pattern.* Norwegian University of Science and Technology, Department of Computer and Information Science. Norway: Norwegian University of Science and Technology.

Ma, W., Campbell, J., Tran, D., & Kleeman, D. (2010). Password Entropy and Password Quality. *Proceedings of the Fourth International Conference on Network and System Security.* Melbourne, Australie: IEEE.

Todorov, D. (2007). *Mechanics of User Identification and Authentication: Fundamentals of Identity Management.* New York, USA: Auerbach Publications, Taylor & Francis Group.

Ye, G., Tang, Z., Fang, D., Chen, X., Kim, K. I., Taylor, B., & Wang, Z. (2017). Cracking Android pattern lock in five attempts. *Proceedings of the 2017 Network and Distributed System Security Symposium (NDSS).* San Diego, CA, USA: Internet Society.

CHAPTER 5

Biometric Authentication

It has been explained in the previous chapter that although passwords or something you know is still the most common authentication method, they are not without problems. In other words, authentication schemes based on passwords or something you know are not considered to be highly secure anymore. This is because they are susceptible to many types of attacks such as password guessing, password dictionary, and even shoulder surfing. There have also been suggestions to create longer and more complex passwords. However, they are considered not usable because they can easily be forgotten.

In order to overcome the issues of the something-you-know authentication method, biometric-based authentication or the something-you-are authentication method has become a focus of research. Biometric-based authentication or biometric authentication is basically the process of verifying a person's identity based on their physiological and behavioral phenomena, which can include their face, fingerprint, and iris.

Biometrics seems to have gained popularity over the past decade, especially with the increasing number of smart phones and mobile devices. This is due to a couple of reasons. First, biometrics is said to be more unique than a password. For instance, there is a smaller chance that two people will have the same fingerprint than them having the same password. The second reason is that biometric systems are apparently more secure than the something-you-know systems. This is especially the case for phishing or social engineering attacks, which are normally used to get hold of a person's password. However, without the actual presence of physiological or behavioral biometric feature of an individual, such attacks will not be successful.

From the mentioned facts, it is, therefore, necessary to understand what biometric-based authentication is, how it works, and how it can be evaluated. This chapter also discusses one particular challenge that biometrics needs in order to function to a level that can be accepted. This challenge is finding a suitable biometric threshold value so that it can be appropriately used. A method, with an example, for determining such value is provided in this chapter.

© Sirapat Boonkrong 2021
S. Boonkrong, *Authentication and Access Control*, https://doi.org/10.1007/978-1-4842-6570-3_5

What Is Biometrics?

The term biometrics or biometry comes from two Greek words. This first is *bios*, which means life. The second is *metron*, which means measure. Therefore, biometrics can simply be defined as *life measurement*. However, in the context of information technology and computer security, biometrics is defined as a means of identifying, authenticating, and controlling access by using measurable human biological data. Therefore, biometric-based authentication is a system that uses a person's biometric data, which are unique and specific only to that person, to check and confirm that person's identity.

Nowadays, there are approximately four billion people on the Internet. The verification of a person's identity is seen as one of the major technological challenges. In order to meet the challenge, biometrics is considered a possibility, led by today's advancement in technology and user-friendly experiences.

Biometrics or the use of human body to verify a person's identity may seem like science fiction, but the concept was first thought of years ago back in 1892 by Sir Francis Galton, a cousin of Charles Darwin. Sir Galton analyzed over 8,000 fingerprints and recognized that it was not likely that; in fact, the chance was smaller than one in four; the print of any person would be exactly like that of any other humans. This work was published in a manuscript called *Fingerprints* and would become the first fingerprint classification in the history of science. An excerpt from the publication is shown in Figure 5-1.

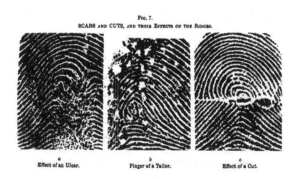

it is a smaller chance than 1 to 4 that the print of a *single* finger of any given person would be exactly like that of the same finger of any other member of the human race.

– *Sir Francis Galton, Fingerprints (1892)*

Figure 5-1. *An Excerpt from Fingerprints by Sir Francis Galton*

Categories of Biometrics

As mentioned previously, biometrics is the measurement of life or the verification of a person's identity using measurable human biological data. Biometrics can be divided into two main categories which satisfy the definition and potential usages. These categories are physiological biometrics and behavioral biometrics.

- Physiological Biometrics – Physiological characteristics of a person are related to the shape of body parts. This means that physiological biometrics is the data and measurement from a part or parts of human body. Examples of physiological characteristics that are used for biometric purposes include fingerprint, the face, palm print, hand geometry, the retina, and the iris.

- Behavioral Biometrics – Behavioral characteristics of a person are related to the pattern of behaviors or actions of a person. This means that behavioral biometrics is the data and measurement from an action of a human. Examples of behavioral characteristics that can be used for biometric purposes include voice, handwritten signature, social media usage pattern, typing pattern (formerly known as keystroke dynamics), heartbeat, and walking pattern (or gait).

The two categories together with their examples are depicted in Figure 5-2.

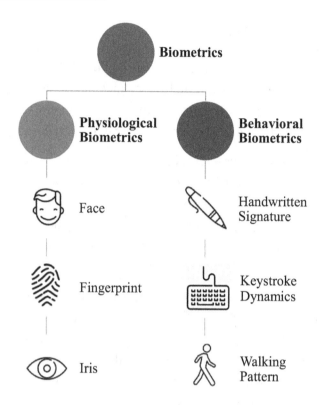

Figure 5-2. *Categories of Biometrics and Their Examples*

Let us get into a little more detail on both categories of biometrics. Physiological characteristics are basically the shape of human body parts, which vary from person to person. As mentioned, they include the face, fingerprint, and the iris. Facial recognition is almost a natural means for verifying a person's identity as in the physical world, a human recognizes another human being by their face. The way it works is that it relies on some specific facial features such as the position of the eyes, nose, and mouth together with the distance between them. Some also attempt to identify other features such as freckles on the face in order to verify the identity of that person. Fingerprint recognition, probably the most commonly used biometric technology today, works by attempting to identify finger ridges and minutia points. It is claimed that some fingerprint technology can provide up to 99% accuracy. As for the iris, it is considered the most unique part of the human body. The iris recognition tries to detect the colors and the geometry around the pupil of the eye.

The main advantage of physiological biometrics is that the data collection process is noninvasive. Many body parts, such as fingerprint, the retina, and the iris, are more stable throughout the life of an individual. However, not all body parts are appropriate due to the fact that they have the potential to change as a person ages, such as their face. Other factors could also affect the performance of facial recognition, for example, the resolution of the collected images, different facial expressions, and lighting conditions. Therefore, an appropriate choice of physiology must be carefully considered.

Behavioral characteristics are the patterns of a person doing something. They include, as mentioned, handwritten signature, keystroke dynamics, and walking pattern. Handwritten signature verification has been proved to be a popular choice over the years. There are two ways that a handwritten signature can be verified. The first is based on the specific features of the image of the signature itself. The second, and more related to the behavioral biometrics, is to look at the features of the actual signing process. The features of the signing process include the signing speed, the pen pressure, the signing directions, and when the pen is lifted during the signing process. Keystroke dynamics is when a human's typing rhythm on a keyboard, a touch screen, or a mobile device is measured and assessed. This method of biometric authentication is nothing new and has been around since the 1990s. The keystroke dynamics works on the principle and belief that it can help verify a person's identity better than a handwritten signature. This is because of the unique features such as the typing pressure, the key press duration, and the typing speed. Recognizing the way a human walks or gait recognition is another example of behavioral biometrics. The method has been developed in order to identify and verify a person by the way they walk. There are two distinct methods that walking pattern recognition can be done. The first is to apply image analysis for extracting unique walking features which helps in the authentication process. The second is to collect walking data such as walking duration and number of steps, which can uniquely identify a person's walking pattern.

The main advantage of behavioral biometrics is that it is difficult to spoof. In other words, what spoofing cannot achieve is to perfectly emulate how a person signs, types, or walks. Therefore, this type of biometrics can help reduce the risk of identity theft. However, the main disadvantage found in behavioral biometrics is its accuracy and performance. What it means is that in order to get behavioral biometrics to work, data need to be collected and analyzed whether it is how a person signs, types, or walks. The accuracy of the verification process is still not as high as that of the physiological methods since it is difficult, even for the genuine entity, to generate the exact same signature, keystroke, and walking patterns.

Biometric Properties

It is necessary to understand that biometric information that can distinguish one individual from another is known as a *biometric modality*. A biometric modality is basically a category or type of human trait, whether it is physiological or behavioral, as explained earlier. No matter what category of biometric information it is, there are a few properties that can help decide which biometric modalities are suitable for real usage. An ideal biometrics should follow these properties:

- Universality – The universality property looks at how common the biometrics is in the general population. That means every person using this system should possess this particular attribute.

- Uniqueness – The uniqueness property simply means that the biometric information used in the system must be able to differentiate one person from others.

- Collectability – The collectability property (sometimes known as measurability) relates to how difficult it is to obtain the required biometric data. Moreover, the obtained data should be easy to extract, evaluate, and measure.

- Permanency – The permanency property means that the biometric information or biometric data used in a system should last a lifetime of an individual. This property reduces the number of times the biometric data has to be collected as a person ages.

- Acceptability – The acceptability property concerns with the willingness of the general public to get into the real usage of the biometric system. In other words, it should not cause any distress, inconvenience, or discomfort to the biometric users.

In order to get some perspective of what the "best" biometrics is for any security applications, Table 5-1 compares some of the biometric technologies based on the biometric properties. For each biometrics, the properties are rated high, medium, and low.

Table 5-1. *Comparison of Biometrics Based on Biometric Properties*

Biometrics	Universality	Uniqueness	Collectability	Permanency	Acceptability
Fingerprint	Medium	High	Medium	High	Medium
Face	High	Medium	High	Medium	High
Iris	High	High	Medium	High	Low
Signature	Medium	Low	High	Low	High
Keystroke	High	Medium	Medium	Low	Medium
Gait	High	Medium	Low	Low	Medium

Table 5-1 shows that there is actually no "best" biometric technologies. However, each of them has some properties that may be attractive to some particular security applications.

Biometric Authentication

As already explained, biometrics allows for the processes of identification and authentication of a person based on some recognizable data which include physiological and behavioral data. In order to understand the process of biometric authentication, it is important to first distinguish between biometric identification and biometric authentication.

Biometric identification is the process of determining the identity of a person. The aim is to answer the "who you are" question. The biometric identification works by capturing a piece of biometric data of a person, such as the person's face, fingerprint, or walking pattern. The data is then compared to those in the biometric database, which already contains many other people's data, in order to identify who that particular person is.

Biometric authentication is a little different in the way that biometric authentication is the process of confirming a person's identity based on their biometric data. That is, when the authentication process is carried out, the person's biometric credential is compared with their previously enrolled biometric data in order to verify or confirm the identity. The detail of biometric authentication is depicted in Figure 5-3.

113

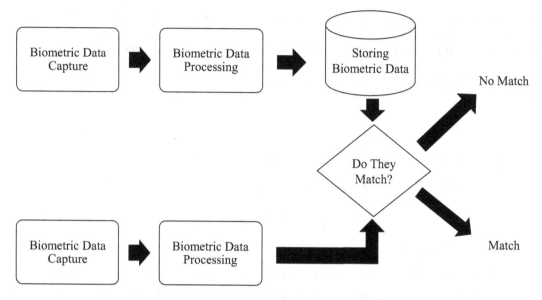

Figure 5-3. *Biometric Authentication Process*

It can be seen from Figure 5-3 that the process is divided into two parts. The first is the registration or the enrolment. The second is the actual authentication. In the enrolment stage, a person must register their identity with the system by having their raw biometric data captured. For example, they could have the fingerprint or iris scanned. In the behavioral biometric case, they could have their signature or walking pattern captured. The captured data is then processed in order to extract unique features that can help distinguish one individual from another. The extracted features can be in the form of baseline values, images, or even binary values. They will then be transformed into a *biometric template* for that particular person. Next, the generated biometric template is stored in a database or any medium where comparisons can be made in the authentication stage.

In the *authentication phase*, the person's biometric data is captured in the same way as in the enrolment stage. The unique features of the captured biometric data are then extracted, which will then be compared to the template stored in the biometric database. If the current biometric data matches with the stored template, it is said that the biometric verification is successful. Otherwise, it is said that the biometric verification fails. In the successful verification cases, the authenticated person is able to confirm their identity to the system. However, in the unsuccessful cases, they fail in the identity confirmation process.

Examples of Biometric Authentication

In order to make the processes of biometric enrolment and authentication clearer, an overview of how they are carried out needs to be given. Therefore, a couple of examples will be provided in this section. The two biometric authentication examples that will be explained here are chosen based on their popularity in the real world. The first is the fingerprint authentication. The second example will be the iris authentication.

Fingerprint Authentication

Fingerprint identification was first introduced in the 19th century as a form of identifying criminals who left their prints at the scene of the crime. Today, it has evolved into a method of authenticating an individual and has become one of the most well-known biometric systems.

Fingerprint authentication captures an image of a person's fingerprint by asking them to place a finger on a scanner. The image of a fingerprint usually appears as a set of dark lines which represent the ridges of the skin and a set of whiter lines which represent the valleys between the ridges. The type of information that can be gathered from a fingerprint is called the fingerprint minutiae, which are practically features of the lines on the fingerprint. Figure 5-4 shows an example of a fingerprint and its common minutiae.

Figure 5-4. *Fingerprint Minutiae*

This leads to the fact that many fingerprint matching algorithms are based on minutiae matching. The recognition of a fingerprint is usually done in two levels. The level 1 detail includes the flow of the ridges on the finger. The level 2 detail deals with the features that are present or absent along the paths of the ridges. Having said that, the feature that is most commonly used for the fingerprint matching purposes is the bifurcation feature. The minutiae matching actually relies on the specific locations of the minutiae and directions of the ridges and valleys.

The minutiae matching algorithms are not the only technique used for matching fingerprints. Pattern matching is another technique that can be used, albeit not as popular. The pattern matching method compares the images of a fingerprint to see how similar they are. The images used in the pattern matching method are the fingerprint template and the one that is being authenticated.

Iris Authentication

Iris authentication is the process of analysis and recognition of the pattern of the iris. The iris authentication system is relatively young compared to the fingerprint authentication system and has only been around since 1994. The iris authentication system is gaining its popularity in security applications. Many studies have claimed that it is one of the most effective biometric methods around due to its high accuracy. However, the main drawback is that, in the context of implementation, it is more complex than the fingerprint authentication system.

The iris authentication system works by capturing an image of a person's iris, which is actually a muscle within the eye surrounding the pupil. The difficulty is that when an image of the eye is captured, there are other parts, considered as noise, present in the frame, too. The noise can include things like eyelash, eyebrow, eyelid, sclera, and pupil. An example of an eye image taken from the CASIA Iris Image Database Version 4.0 displaying parts of the eye is shown in Figure 5-5.

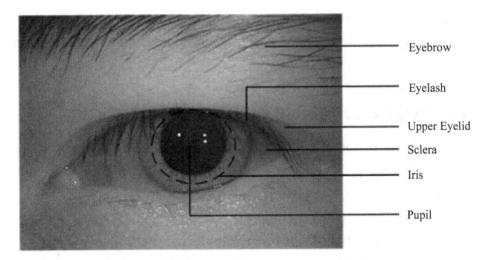

Figure 5-5. *Parts of the Human Eye*

Before recognition of the iris can take place, an algorithm which helps reduce the noise and extract features of the iris needs to be applied. One effective and commonly used algorithm for such purposes is called the Circular Hough Transform (CHT) method. Circular Hough Transform works in two steps. The first is the segmentation step, which divides and separates the eye image into different parts with the iris being the main segment. The second step is normalization or localization, which reduces noise and extracts the main features from different parts of the eye.

The data extracted from the eye, especially the iris, is usually represented in a series of binary bits. That means the iris authentication system verifies the identity of a person by attempting to compare the binary values of an iris image with the binary values of the iris template. For the comparison of the image and template, Hamming Distance (HD) algorithm is applied as a test of statistical difference between the two values. Therefore, the iris authentication is essentially the attempt to determine the proportion of binary bits of the captured iris image that match the binary bits of the iris template.

Performance Metrics of Biometric Authentication

As shown in the previous sections, biometric authentication systems work on the basis of comparing the captured or test biometric information with the existing biometric template. Some metrics or criteria need to be established and explained in order to properly evaluate biometric systems. The common metrics for measuring the performance of biometric authentication are categorized into fundamental performance metrics and authentication performance metrics.

Fundamental Performance Metrics

The fundamental performance metrics are normally concerned with the registration or enrolment process. Two metrics are measured at this stage:

- Failure-to-Enroll Rate (FTE) – The failure-to-enroll rate measures the number of people or the proportion of people from whom a biometric registration system fails to capture or extract biometric information. This usually occurs when a person's biometric data such as a fingerprint or an iris cannot be properly obtained as a sample or a template by the system. The FTE is basically when the biometric system cannot create an enrolment record for a person, which implies that the person will not be able to use the biometric system. The FTE can be calculated by

$$FTE = \frac{Number\ of\ Users\ who\ Failed\ to\ Enroll}{Number\ of\ Users\ who\ Attempt\ to\ Enroll} \qquad (5\text{-}1)$$

- Failure-to-Acquire Rate (FTA) – The failure-to-acquire rate measures the number of people or the proportion of people from whom a biometric system fails to extract any biometric data deemed usable for identification purposes. The FTA usually occurs when a biometric system fails to find a biometric sample of sufficient quality to be used in the authentication purposes. For example, in a facial authentication system, the FTA may be a result from the subject not looking directly at the camera.

These two measurements are considered the main ones during the registration and the beginning of the authentication phases. In addition to these metrics, there are others that can also be considered. They include the average time taken to enroll a biometric record and the average or the maximum size of biometric templates.

Authentication Performance Metrics

The authentication performance metrics are concerned with the accuracy of the authentication process. The three principal metrics used for the measurement of authentication performance are as follows:

- False Acceptance Rate (FAR) – The false acceptance rate or FAR is sometimes known as the false negative rate or FN. This is when a biometric authentication system incorrectly allows an unauthorized person an access. In other words, it is defined as the number of the proportion of unauthorized users or adversaries accepted by the biometric system. It simply means that a person not enrolled in the biometric system is given permission to access a system. The FAR can be calculated by

$$FAR = \frac{Number\ of\ Successful\ Authentications\ by\ Unauthorised\ Users}{Number\ of\ Authentication\ Attempts\ by\ Unauthorised\ Users} \qquad (5\text{-}2)$$

- False Rejection Rate (FRR) – The false rejection rate or FRR is sometimes known as the false positive rate or FP. This is when a biometric authentication system incorrectly denies an authorized person an access. In other words, it is defined as the number or the proportion of genuine or authorized users that are wrongly denied an access by the biometric system. This simply means that a person enrolled in the biometric system is not allowed to access a system. The FRR can be calculated by

$$FRR = \frac{Number\ of\ Failed\ Authentication\ Attempts\ by\ Authosied\ Users}{Number\ of\ Authentication\ Attempts\ by\ Authorised\ Users} \qquad (5\text{-}3)$$

- Genuine Acceptance Rate (GAR) – The genuine acceptance rate or GAR is sometimes known as the true positive rate or TP. This is when a biometric authentication system correctly allows an authorized person an access. In other words, it is defined as the number or the proportion of genuine or authorized users that are accepted by the biometric system. The GAR can be calculated by

$$GAR = 100 - FRR \qquad (5\text{-}4)$$

The preceding are the main metrics for evaluating the performance of a biometric authentication system. Sometimes a fourth metric called the true negative rate or TN is also used. The true negative rate is when a biometric authentication system correctly denies access to an unauthorized person. In other words, it can be considered as a proportion of unauthorized users who are correctly not given a permission to access a system.

Biometric Threshold

As described previously, a biometric authentication system works by comparing biometric data from a person to be authenticated with their biometric template. It needs to be understood that a biometric match is never exact or there will never be 100% match between the biometric template and the authenticating biometric data. That means a match score or the proportion of matched biometric patterns is derived. In order to make a decision whether or not to accept the person being authenticated, a level of acceptance or the proportion of matched patterns needs to be established. This number is called the *biometric threshold*. It is simply a level or a point at which the biometric system is certain that the authenticating data matches the existing template.

Once a threshold is specified, if the match score exceeds the threshold, the authentication attempted by a person is a success. On the other hand, if the proportion of the matched patterns is lower than the established threshold, the authenticating person is rejected by the biometric system.

The biometric threshold is considered a very important value because it relates to and affects the authentication performance metrics explained in the previous section. The ways that the threshold can impact the authentication performance metrics can be explained as follows.

If the threshold is set at a high value, such as the authenticating biometric data must match at least 90% of the biometric template, it is likely that a high number of genuine users will be rejected. This is because it is not easy to have that many bits or patterns matched the stored template due to different conditions and noises that may occur during the authentication. When the threshold value is set too high, what happens is that the genuine acceptance rate (GAR) will be low, while the false rejection rate (FRR) will be high. This, of course, affects the accuracy of the biometric system.

In contrast, if the threshold value is set at a low value, such as the authentication biometric data must only match 40% of the stored template, it is very likely that unauthorized persons will be accepted by the biometric system. That is, it will not be difficult for adversaries to successfully be authenticated and accepted by a system. Specifying a low threshold value can cause the false rejection rate (FRR) to be low, while the false acceptance rate (FAR) will be high. Again, setting the threshold to a low value has an impact on the accuracy of the biometric system.

It can be seen that the biometric threshold value has a direct impact on both the security level and usability of a biometric system. From the explanation above, a high threshold value implies a higher security level and lower usability. This is because it will be very difficult for any user, including a genuine person, to have their biometric data matched the template at the specified proportion. On the contrary, a low threshold value leads to a lower security level but higher usability. This is because it will be easier for any person, including an unauthorized person, to have their authenticating biometric data accepted by the system.

It is, therefore, important to establish a suitable threshold value which will provide appropriate levels for both security and usability.

Equal Error Rate

One way to establish a value for a biometric threshold is to understand how the false acceptance rate (FAR) and the false rejection rate (FRR) can impact one another. It should be understood from the explanation in the previous section that if the biometric threshold is at a low value, few users will be rejected, which means that the FRR will be low. This, in turn, implies that many adversaries or impersonators will be accepted. Hence, the FAR will be high.

In order to reduce the number of impostors being accepted, the threshold value of a biometric system should be increased. As the biometric threshold increases, the number of authorized persons rejected by the biometric system will also increase, which means the FRR will go up. At the same time, the number of unauthorized persons being accepted will decrease, which means that the FAR will go down.

On the whole, if the number of false acceptance rate goes down, the number of false rejection rate will go up. In the opposite direction, if the number of false acceptance rate goes up, the number of false rejection rate will go down.

If the FAR and FRR were to be plotted on the same graph with the x axis being the level of security and the y axis being the amount of FAR and FRR, there would be a point where the FAR and FRR are equal to each other. This is the intersection of the FAR and FRR lines. The point at which the FAR and FRR are equal is called the *equal error rate* or *EER*. This is basically the point where the amount of false acceptances and false rejections are the same. The intersection of the FAR and FRR lines which represents the equal error rate of the EER is illustrated in Figure 5-6.

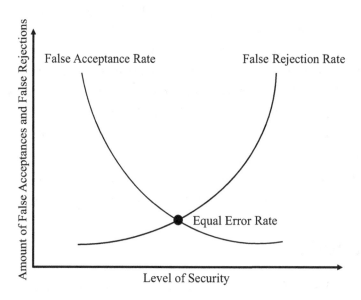

Figure 5-6. *Relationship Between FAR, FRR, and EER*

The equal error rate or EER actually provides a balance between the FAR and FRR. However, in the security perspective, the EER value is rarely used. This is because it is also important to consider what is really required – security or usability. From Figure 5-6, it can be seen that if the FAR value is reduced, it is likely that the FRR value will rise. What this means is that if the biometric system is more secure in the sense that some legitimate users can be falsely rejected, the less convenient the system will be. The same also applies in the other direction. That is, the biometric authentication system becomes more convenient to use with the expense of the level of security.

It is, therefore, necessary to determine whether to keep more adversaries out albeit with the expense of rejecting authorized persons or to try to avoid rejecting as many authorized users as possible.

Although an EER value provides a simple guideline for the threshold value of a biometric authentication system, it still does not seem adequate enough. That is why there has been a study which attempted to provide a method for finding a suitable threshold value.

Finding a Biometric Threshold

As explained, a biometric threshold is the point at which a biometric system is certain that the acquired biometric data matches the available biometric template. This value is usually configured or chosen by the biometric system administrator. However, whatever threshold value is chosen, it will affect all the biometric metrics, namely, genuine acceptance rate, false acceptance rate, and false rejection rate, in some way. Even though the EER value could be used as a rule of thumb, some issues still remain. This section, therefore, provides an attempt to explain a method that could be applied so that a more suitable biometric threshold can be determined.

It needs to be understood that, in obtaining a biometric threshold, three values must be measured. They are genuine acceptance rate (GAR), false acceptance rate (FAR), and false rejection rate (FRR). If the threshold value is low, this will result in a high GAR, a high FAR, and a low FRR, which implies high usability but low security. In contrast, if the threshold is high, it will result in a low GAR, low FAR, and high FRR. This implies lower usability but higher security. Thus, when choosing a biometric threshold, both security and usability must be considered.

A recommended method for finding a biometric threshold is to first specify several threshold values, such as 60% match, 65% match, 70% match, 75% match, 80% match, and 85% match, which can be experimented to compute the GAR, FAR, and FRR values. In other words, one could have a set of biometric data used for testing and another set acting as biometric templates. The two sets of data are then compared based on a specified threshold value. The GAR, FAR, and FRR values for this particular threshold are calculated and recorded. The same process is done for all specified threshold values. Of course, the required and desired performance metrics are high GAR, low FAR, and low FRR. The process is explained in Figure 5-7.

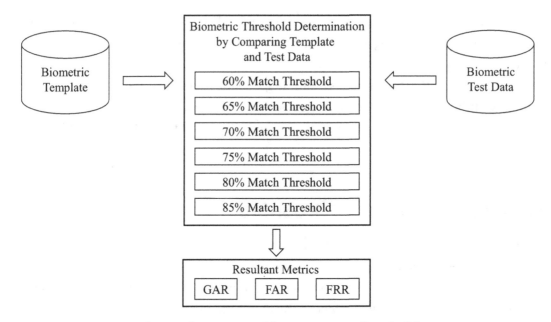

Figure 5-7. *Process for Finding a Suitable Biometric Threshold*

Once the GAR, FAR, and FRR are obtained for each biometric threshold, all the values are plotted on a graph whose x axis is the experimented threshold values and y axis is the amount of GAR, FAR, and FRR. The analysis on the graph, specifically the intersection of the GAR and FRR lines, will determine a suitable biometric threshold under the security and usability conditions.

Finding Biometric Threshold: Iris Case Study

In order to ensure that the process of finding a biometric threshold is more intuitive, a case study of iris authentication system is provided here. The experiment was carried out as follows.

Two sets of iris data were used as biometric templates and authentication biometric data. There had actually been a study that stated that a suitable threshold value for an iris authentication system was having a match of 60%. However, another study disagreed and gave an explanation that this threshold would still give a high value of the false acceptance rate. Therefore, this particular iris case study specified the biometric thresholds to be tested by having a biometric matching pattern of 50%, 55%, 60%,

65%, 70%, 75%, and 80%. Three biometric performance metrics in GAR, FAR, and FRR were measured and compared for all the specified thresholds. For this particular iris authentication case study, the obtained results for the performance metrics of each threshold are shown in Table 5-2.

Table 5-2. *Resultant Performance Metrics for Specified Thresholds*

Metric	Specified Threshold						
	50%	55%	60%	65%	70%	75%	80%
GAR	92.36	80.64	72.08	64.18	55.46	44.53	40.85
FRR	7.73	19.35	27.91	35.81	44.53	55.46	59.14
FAR	70.84	39.26	24.93	17.03	12.67	9.13	6.13

For security purposes, in this case study, the value of FAR should be low. In terms of correctness or accuracy of any biometric authentication system, the GAR value should be higher than the FRR value. It is, therefore, evident from Table 5-2 that the specified threshold values of 65% and 70% satisfied the security and correctness criteria. The threshold of 65% obtained the values of 64.18, 35.81, and 17.03 for GAR, FRR, and FAR, respectively. At the same time, the threshold of 70% had the GAR, FRR, and FAR of 55.46, 44.53, and 12.67, respectively. However, the threshold value of 75% could not be ignored due to the very low value of FAR and the closeness of the GAR and FRR values.

According to the method of finding a biometric threshold, the values obtained in Table 5-2 were plotted. The resultant graph was illustrated in Figure 5-8.

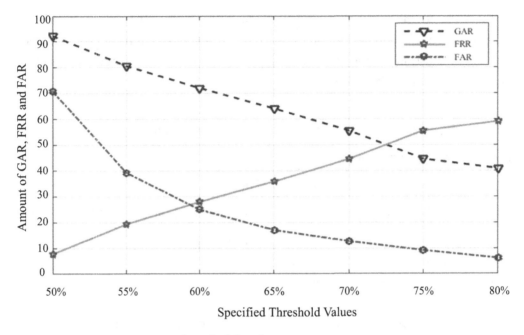

Figure 5-8. *Determining a Threshold Value*

Figure 5-8 displays two intersections. The first is the intersection of the FAR and FRR, which, according to a theory, is actually the equal error rate or EER. Despite that, the EER could not be used as a suitable threshold in this case. The reason was that the intersection occurred at a threshold value lower than 60% where false acceptance rate was very close to 30 which, in turn, would mean that it would be likely that unauthorized persons would be accepted by the system.

The other intersection was created by the GAR and FRR and occurred at the threshold value of around 72%. Looking at this intersection, it appeared that this specific threshold value would be more appropriate because of its very low FAR and high GAR which satisfied the important aim of security.

It is clear and has been confirmed by this iris authentication system case study that a biometric threshold does not always have to be the equal error rate or the EER value. Studying and investigating a few different thresholds can also yield a better result in terms of both security and usability.

Biometric Authentication Use Cases

The concept of biometrics has been around for over a century. In the 19th century, some specific anatomical characteristics were used for the purpose of criminal identification. Later on, the British and French police adopted the idea and used biometrics for identification of both criminals and police personnel. Even the FBI started using biometric identification a little later in 1924. Since then, biometric identification came under research and development, and fingerprints were not the only body part used for identity authentication. Many more unique physical, biological, and behavioral characteristics have been identified as candidates for biometric identification and authentication, although fingerprints are still the most commonly and extensively used in many situations. Due to the gain in awareness and acceptance of biometrics in recent years, this section will provide an overview of where biometric identification and authentication is used in the real world.

Smart Phones

First of all, it has been acknowledged by many smart phone manufacturers that a stronger form of authentication is needed in place of a traditional PIN code. Biometric authentication has, therefore, become a solution of choice. Nowadays, it is common to see a smart phone come equipped with a biometric authentication function, which actually allows biometric technology to become a lot more accepted.

With the more recent updates or versions of smart phones, it is possible to choose from a selection of biometric authentication options, which include fingerprint recognition (some call it the Touch ID), facial recognition (sometimes known as the Face ID), and some even have keystroke dynamics option. The available biometric authentication features not only allow users to unlock their devices, they have also become a part of many mobile applications on the phones. For example, many banking applications have integrated a biometric authentication function for users to carry out some sensitive transactions such as making fund transfers and payments.

Access Control and Clocking System

The second biometric use case is access control. Biometric authentication for access control has an aim of preventing unauthorized persons from accessing the premise, networks, systems, or some facilities. Many organizations have adopted biometric technology to achieve this purpose rather than using passwords or pin codes which can be forgotten. Access cards, although still popular, have decreased in the number of usage due to the possibility of them being lost and stolen.

Together with physical access control, biometric technology can also be used as a time and attendance system. In this case, the employees use their fingerprint to verify their identity when clocking in and clocking out of the office. The biometric clocking system is said to be a better alternative than an access card, because there have been cases where an employee asks their colleague to scan the card on their behalf. When biometrics is used, this favor cannot be asked, however.

Military

The third use case of biometric technology is, of course, the military. This is especially the case in the United States of America where a large database containing approximately 7.4 million identities was set up by a Department of Defense agency. The vast majority of the biometric data stored in the database is said to be from the operations in Iraq and Afghanistan. It has also been reported that over the ten-year period between 2008 and 2017, almost two thousand individuals were either arrested or killed based on the biometric data stored in this particular database. This implies that biometric identification has been used by the American military to identify enemies on the battlefield.

Border Control

The next use case is the biometric identification and authentication for border control, travel, and immigration. Today, approximately 1.2 billion electronic passports or e-passports have been deployed around the world. The most widely used are the second-generation passports, which store two fingerprints in addition to a photograph of the passport holder. The flow of how the automated border control works is as follows.

An individual entering or leaving a country places their passport in a provided slot where the stored information is read by the system. The individual then has their fingerprint scanned by a scanner and their face captured by a camera. If the biometric information, that is, fingerprint and the face, match the biometric information stored in the passport, they are allowed to enter or leave the country. This type of automated border control which applies biometric technology can now be seen on all continents especially in the United States, the EU countries, Australia, and Asia.

Financial Sector

The fifth use case is in the financial sector. KYC or know your customer has become an obligation for the financial industry with an objective of identifying customers in order to fight against financial crime and money laundering. KYC is the process of customer identification and authentication when they open an account. This basically means that a bank or a financial institution must be sure that their customer is genuinely who they claim to be. Without being able to meet basic KYC requirements, the customer would be refused to have their account opened.

The KYC procedure comes in two different formats. The first is paper based which requires customers to fill in a form and to attach their photo identification documents such as an ID card or a passport. The other format is digital based, which, a lot of the times, involves the use of biometric authentication such as fingerprint or facial authentication. An example of the digital-based KYC is known as E-KYC or electronic know your customer. E-KYC allows customers to open an account without having to go to a physical bank branch. This feature allows a mobile banking application to capture the customer's biometric data, in this particular case the customer's face, in addition to either a national ID card or a passport. The customer's face will then be used as a part of an authentication process for future activities and transactions.

In more detail, the E-KYC works by a customer wanting to open an account accesses their mobile banking application. The customer fills in the required information, which includes attaching a photo identification document such as a national ID card or a passport and capturing a photograph of their face. The bank's facial recognition system, together with human assistance, then compares the photograph on the ID card or passport with the captured photograph of the customer. If they match, it will mean that the customer has successfully opened their account.

Concerns and Future of Biometrics

Biometrics is not without concerns. It needs to be understood that biometrics is not secret and cannot be replaced. This is especially the case with the physiological biometric data. There have also been cases where biometric databases have been compromised. This presents a bigger problem than when a password database is breached. The reason is that people can always change their passwords. However, when there is a leakage of biometric data, it is very difficult, in some cases impossible, to change users' physiological characteristics such as their fingerprints, their irises, or their faces.

On a more technical note, a popular attack on biometrics, especially physiological biometrics, is known as the hill climbing attack. In the case of physiological biometric authentication, features of biometrics are stored as a template in a database. When carrying out a hill climbing attack, an attacker begins by constructing a biometric sample and iteratively modifying it until a certain threshold is reached. The goal of the hill climbing attack is for an attacker to be falsely accepted into the system. Fortunately, one simple method that can be used to prevent this type of attacks is to limit the number authentication attempts which can reduce the probability of the iteratively modified biometric data being falsely accepted.

Many countries, such as China and the United Kingdom, have deployed a facial recognition system in a surveillance network across many major cities for many purposes. They include calculating social score, catching criminals, and identifying illegal immigrants, for example. With this application of biometric identification and authentication, there are people who are against this idea. Some argue that this is the invasion of privacy. Others have suggested that the accuracy of the facial surveillance system is as low as 20%.

Speaking of accuracy of biometric authentication, there are ways that can be done in order to increase the rate of correctness or genuine acceptance rate. One method is called multimodal biometrics, which combines at least two different types of biometric information for identification and authentication purposes. For example, instead of just using a fingerprint when carrying out an authentication process, an iris scan is also done. Due to the requirement of presenting more than one biometric credential, multimodal biometrics can increase both security and accuracy of biometric authentication. Another method for improving the accuracy of biometric authentication is the application of machine learning algorithms. Some have applied the K-Nearest Neighbors (KNN) to fingerprint authentication. Some have used deep learning and convolutional neural network (CNN) in facial and iris authentication. Others have suggested that support vector machine (SVM) could improve the performance of keystroke dynamics and signature authentication.

Even though the genuine acceptance rate has been increased through the use of machine learning algorithms, more work is still needed, in particular in the real-world applications like the facial surveillance system, mentioned previously. Furthermore, many other anatomical parts and characteristics can still be explored and investigated so that the options that could be better suited to some particular situations can be available.

Summary

Biometric authentication or the something-you-are method is another authentication scheme, which has exploded in its popularity over the years. This chapter provides a detailed explanation of what a biometric authentication is and how it works. In addition, it has been clarified that there is a main issue with biometrics. In other words, the security and usability of a biometric authentication system depends on the biometric threshold, which can directly affect the biometric performance metrics in GAR, FRR, and FAR. In order to determine an appropriate value of the biometric threshold, two methods are illustrated in this chapter. The first is the use of the EER value, while the second method is done through a threshold experiment.

After the technical aspects of biometric authentication have been elucidated, examples of real-world biometric use cases are given. The chapter then ends with the description of concerns and future opportunities of biometric development.

Bibliography

Buriro, A. (2017). *Behavioral Biometrics for Smartphone User Authentication.* Ph.D. Thesis, University of Trento, International Doctoral School in Information Engineering and Communication Technologies (ICT), Italy.

El-Abed, M., & Charrier, C. (2020). Evaluation of Biometric Systems. *New Trends and Developments in Biometrics*, 149–169.

FBI. (2020, March). *Biometric Modalities.* Retrieved April 4, 2020, from FBI: www.fbi. gov/services/cjis/fingerprints-and-other-biometrics/biometric-center-of-excellence

Gemalto. (2020). *Biometrics: Authentication and Identification - 2020 Review.* Retrieved April 4, 2020, from Gemalto: www.gemalto.com/govt/inspired/biometrics

Hitchcock, D. C. (2003). *Evaluation and Combination of Biometric Authentication Systems.* Master Thesis, University of Florida, The Graduate School of the University of Florida, Florida, USA.

Koong, C.-S., Yang, T.-I., & Tseng, C.-C. (2014, July). A User Authentication Scheme Using Physiological and Behavioral Biometrics for Multitouch Devices. *The Scientific World Journal, 2014*, 1–13.

Kothavale, M., Markworth, R., & Sandhu, P. (2004). Lecture Notes in Computer Security SS3: Biometric Authentication. Birmingham, UK: University of Birmingham.

Vacca, J. (2014). *Cyber Security and IT Infrastructure Protection*. Science Direct.

Wangkeeree, N., & Boonkrong, S. (2019, October). Finding a Suitable Threshold Value for an Iris-Based Authentication System. *International Journal of Electrical and Computer Engineering, 9*(5), 3558–3568.

CHAPTER 6

Multi-factor Authentication

Today, there are over 3.5 billion people online and have access to many online services such as banking, shopping, student records, and social media. In order to access these services, they have to carry out and pass a login or authentication mechanism, which usually requires a username and a password. In the previous chapters, we have learned a username and a password are not the only credentials that can be used during the login process.

As explained earlier, there are actually three major methods of authentication. They are something you know, something you have, and something you are. Any one of these methods is one authentication factor. There are, however, problems with any authentication system that only uses one factor of authentication. Something you know or a password is not enough to secure a system. If it is known by an adversary, it becomes useless in keeping information private and preventing unauthorized access. Something you have or an authentication token is not much better. If it is lost or stolen, anyone who gets hold of it can easily impersonate the owner and access the system. Something you are or biometrics, although claimed to be more secure, is not without security issues. Losing control of a biometric database is said to be even worse than losing a password database. The reason is that changing a password does not require a lot of effort, but changing biometric data is not as easy, whether it is physiological or behavioral.

Many organizations and users have now realized how important it is to have a more secure mechanism that can prevent their data from being exposed as easily as it has been. This has led to an increase in the adoption of two-factor authentication (2FA) and multi-factor authentication (MFA) mechanisms.

© Sirapat Boonkrong 2021
S. Boonkrong, *Authentication and Access Control*, https://doi.org/10.1007/978-1-4842-6570-3_6

This chapter explains what 2FA and MFA actually are, how they work, and how they can be evaluated. Moreover, the chapter considers examples of applications of 2FA and MFA in real scenarios so that it is possible for us to see how they can help increase the security of traditional one-factor authentication.

Issues with Traditional Authentication

Before answering the question of what two-factor authentication or 2FA is, let us establish why it is important to improve the security of a traditional authentication system. Today, so much of our lives are spent on mobile devices, laptops, and online, our digital accounts have become a target for cybercriminals. There have been attacks on multinational organizations, enterprises, governments, and individuals. Unfortunately, the number of attacks does not appear to go down any time soon. It is, therefore, necessary to have an additional level of protection to a traditional password authentication system.

Let us remind ourselves by talking a little bit about the insecurity of the traditional password authentication systems. Passwords, despite their security issues, are still the most commonly used form of user authentication. Of course, although having passwords is better than no passwords, they are vulnerable due to the following reasons.

The first, and perhaps the worst, culprit is the fact that humans' memories are not as good as we think. Every year, a list of the top 25 or top 50 bad passwords is published, and they are embarrassingly bad. Among the worst of the bad lot include "123456", "12345678", "letmein", and "password". People choose to use these as their passwords because they are easy to remember. However, the problem is they can be cracked in no time.

The second reason is the fact that today, people tend to have more than one account. In other words, it has become more and more simple to do things on mobile devices, computers, and online. People, therefore, open more and more accounts. With each account, a login detail including a password is required. This eventually means more passwords to remember. A solution that many people have chosen to avoid memorizing too many passwords is password reuse, which leads to an attack called credential stuffing. This means that if an attacker gets hold of a username and corresponding password, it is likely that many more accounts of this particular user can be unlocked.

Many people have now realized the needs for stronger passwords and have tried to create more complex passwords that are harder to crack. However, with so many accounts to look after and use, many have given up and gone back to using weaker passwords anyway. When this occurs, it is sometimes known as *security fatigue*, which is when a user becomes tired of trying to keep their systems and accounts secure.

Two-Factor Authentication

Due to the vulnerability of the traditional password authentication system, attentions have turned to two-factor authentication or 2FA. Two-factor authentication is also an authentication mechanism, which has the objective of proving the identity of an individual. The two-factor authentication is said to provide an extra level of security to ensure that the authentication process is more secure. There are other names used in place of two-factor authentication, which include two-step verification and two-step authentication.

In a typical scenario, a person first enters their username and password. They will then be asked to provide another piece of information before being able to gain access to the account or the system. This extra piece of information is known as the second factor of authentication with the first being the password, in this scenario. In truth, any of the two factors could come from any of the following categories:

- Something You Know – This could be a password, a personal identification number (PIN), or even an answer to some secret questions.

- Something You Have – An individual could use something in their possession, such as an authentication token, a smart phone, or a smart card.

- Something You Are – This is the biometric information of an individual including a fingerprint, an iris, a typing pattern, or a walking pattern.

An example of a two-factor authentication process is illustrated in Figure 6-1. The figure shows that in order to log into a system, an individual has to enter their username and password as the first factor of authentication. They will then be provided with a newly generated secret code on the mobile device. Next, the secret code is entered into the system as the second authentication factor. If the password from the user's memory (something you know) and the secret code from the mobile device (something you have) are both correct, the user will be granted an access to the system.

| A user enters his/her username and password. | A secret code is sent to the user's mobile device. | The secret code is entered as a second factor and the access is granted. |

Figure 6-1. *An Example of a 2FA Process*

We need to make it clear that two-factor authentication requires two pieces of information from two different authentication categories. For example, if a password and a PIN are used during the authentication process, this is not classified as two-factor authentication. This is because the password and PIN belong to the same authentication factor category, namely, the something-you-know factor. In another situation, a password is needed to be entered, and a fingerprint is also needed to be scanned. This would be classified as two-factor authentication, because the password is in the something-you-know category and the fingerprint is in the something-you-are category. Another scenario would be when a user enters their password into a system, together with a random code sent to them via an SMS on a smart phone. This also would be called two-factor authentication, because the password and the SMS code are from the something-you-know and something-you-have categories, respectively.

Common Authentication Factors

Although anything belonging to any category can be used as authentication factors, there are only few interesting and practical forms of two-factor authentication that are in use today. Admittedly, some are stronger and some are more complex than others. However, all of them provide better security and protection than password-only authentication. Let us now take a look at some common forms or factors that are used as a part of two-factor authentication.

Hardware Authentication Token

A hardware authentication token or authentication token, in short, was actually the device that was most commonly used as the second authentication factor. An authentication token physically looks like a crossbreed between a key ring and a USB flash drive, with a screen on it. Some of them even have a numeric keypad. The main function of the authentication token is to produce a new numeric code each time the owner of the token wants to log in.

There are two types of authentication tokens that are used today. They are called synchronous token and asynchronous token. The former type synchronizes its time with an authentication server. A numeric code is generated according to the current time. The latter type receives a random set of numbers from an authentication server. The numbers are then entered into the token, which uses them to generate a numeric code for the user. The detail of how the synchronous and asynchronous authentication tokens work is explained in the "Something You Have" section in Chapter 3. For both types of the tokens, once the numeric code has been generated on the token's screen, the user has to enter it into the system or application that is authenticating the user.

A newer version of the authentication token comes in a form of USB, known as the USB authentication tokens. They can automatically transfer the numeric code into the system or application, in which an individual is logging, when plugged into a USB port on a computer or a laptop. A typical scenario when using a hardware authentication token is shown in Figure 6-2.

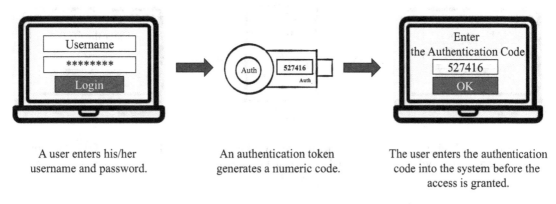

| A user enters his/her username and password. | An authentication token generates a numeric code. | The user enters the authentication code into the system before the access is granted. |

Figure 6-2. *A Typical Scenario for a Hardware Authentication Token*

One positive point of the authentication token is that a numeric code is freshly generated each time, which makes it difficult for an attacker to guess or crack. However, there are a couple of downsides, which are the additional cost and the possibility of the loss of the token.

Short Message Service (SMS)

The SMS factor of authentication is nothing new. It was invented long before the birth of smart phones and is still popularly used today. The way the SMS-based two-factor authentication works can be explained as follows.

After a username and a password are entered into a system, an application, or a website, a unique one-time password (OTP) is generated and sent to the user in the form of a text message (SMS). Similar to the hardware authentication token, the user has to enter the received OTP back to the system, application, or website before being granted an access. The value of the OTP is usually computed based on an algorithm known as the HMAC-based one-time password algorithm or the HOTP, whose detail can be studied in the RFC 4226 document.

Even though the received SMS is considered a one-time password, this factor of authentication is not the something-you-know factor. This is because the OTP is not something that the user has to remember. Rather, the SMS factor falls into the something-you-have category as a result of the user obtaining the OTP value from their phone. The SMS-based two-factor authentication can be visualized in Figure 6-3.

| A user enters his/her username and password. | A one-time password is sent to the user's mobile device via SMS. | The received OTP is entered before the access is granted. |

Figure 6-3. A Typical SMS-Based 2FA

The SMS-based authentication, although very popular, does not come without any flaws. One problem with this scheme was realized by the National Institute of Standards and Technology (NIST). NIST stated that when an OTP in the form of an SMS is sent to a user's mobile device, there is no way for the OTP transmitter, in this case a system, an application, or a website, to know whether or not the OTP actually arrives at the intended destination.

Another potential problem may be caused by a vulnerability in the Signaling System Number 7 (SS7) protocol, which is also known as Common Channel Interoffice Signaling 7 (CCIS7). The SS7 protocol is primarily used for connecting one mobile phone network to another. More specifically, it allows the mobile phone networks to exchange information required for passing phone calls and text messages between each other. If an adversary has an access to the SS7 protocol, they will be able to listen to phone calls and read SMS messages. This means that it is possible for the SMS-based OTP to be compromised in this way.

This is why today, many researchers and organizations have considered the SMS authentication factor to be the least secure way to authenticate users. Having said that, it is still commonly used especially by financial institutions.

Software Authentication Token

Since there is a vulnerability in the SMS authentication factor, many people and organizations have begun to find alternatives. One of the more popular choices uses a software-based time-based one-time password. This is sometimes known as TOTP or soft token.

In order to use the software authentication token, a user has to download and install a two-factor authentication application on their mobile device. The most highly downloaded and recommended applications include Google Authenticator and Authy. The user can then use this application with any website or system that supports the use of two-factor authentication.

During the user authentication process, the user enters their username and password as per usual. They will then be prompted with a text box asking for an authentication code. At this stage, the two-factor application will compute and generate a numeric code, based on the current time, and displays it on the user's mobile device. The user then enters the generated authentication code in the text box in order to gain access into the website or the system. An example of how the code can be entered into the system or on a website is shown in Figure 6-4. It can be observed in the figure that the software authentication token generates a unique code, "478 724" in this case, which is then entered in the provided space for the two-step verification process.

The way the two-factor authentication application generates the authentication code is based on the algorithm known as the time-based one-time password or the TOTP algorithm. The detail of how the algorithm is designed and can be implemented can be studied further in the RFC 6238 document. However, to put it simply, the time at authentication is used as an input of the authentication code generation function. This is the reason why the code is typically only valid for less than 60 seconds. That means once the code has been generated, it must be used within 60 seconds. If the authentication code is not entered within the specified time, a new one will have to be generated by the application.

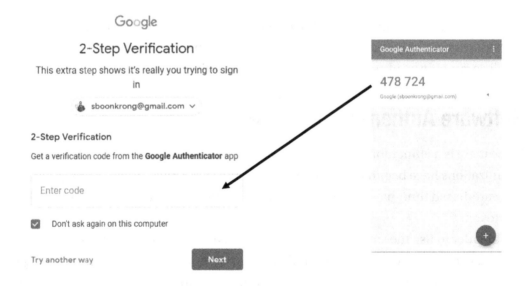

Figure 6-4. *An Example of How Software Authentication Token Can Be Used*

The software authentication token has an advantage over the traditional SMS-based OTP because the authentication code is generated and displayed on the same device. In other words, the code will never have to travel through any insecure network. The risk of the authentication code being intercepted in the same way as the SMS interception is, therefore, removed.

The convenience of the software authentication token cannot be argued since anyone can download, install, and use it on their devices. Unfortunately, not all TOTP applications are secure. There is a piece of Android malware called Cerberus, which has recently been reported, at the time of writing, to have the capability of stealing the time-based one-time password generated by one software authentication token.

The malware of the Trojan type abuses the weakness of the application to gain privileges so that when the application runs, the Trojan can obtain the content of the application's interface and send it back to the attacker's server. The good news, according to the report, is that the Cerberus malware is not out in the wild yet. This will probably give the application owner some time to patch things up to make it more secure.

Biometrics

What we have seen so far is that the second factor of authentication is from the something-you-have category. Another category that has been studied and applied as an addition authentication factor to the something you know is the something-you-are factor or biometrics. Biometric factor has only recently been considered as a candidate for the second factor of authentication because of the issues with the something-you-have factor, including security flaws and extra effort in entering more credential. This reflects in the fact that only 10% of all active Gmail users have adopted to use two-factor authentication.

An organization called IDSquared has realized this and has attempted to provide an alternative to the troublesome something-you-have factor. Biometric factor, specifically the keystroke dynamics, has been seen as a solution that can smooth out the two-factor authentication process. The way that this two-factor authentication system works is seamless to the user. In other words, when the user types their username and password, the authentication system will capture the keystroke dynamics in order to verify their unique typing pattern. This means that in order to be successfully authenticated, the user will have to both enter the correct password and demonstrate the precise-enough typing pattern.

Despite the fact that this type of biometric-based two-factor authentication is seamless and does not require any extra device or effort from the user, its accuracy in detecting the correct keystroke dynamics is still being questioned.

Another example of using biometrics as the second factor of authentication is called voice-based two-factor authentication. Due to the availability of smart phones and voice recognition services over APIs, it is not difficult to implement a two-factor authentication system, which requires the something-you-know factor or a password and the something-you-are factor or the user's voice.

In a typical scenario of the voice-based two-factor authentication, the user provides their username and password and is asked to speak an authentication phrase. The voice recognition is then processed in order to decide whether or not the user is to be granted an access into the system, application, or website. This type of authentication is admittedly still in the implementation and testing phases. Some work is required for the accuracy to be improved. An example scenario is illustrated in Figure 6-5.

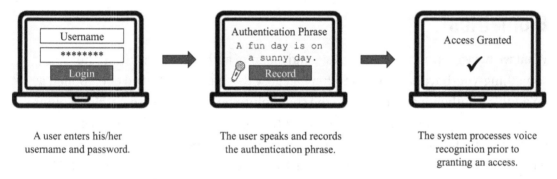

Figure 6-5. *An Example of Voice-Based Two-Factor Authentication*

Even though biometric factor is believed to be a convenient alternative to the vulnerable OTP-based authentication factor, many researchers are still against the use of biometrics as a factor in two-factor authentication. This claim is specifically for the client–server environment. The reason is that biometric information is not secret and is irreplaceable. That is, once the biometric information of an individual is compromised, it is compromised forever. In the case of the client–server environment where biometric information is transmitted from one device to another over the network, it is possible for an adversary to intercept the biometric information. This could lead to an impersonation attack on this particular user that the captured biometrics belongs to for the rest of their life since the biometric data is not revocable.

Hand-Drawn Image

There has been an interesting research that designed a two-factor authentication which combines the use of a traditional password and a hand-drawn image. The researcher claimed that this was different from an image authentication where an individual was asked to pick an image available on a pane. In this particular two-factor authentication, an individual was allowed to create their own image as part of the authentication process.

In this two-factor authentication system, a user registers their username and password in a similar way to any traditional password-based authentication system. An additional piece of information that needs to be registered and stored as a template is their hand-drawn image. This particular system restricts the drawing area to 80 x 80 pixels since any larger areas would put a burden on the memory and processor of the computer. The image, once drawn either by an electronic pen or even by a mouse, is converted into an array of bytes which are then stored as a template in the database. Figure 6-6 shows an example of a grid in which a user is asked to hand-draw an image. In this example, once the user is given an empty grid, they decide to draw an image of a mountain with two peaks. It is to be noted that a user is allowed to draw absolutely anything as long as the image stays in the provided area.

When authenticating into the system, the user enters their username and password. If they match the information stored in the database, they will be presented with an empty grid. The user is then required to draw their image into the given area in such a way that it matches the template of the image.

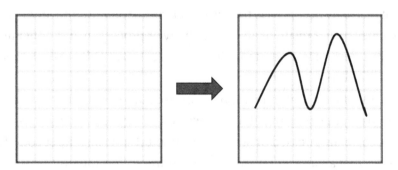

Figure 6-6. *An Example of a Hand-Drawn Image on a Grid*

One important challenge that must be overcome by this two-factor authentication is how to correctly match the user's hand-drawn image with the existing template. Similar to biometric-based authentication, it is near impossible to have an exact match. Therefore, an appropriate threshold, which specifies the acceptable level of correctness, is required.

The appropriate threshold value for this method of authentication was determined by the evaluation of user satisfaction and the failure rate of matching the authenticating image with the template. It was found that the suitable threshold value was approximately a 45% match, which works but admittedly on the low side, because it could allow for a high value of false negative.

The two-factor authentication using the combination of a password and a hand-drawn image, although not currently popular, will be another choice to choose from if the threshold value can be pushed higher without having to trade off with the satisfaction of users. This is still a challenge which needs to be addressed.

Another point that needs to be considered is the performance. Since this two-factor authentication also requires the user to hand-draw an image, the time taken to complete the authentication is around 60% higher when compared with the authentication requiring only a password. However, the improvement of the performance, specifically the speed of authentication, is not seen as a big issue compared with the challenge of the accuracy of image matching.

Is Two-Factor Authentication More Secure?

One thing that has to be accepted is the fact that two-factor authentication causes minor inconvenience as a result of an extra activity or process of authentication and verification. The question is: does it provide better security? This section tries to provide an answer to this question.

In practice, two-factor authentication means that there is another thing that an individual has to do after entering their password into a system. The idea is that if a password were correctly guessed or stolen, there would still exist the second factor of authentication that an attacker needs to compromise. This means that with two-factor authentication, it has become more difficult for an attacker to impersonate any individual since two elements will have to be compromised rather than just one password.

Let us elaborate this argument with an example. An ordinary email account is logged in by the use of a password only. If that password is known by an unauthorized person, the owner of the email account is said to be impersonated straight away. In other words, the unauthorized person who possesses the password can easily log into the email account as the account owner. On the other hand, suppose two-factor authentication is enabled on an email account with the use of a password and a software authentication token. Using a similar scenario, if an unauthorized person gets hold of the password of this particular email account, it does not mean that they will be able to impersonate the account owner and log into the email. This is because in order to be successfully authenticated by the email system, the second factor of authentication is required. In this case, the software authentication token, which effectively means the smart phone of the email account owner, needs to be in the hand of the adversary, too.

It can be seen from this simple but practical example that comparing with one-factor authentication, two-factor authentication is more secure since it requires more effort from the attacker to compromise both factors before being able to successfully impersonate an individual.

Unfortunately, there is a counterargument from some sectors that two-factor authentication, although more secure than the traditional password-only authentication, may not be bulletproof. As we say in the field of security that no security system is perfect, two-factor authentication is no exception. One example of a flaw that can affect the security of two-factor authentication is SMS hijacking, which is the case for the code sent to a user via SMS. However, a more common method that two-factor authentication can be compromised is phishing.

As explained in the earlier chapters, phishing is a form of social engineering which lures a victim to a counterfeit login page. The victim is then tricked into entering their credentials, including a password and a two-factor authentication numerical code from either an SMS message or a software authentication token. The attacker can catch both credentials and use them on the legitimate website, which results in a successful impersonation of the victim. This is also the case for the account recovery situation where some company sends a confirmation code via either an SMS message or an email. The person trying to recover the account can be tricked by the attacker to a fake account recovery page, which can result in their account recovery code being stolen.

This attack method on two-factor authentication is admittedly very difficult to defend against since it is an attack on humans rather than on the authentication technology itself. It is the flaw within humans.

Even though there are flaws and drawbacks in two-factor authentication, it does not mean that two-factor authentication is obsolete. It is obvious that two-factor authentication is still massively useful and is stronger than the traditional one-factor authentication. This is why many organizations have adopted the technology.

Where Is Two-Factor Authentication Used?

Security has been a major concern for many organizations for a long time. However, not until a few years ago that two-factor authentication caught their attention. Not only those in the financial sector and healthcare industry who appear to possess sensitive information have adopted two-factor authentication technology, many other sectors including higher education and social media are now relying on the same or similar methods. This section provides an overview of where two-factor authentication is used and which factors of authentication, other than a password, have become a part of it.

Finance

The first prime example of the application of two-factor authentication has to be in the financial sector, which also includes the banking and investment sectors as its subsets. The financial industry possesses many sensitive computer systems and a lot of sensitive information that belongs to their clients. It is, therefore, inevitable that the industry is under the surveillance of attackers. Consequently, many financial institutions have to find a way to defend against potential hacking attempts.

Not all financial institutions have adopted two-factor authentication, but there are many that have. A research by twofactorauth.org shows that some organizations even provide choices of the second authentication factors for their customers to select. Out of those who have applied two-factor authentication as part of identity verification, nearly all of them have the SMS factor as their main option. Hardware authentication token is the second popular choice with software authentication token being closely in the third place. Other authentication factors provided by several financial institutions include email and phone call.

Healthcare

Healthcare is another industry that possesses a lot of sensitive data that belong to both the patients and the physicians and nurses. Moreover, the healthcare organizations are required to meet a number of security standards. For example, in the United States, they are required to meet the HIPAA and NIST standards, while in Europe, GDPR is the law that must be complied. In Thailand, the Personal Data Protection Act or PDPA is now effective.

Weak authentication is considered a threat to healthcare organizations. Thus, it is necessary to increase the security of the authentication process for the physicians, nurses, and administrative staff to access the sensitive patient data so that the risk of unauthorized access can be reduced. However, the number of healthcare organizations that have adopted the two-authentication factor technology is still relatively small when compared with the financial institutions. Statistically, out of the ones that use two-factor authentication, software authentication token appears to be the most popular choice. The SMS factor and hardware authentication token are the second and third most commonly used authentication factor, respectively.

Today, there have been reports that many healthcare organizations have adopted a relatively newer technology called U2F or Universal 2nd Factor. With U2F, a doctor, a nurse, or a member of administrative staff initiates an authentication session on their computer by entering username and password; the authentication process is completed by them approving it with the activity confirmation, usually just a tap on a button, on their smart phone. The U2F works as two-factor authentication under an assumption that the smart phone is only associated with its owner, which should be able to prevent an impersonator to gain access to the patient records even if the password is known.

Education

All higher education institutions around the world hold and manage a vast amount of data that belong to academic staff, nonacademic staff, researchers, and students. Many institutions even run hospitals, which mean additional amount of data to manage. The data that a higher education institution possesses vary from financial to personally identifiable information (PII). This has made it a prime target for attackers to try to breach the data.

The culture and the way that academic staff, nonacademic staff, and students work today is massively different from what it was in the past. Now there is a need to access data and information anytime, anywhere, and from any device, which creates a new security challenge for universities and colleges. In many parts of the world, governments have issued guidelines and standards that should be followed when implementing two-factor authentication for reducing the risk of data breaches. In the United States, there is a set of regulations called the NIST SP-800-171, which requires universities and colleges to comply and meet the requirements if they are to receive grants from the Department of Defense (DoD). Many of the regulations even order the use of two-factor authentication to ensure that only authorized persons can access sensitive information.

In the United Kingdom, the National Cyber Security Centre (NCSC) provides a guideline for higher education institutions on how to implement two-factor authentication and which factor to choose. The guideline suggests that an extra factor of authentication should be applied whenever possible, especially for the services that are cloud based and are connected to the Internet. The NCSC does not specifically state which extra factor of authentication to use, but a generic advice is given. The NCSC's suggestions for an additional authentication factor include software authentication token, hardware authentication token, a smart card, a second password in the form of SMS, and another piece of knowledge known only by the user.

Social Media

Another industry that appears to hold a massive amount of personal data is the social media industry. Facebook has approximately 2.5 billion active accounts, while Twitter has around 330 million active users per month. WhatsApp holds 1.5 billion accounts in over 180 countries, which makes it the most popular chat application in the world. Even WeChat, which is primarily used in China, has approximately one billion active users monthly. It can be said that social media has now become a place where people spend their time and share many things, a lot of the time private information, with other people. As the amount of usage grows, cybercriminals see social media as a target for data breaches. It is, therefore, essential for these social media companies to find a way to protect personal data of their users.

Fortunately, many large social media companies also see the problems and have provided their users with an extra layer of security in the form of two-factor authentication. They have made it simple for their users to enable two-factor authentication on their account. Facebook, Instagram, LinkedIn, Pinterest, and Twitter have all added an option for their users to use two-factor authentication. All of them seem to have adopted the use of software authentication token as the second authentication factor, which makes it the most commonly used factor on the social media platform.

Many social media companies previously required a mobile phone number of an account owner in order to set up two-factor authentication. Now, as mentioned, nearly all major social media companies have turned to third-party authentication applications such as Google Authenticator, Authy, and Duo Security instead.

Although the social media companies claim that it is easy to set up two-factor authentication for additional account security, the majority of social media users still ignore it. Statistically, only around 30% of the active accounts have enabled two-factor authentication. The reason is that many still find two-factor authentication cumbersome and time consuming. This is something that social media companies will have to work hard on in order to convince more users to see the importance of the technology.

Multi-factor Authentication

Multi-factor authentication or MFA can be seen as an extension of two-factor authentication. As the name suggests, multi-factor authentication is an authentication process that uses two *or more* authentication factors. It is now considered as a de facto standard for any systems that require strong security. The previous sections focus on two-factor authentication, which require two authentication factors from different authentication categories. This section will put an emphasis on the authentication process that requires three or more factors for confirming the identity of an individual.

Due to the development of new information systems, there are many challenges as well as opportunities for authentication systems. It has been claimed that the trust and security of authentication increase exponentially when more factors are applied as a part of the identity verification process. Although two-factor authentication has increased the level of protection for the access control mechanism, it is still interesting to see how a stronger authentication scheme in multi-factor authentication can be utilized.

First, let us remind ourselves that an authentication factor is a piece of credential information that is used to verify an individual's identity. For two-factor authentication mechanisms, they combine two factors from different categories, which include something-you-know factor, something-you-have factor, something-you-are factor, and occasionally something-you-process factor. Since multi-factor authentication requires more than two factors, a lot of researches have been done to introduce new authentication factors which will be potentially considered and used by security professionals. These relatively newer factors of authentication include the following:

- Time Factor – The time factor authenticates an individual based on an assumption that their login behavior occurs within a specific range of time. If an authentication attempt happens outside the specified time interval, they are likely to be denied an access to the system. In order for this factor of authentication to function properly, it is required that the time on the system and the authentication server are synchronized.

- Location Factor – The location factor authenticates an individual based on their physical location. If a user had registered their account in a part of the world, but carries out an authentication attempt in another location, the location factor will be triggered and at the very least warn the user of this authentication attempt. IP address and GPS technology have been the chosen methods for the location identification purpose.

- Ambient Sound Factor – The ambient sound factor works on the fact that every smart phone transmits a distinct ambient sound. That means the authentication process verifies the presence of a user's smart phone near the main device such as a laptop computer on which they are being authenticated. Apart from verifying the actual device, the ambient sound factor, also known as the *soundproof* factor, is used to determine the proximity between the two devices.

Multi-factor authentication can increase the level of security for access control mechanisms due to the higher number of factors required when verifying an individual. However, it has to be kept in mind that the convenience and usability are still an issue that needs to be addressed. Having said that, it is still essential that a more secure authentication scheme is implemented to protect a system from attackers. With the availability of different types of authentication factors, it is possible to design and construct multi-factor authentication protocols that could potentially be used in the future. The subsequent sections will, therefore, provide a couple of examples of multi-factor authentication protocols. The first has been specifically designed for the Internet banking service, while the second is more generic and can be applied anywhere provided that the factors are available.

Multi-factor Authentication for Internet Banking

In order to illustrate how multi-factor authentication works, an example of our research on Internet banking login process will be explained. Internet banking is a service provided by financial institutions and has gained popularity over the years. With the increasing number of users, Internet banking has become a target for attackers with authentication being one of their focuses.

Users need to be authenticated by the bank or financial institution before being able to carry out financial transactions. The authentication process adopted by many banks is either a password-only scheme or a two-factor authentication scheme. Unfortunately, the password-only authentication has been found not to be secure enough, while some two-factor authentication schemes also have their vulnerabilities, such as SMS hijacking.

One interesting authentication protocol for Internet banking has, therefore, been proposed to contain multiple authentication factors with an aim of improving the security of the login process. However, the details of computations and message generation will be omitted in this section because we would like to concentrate more on the different factors of authentication. The multi-factor authentication mechanism can be described as follows.

Authentication Factor Generation

Similar to any systems, prior to using an Internet banking service, it is mandatory for an individual to register with the financial institution. For this particular multi-factor authentication, the registration process is very much the same as any normal registration, but is a little different in the background process of authentication factor generation. That is, in addition to the user choosing a password as the first authentication factor, other factors are also generated in this registration phase.

Once a password has been chosen, it needs to be securely stored. One way to achieve that is with the use of a salt value, as explained in the "Hashed Passwords" and "Salted Passwords" sections. The salt value can, therefore, be considered as the second factor of authentication here because if an invalid salt value is used, the user will not be successfully authenticated.

During this registration process, a public key and a private key for this particular user are generated as the third and fourth authentication factors, respectively. As the names suggest, the public key is available to anyone, including the bank, while the private key is to be kept secret and only known by the user. One possible way to accomplish the secrecy of the private key is to use symmetric cryptography, which will be used to encrypt the private key. This means that a symmetric key needs to be produced and will only be available to the user. The symmetric key will be the fifth factor of authentication.

After the private key has been encrypted, the information created during the registration process is ready to be transmitted to the bank. The information to be sent includes (1) username, (2) salt value, (3) the hash value of the salted password $H(salt \| password)$, (4) the user's public key, and (5) the user's encrypted private key. Everything is, of course, encrypted using the bank's public key which can be obtained from the bank's digital certificate. The message containing the information from the user to the bank can be constructed as follows:

$$User \rightarrow Bank : \{username, salt, H(salt\| password), +K_{User}, \{-K_{User}\}_K\}_{+K_{Bank}}$$

where $+K_x$ means a public key of an entity x,

$-K_x$ means a private key of an entity x,

K means a symmetric key,

$\{M\}_K$ means a message M is encrypted using the key K,

$\{M\}_{+K_x}$ means a message M is encrypted using the public key of an entity x, and $H()$ means a cryptographic hash function.

After all the information arrives at the bank, everything will be stored on the bank's server for the authentication phase.

Authentication

One thing to be noted is the fact that an ordinary authentication process for the Internet banking service does not take mutual authentication into consideration. That is, it appears that a bank authenticates its customers but not the other way around. It is, therefore, necessary that two-way authentication is accomplished. Multi-factor authentication can certainly help achieve this goal.

The multi-factor authentication protocol for Internet banking consists of two parts. The first is for the user to fetch their encrypted private key from the bank's server. The second is the two-way authentication process.

When an individual visits a bank's website, the bank sends its digital certificate to the individual's device while recording the IP address of the user's device. The user's machine verifies the received certificate. Assuming that the verification is a success, the following proceeds:

Message 1. $User \rightarrow Bank : Req, UserID, \{UserID, Nonce_{User}\}_{+K_{Bank}}$

Message 2. $Bank \rightarrow User : \{BankID, Nonce_{User}, Nonce_{Bank}\}_{+K_{User}}, \{-K_{User}\}_K, Salt,$

$\{H(Bank \rightarrow User : \{BankID, Nonce_{User}, Nonce_{Bank}\}_{+K_{User}}, \{-K_{User}\}_K,$

$Salt, IP_{Bank})\}_{-K_{Bank}}$

Message 3. $User \rightarrow Bank : \{UserID, Nonce_{Bank}, H(Salt\|Password)\}_{+K_{Bank}},$

$\{H(UserID, Nonce_{Bank}, H(Salt\|Password)\}_{+K_{Bank}}), IP_{User}\}_{+K_{User}}$

where $Nonce_x$ means a random set of characters from an entity x,

$+K_x$ means a public key of an entity x,

$-K_x$ means a private key of an entity x,

K means a symmetric key,

$\{M\}_K$ means a message M is encrypted using the key K,

$\{M\}_{+K_x}$ means a message M is encrypted using the public key of an entity x,

$\{M\}_{-K_x}$ means a message M is encrypted using the private key of an entity x
      or a digital signature of an entity x,

$H()$ means a cryptographic hash function,

Salt means the salt value generated during the registration phase, and

IP_x means the IP address of an entity x.

The multi-factor authentication mechanism for Internet banking begins by the user sending their username to the bank, who then replies with the salt value and the encrypted private key of the user with its digital signature attached to the message. Having received the information, the user verifies the bank's signature and generates their symmetric key by using their password as well as the received salt value as inputs to the key derivation function.

After the symmetric key is computed, the key can then be used to decrypt the encrypted private key. The user can now use the private key to generate their digital signature for the subsequent messages in the authentication protocol.

The next step of the multi-factor authentication is that the user transmits the hash value of their salted password before encrypting it with the bank's public key, which has already been obtained from the bank's certificate in the earlier stage. Moreover, the user generates their digital signature and appends it with the rest of the information.

Next, the bank verifies the user's digital signature by using the user's public key that is already stored on the server during the registration process. If the verification succeeds, the bank decrypts the message and verifies the hash value of the salted password. Furthermore, the bank checks the IP address of the user. If the password and IP address match with the ones recorded on the server, then the authentication is said to be complete and successful.

Evidently, this example of multi-factor authentication mechanism for Internet banking applies many authentication factors. They include an individual's password, symmetric key, public key, private key, digital signature, and IP address. All of them are unique to each user. They are also kept confidential to each user, except for the salt value (used with the password) and the public key which is by definition available to anyone anyway.

On the whole, this section illustrates how many factors of authentication can be put together and applied in a real-world scenario. Even though this is just an example, a case study, or a proposition, it can be seen that the future of authentication will be relying on the idea of multi-factor authentication.

Multi-factor Biometric-Based Authentication

Another interesting example of multi-factor authentication is biometric based. This is different from the previous example, which does not contain any biometric information. We have already seen what biometric authentication is and how it is believed to provide better security than a password-only scheme. Unfortunately, it has also been discovered that biometric authentication is not without flaws since some physiological biometrics such as fingerprints and even some behavioral biometrics such as written signature can be forged. It is, therefore, necessary to add other authentication factors to biometric-only authentication mechanisms in order to produce a multi-factor biometric-based authentication.

This example of multi-factor biometric-based authentication has been around for some time and has been improved by many researchers so that it provides better security for a more general usage. In other words, this multi-factor biometric-based authentication allows for mutual authentication and an establishment of a session key between two entities, usually a client and a server.

Authentication Factor Generation

The authentication protocol begins with an individual completing their registration at a registration center remotely. During this stage, the individual chooses their username and password and imprints their biometric information which could be a fingerprint. All of the information is then stored on a smart card, which is later delivered to the user. The information storing and smart card creation are done by the registration center. The registration process, which is practically the generation of authentication factors, is illustrated in Figure 6-7.

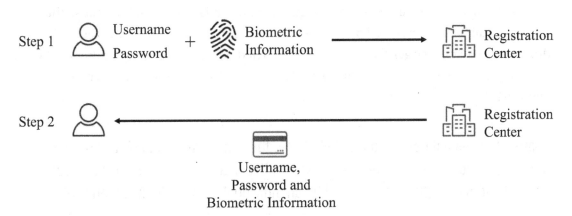

Figure 6-7. *Registration Process and Authentication Factor Generation*

On the whole, the factors of authentication generated during the registration stage include a password, user's biometric information, and a smart card. This scheme is an attractive proposition as it applies all three authentication factors, namely, something you know, something you have, and something you are.

Authentication

For the user to be authenticated, they first must compare their biometric information with the one stored on the smart card. If it is valid, the user enters their username and password into the smart card. The biometric information, username, and password all become a part of a computation to produce a dynamic identity on the user's side. The newly computed dynamic identity is then transmitted to the authentication server as a login request.

Once the login request arrives at the authentication server, a similar computation is carried out as a part of the authentication process. In other words, the authentication server uses the stored information, including the username, password, and biometric credential, to compute a dynamic identity for this particular user. If the dynamic identity received from the user matches with the one computed by the authentication server, it will mean that the identity verification is a success. Otherwise, the verification process fails and the authentication process is terminated.

If the dynamic identity verification succeeds, the authentication server makes some computation, and a challenge-and-response mechanism is applied to the user so that the server can be authenticated by the user. Hence, mutual authentication is achieved. Moreover, a session key generation process is carried out once the server authentication is accomplished to complete this protocol. The authentication process is summarized in Figure 6-8.

Note   We will not get into the detail of how the computation and challenge-and-response mechanism are carried out here in this chapter because our main focus is the factors of authentication used by an individual in the authentication process.

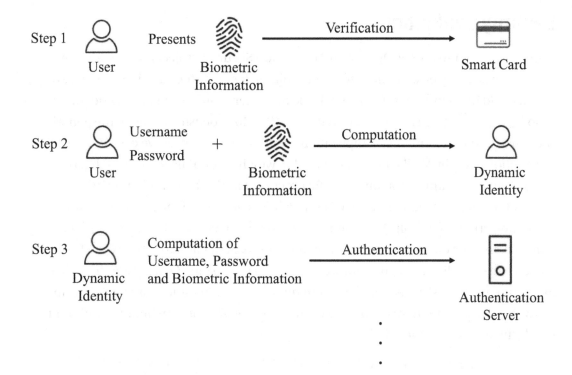

Objectives Reached: Mutual Authentication and Session Key Establishment

Figure 6-8. User Authentication via the Use of Multiple Authentication Factors

It can be observed in Figure 6-8 that in order to carry out a successful user authentication process, an individual must have valid biometric information, must hold a smart card, and must be able to recall a correct password.

Multi-factor Authentication Evaluation

Not only that we are able to understand and design multi-factor authentication schemes, it is essential that some evaluation is done. It is recommended that evaluation is done in two critical areas. The first is, of course, the security of the authentication. The second area is user acceptance.

Security Evaluation

A few years ago, OWASP or Open Web Application Security Project had a guideline defined for security evaluation criteria for multiple factor authentication system (MFAS), which could be found in the OWASP-AT-900 document. Unfortunately, the document is no longer available. The reason is that OWASP is now focusing more on the generic standards and requirements of application security verification as we can see in their Application Security Verification Standard 4.0, which was published in March 2019, rather than concentrating on one specific process of multi-factor authentication.

For the sake of explanation, we will give a brief overview of the OWASP security evaluation criteria for multi-factor authentication. First, we have to understand that doing an analysis on a multi-factor authentication system based on the OWASP criteria had an aim of finding strengths and weaknesses of the system. OWASP identified five major threats and risks that could occur in multi-factor authentication, especially in the web environment. It was known, back then, as the 5T model (where T stands for the word "threat"), which included

- Credential Theft – OWASP stated that the prevention of credential theft was considered as a strength of the system, especially if either symmetric or asymmetric encryption was applied to make eavesdropping more difficult to accomplish.

- Weak Credentials – OWASP stated that it was easy for any user to use weak credentials, especially a weak password. The authentication system must, therefore, provide a method which allowed for credential strength checking.

- Password Reuse – OWASP knew that password reuse would create a security problem for any authentication system. It was, therefore, recommended that a method for encouraging users to change their passwords should exist. This included the use of any one-time password mechanism such as SMS, hardware, and software authentication token.

- Session-Based Attack – This threat stated by OWASP focused on the replay attack, which was when an attacker reused an old session. The authentication system must, therefore, have a mechanism that would prevent this from happening. Such mechanism included the use of a timestamp or a randomly generated string for each authentication session.

- Malware – It was and is a well-known fact that some malware
  had an ability to modify information exchanged between a client
  and a server. OWASP, therefore, suggested that the authentication
  system must be able to at least detect when changes were made to
  authentication messages.

We have to accept the fact that with the ever-changing threat landscape, it is not an easy task to evaluate the level of security provided by any multi-factor authentication scheme or even any authentication system, for that matter. Fortunately, the OWASP criteria, albeit no longer downloadable from their website, can still be thought of as a basic guideline for security consideration for multi-factor authentication systems.

Usability Evaluation

One major challenge for any information system including multi-factor authentication is to ensure that users are not resistant to the new process. That means the system must be considered usable from the users' perspective. The term *usability* is defined by ISO/IEC 9241-11 as the "extent to which a product can be used by specified users to achieve specified goals with effectiveness, efficiency and satisfaction in a specified context of use." Based on this definition, the National Institute of Standards and Technology (NIST) has explained that the aim of users is to access an information system in order to perform and complete a task. The problem is they see authentication as an obstacle. As a result, NIST has suggested that an effective authentication system should "make it easy to do the right thing, hard to do the wrong thing, and easy to recover when the wrong thing happens."

With this statement, usability evaluation is, therefore, essential because poor usability can result in users trying to find a workaround which can decrease the level of security of the authentication system. When designing and implementing a multi-factor authentication system, factors of authentication are the ones to be evaluated. NIST provides a guideline for evaluating the usability of authentication factors as follows:

- Availability – Authentication factors should be readily available
  for users to use when carrying out an authentication process. The
  case where the factors may not be available such as loss or damage
  should be considered so that users are not negatively affected by such
  situation. An alternative factor could be considered as a backup.

- Usage and Maintenance – During the first-time usage, the requirements should be clearly stated. The initialization steps should be easy to follow. In case of loss, stolen, or damage, there should be a clear instruction of what to do to solve this problem.

- User Experience – NIST appears to put an emphasis on the experience of the user during the authentication process. It is suggested that a clear and meaningful feedback is a must so that users know what is going on and are not lost. The number of attempts is another important criterion to be considered. If more authentication factors are involved, the more likely that mistakes will be made. Therefore, a higher number of allowed attempts may be required.

- User Interface – NIST recommends that good user interface design should be followed. For example, a larger area for text entry can increase usability, while a smaller area is more difficult to type.

One other element considered important today is the portability of the authentication system. Nowadays, users want to be able to log in from any device, at any location, and on any type of network. Therefore, this level of flexibility must also be considered so that the system can be claimed to have high usability and high user satisfaction.

Overall, when designing and implementing a multi-factor authentication system, security concerns and authentication needs should be the first to be addressed. However, it is also unavoidable that the multi-factor authentication solution provides acceptable user experience.

Summary

A challenge for any authentication mechanism is to provide protection to information systems. One-factor authentication has been proved to have many security concerns such as password attacks and biometric forgery. As a result, multi-factor authentication or MFA is a scheme that has been gaining popularity over the past few years.

Two-factor authentication or 2FA, considered a subset of multi-factor authentication, combines two different authentication factors from two different authentication categories, while multi-factor authentication is an extension to it as it combines three or more authentication factors. Both two-factor authentication and multi-factor authentication have an objective of increasing the security of authentication systems. Consequently, multi-factor authentication, especially the two-factor authentication, has been adopted in many industries such as the financial sector, the healthcare sector, the higher education, and the social media industry.

Even though, theoretically, multi-factor authentication can increase the level of security, there are still some criteria such as the OWASP's 5T model that need to be evaluated in order to really ensure that the required level of security is achieved. In addition, user experience or usability is something that cannot be overlooked and must be taken into consideration when designing, implementing, and deploying a multi-factor authentication system.

Bibliography

Abhishek, K., Roshan, S., Kumar, P., & Ranjan, R. (2013). A Comprehensive Study on Multifactor Authentication Schemes. *Advances in Computing and Information Technology, 177,* 561–568.

Boonkrong, S. (2017, January). Internet Banking Login with Multi-Factor Authentication. *KSII Transactions on Internet & Information Systems, 11*(1), 511–535.

Boonkrong, S. (2019, November). Security Analysis and Improvement of a Multi-Factor Biometric-Based Remote Authentication Scheme. *IAENG International Journal of Computer Science, 46*(4).

Choong, Y.-Y., Greene, K. K., & Theofanos, M. F. (2017). *Digital Identity Guidelines: Usability Consideration.* Technical Report, National Institute of Standards and Technology (NIST).

Huseynov, E., & Seigneur, J.-M. (2017). *Context-Aware Multifactor Authentication Survey in Computer and Information Security Handbook* (3rd ed.). Science Direct.

International Standards Organization. (1998). *Ergonomic requirements for office work with visual display terminals (VDTs) - Part 11: Guidance on usability.*

Li, C. T., & Hwang, M. S. (2010, January). An efficient biometrics-based remote user authentication scheme using smart cards. *Journal of Network and Computer Applications, 33*(1), 1–5.

Mahitthiburin, S., & Boonkrong, S. (2015, March). Improving Security with Two-factor Authentication Using Image. *Applied Science and Engineering Process, 8*(1), 33–43.

National Cyber Security Centre. (2018). *Multi-factor authentication for online services.*

Open Web Application Security Project (OWASP). (2014). *Testing Multiple Factors Authentication (OWASP-AT-009).*

Park, Y. H., Park, K. S., Lee, K. K., Song, H., & Park, Y. H. (2017, August). Security analysis and enhancements of an improved multi-factor biometric authentication scheme. *International Journal of Distributed Sensor Networks, 13*(8), 1–12.

Schneier, B. (2015, April). Two-factor authentication: too little, too late. *Communications of the ACM, 48*(4), 136.

Stanislav, M. (2015). *Two-Factor Authentication.* IT Governance Publishing.

CHAPTER 7

Authentication and Key Establishment Protocols

The first chapter shows that it is possible to achieve data confidentiality through the use of encryption, which could either be symmetric or asymmetric cryptography. We also know from the same chapter that the integrity of data or the loss of it can be detected with the use of cryptographic hash functions. However, higher level of security can be achieved via the use of access control mechanism in which authentication is a major part.

What we learn from the previous chapters is different authentication methods, namely, something you know, something you have, and something you are. In addition, it is recognized that a combination of two or more categories of these authentication methods can provide better security. They are known as two-factor authentication when using two different types of authentication and multi-factor authentication when using three or more different authentication categories.

What we have not looked at, however, is how cryptography can be applied in order to produce authentication mechanisms. When cryptography is used in the authentication domain, it is sometimes known as a *cryptographic protocol* or an authentication protocol. The way cryptography is applied so that authentication or identity verification can be accomplished is the focus of this chapter.

The chapter first presents two categories of authentication protocols, which are classic and real-world protocols. The classic protocols which now act as the basis of today's authentication protocols are explained and analyzed. The two real-world authentication protocols that will be looked at are secure socket layer and Kerberos, which are the most commonly used authentication protocols today. Next, the lessons learned from these protocols, specifically the reasons for the existence of vulnerabilities in the classic protocols, are analyzed, and design principles will be provided so that future protocols do not contain the same security mistakes.

© Sirapat Boonkrong 2021
S. Boonkrong, *Authentication and Access Control*, https://doi.org/10.1007/978-1-4842-6570-3_7

Authentication Protocols

Before illustrating authentication protocols that are commonly used in the real world today, the word "protocol" needs to be defined. *Protocols* are the rules that must be followed by participants or entities in some particular interactions. Thus, *network protocols* are the rules followed in networked communication systems. *Security protocols* are the communication rules followed in security applications. *Cryptographic protocols* are the rules that apply cryptographic techniques so that participants or entities can communicate securely. *Authentication protocols* fall into the security and cryptographic protocol categories and can be defined as a set of rules that must be followed for entities to prove or confirm their identity. That is, Alice must prove to Bob that she is really Alice, or Bob must prove to Alice that he is really Bob.

Authentication, in many cases, only requires that Alice proves her identity to Bob without Bob proving his identity to Alice. This is called *one-way authentication*. Sometimes, though, it is necessary for both Alice and Bob to prove their identity to one another. In other words, Alice proves that she is Alice, and Bob, in turn, proves that he is Bob. This is known as *two-way authentication* or, more formally, *mutual authentication*. In some situations, the use of symmetric cryptography, asymmetric cryptography, or cryptographic hash functions might be required, as will be seen in the following sections.

Before going into the details of well-known authentication protocols that have been designed, it is necessary to explain the concept of one of the most commonly used components in authentication protocols. The component is known as a *nonce* or a *cryptographic nonce*. In cryptography, the term "nonce" stands for "number used once." It is an arbitrary number that is usually created randomly and can only be used once in a cryptographic protocol or cryptographic communication.

In authentication protocols, nonces are used to ensure that protocol messages cannot be reused in replay attacks. A replay attack is when an attacker eavesdrops a protocol message and retransmits it. A replay can be explained with a simple example shown in Figure 7-1, which shows that Eve sniffs a message that Alice is sending to Bob. Eve then resends the exact same message to Bob, who might think that it is Alice who has sent it.

One way that this problem can be solved is to apply a nonce to a message. In the example, if a nonce is added to the message that Alice sends to Bob and then Eve replays the same message, Bob will be able to notice that Eve's message is a replay. This is because Bob will notice that the nonce in Eve's message is exactly the same as the one in Alice's message.

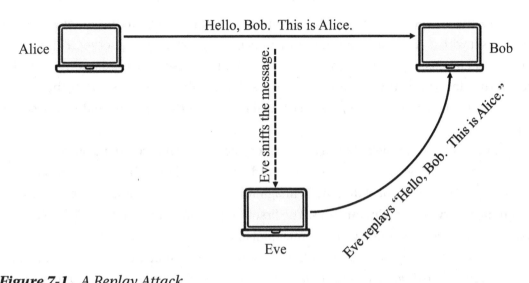

Figure 7-1. *A Replay Attack*

In reality, apart from using nonces to prevent replay attacks, they can serve other purposes, too. One purpose is that they can serve as a *challenge-and-response* mechanism. A challenge-and-response mechanism is basically a protocol where one entity presents a question (called a "challenge"), while the other provides an answer (called a "response"). The most simple challenge-and-response mechanism is actually when a server asks a client for a password. This is a challenge. The client then replies with their password. This is a response.

However, when a nonce is used in the challenge and response, it is a little different. In an authentication protocol where a server would like to prove whether or not a client possesses the same symmetric key, a nonce can be used as follows:

$$Server \rightarrow Client : Nonce_S$$

$$Client \rightarrow Server : \{Nonce_S\}_{K_{SC}}$$

where $Nonce_S$ is the nonce value belonging to the server,
K_{SC} is the symmetric key shared between the server and the client, and
$\{M\}_K$ is when the message M is encrypted with a symmetric key K.

From the preceding example, the server sends a nonce value to the client who then encrypts it with a symmetric key and transmits the ciphertext to the server. This way the server can easily prove whether or not the client is possessing the same symmetric key by just decrypting the ciphertext. If the resultant plaintext is the same as the nonce value he has sent earlier, the server will know that the client is holding the same symmetric key.

This is just an example of how a nonce or cryptographic nonce can be used in authentication protocols. How nonces are used and applied in authentication protocols is actually up to the protocol designer's imagination. However, it is important to know that nonces serve two main purposes. The first is to prevent replay attacks. The second is to be used in challenge-and-response mechanisms.

Let us now take a look at some authentication protocols that are deemed interesting and thought provoking. Some are actually very commonly used in the real world, while some are considered classic albeit not the most secure.

Andrew Secure RPC Protocol

RPC stands for Remote Procedure Call which is a method used for causing a function to be executed at another place or on another machine. RPC can either be done by calling a function at a different address space on the same machine or on another machine on a network and even over the Internet. In order to make this procedure more secure, Andrew Secure RPC was proposed as a protocol that allowed two entities, usually a client A and a server B, who already shared a secret key K_{AB} to carry out authentication and establish a new session key K'_{AB}. The Andrew Secure RPC consists of four messages that constitute two main parts. The first three messages make up the handshake, while the fourth message is the session key establishment. The protocol messages are as follows:

$$A \rightarrow B : A, \{N_A\}_{K_{AB}}$$

$$B \rightarrow A : \{N_A + 1, N_B\}_{K_{AB}}$$

$$A \rightarrow B : \left\{ N_B + 1 \right\}_{K_{AB}}$$

$$B \rightarrow A : \left\{ K'_{AB}, N'_B \right\}_{K_{AB}}$$

From the above protocol, N_A is the nonce generated by the client A. The nonces N_B and N'_B are generated by the server B. The notation $\{M\}_K$ means the message M is encrypted with the symmetric key K.

Unfortunately, the original Andrew Secure RPC has been found to be insecure. The first problem is that the second message could be substituted for the fourth message making the client believe that the component $N_A + 1$ is actually the new session key. Looking at another angle, the fourth message could easily be a replay of the second message. Another problem is concerning the *freshness* of the new session key K'_{AB} because there is no guarantee that the key is really fresh or newly generated. There are also other issues including the lack of message integrity detection mechanism and mutual authentication.

Various researchers have made an attempt to improve the protocol with the following being the latest and most secure version:

$$A \rightarrow B : A, \left\{ N_A \right\}_{K_{AB}}, MAC_{K_{AB}} \left(A, \left\{ N_A \right\}_{K_{AB}} \right)$$

$$B \rightarrow A : \left\{ N_A, N_B, K'_{AB}, B \right\}_{K_{AB}}, MAC_{K_{AB}} \left(\left\{ N_A, N_B, K'_{AB}, B \right\}_{K_{AB}} \right)$$

$$A \rightarrow B : \left\{ A, N_B + 1 \right\}_{K'_{AB}}, MAC_{K_{AB}} \left(\left\{ A, N_B + 1 \right\}_{K'_{AB}} \right)$$

The notations are as described earlier with the addition of MAC_K which means a cryptographic hash function MAC being computed with the secret key K.

The most recent version of the Andrew Secure RPC protocol accomplishes all the objectives in mutual authentication and secure key establishment. It is also secure against replay attacks and message modification attacks.

Needham–Schroeder Protocol

The Needham–Schroeder authentication protocol is probably one of, if not, the best-known security protocols. This authentication protocol is considered important to the field of authentication protocols because it has influenced the design of a significant number of authentication protocols existing today. The Needham–Schroeder authentication is different from the Andrew Secure RPC because it requires the use of a trusted third party (TTP) to complete the authentication and session key establishment.

The aim of the Needham–Schroeder protocol is for two entities A and B to be provided with a new session key K_{AB}. The protocol requires a trusted authentication server S, which shares common secret keys with all potential participants, A and B in this case. The server S also has the ability to generate a secure session key for any two entities wanting to have a secret key shared between them. The Needham–Schroeder protocol consists of the following five messages:

$$A \rightarrow S : A, B, N_A$$

$$S \rightarrow A : \left\{ N_A, B, K, \{K, A\}_{K_{BS}} \right\}_{K_{AS}}$$

$$A \rightarrow B : \{K, A\}_{K_{BS}}$$

$$B \rightarrow A : \{N_B\}_K$$

$$A \rightarrow B : \{N_B - 1\}_K$$

where N_i is the nonce value belonging to an entity i,
K_{ij} is the symmetric key shared between the entities i and j, and
$\{M\}_K$ is when a message M is encrypted with a symmetric key K.

It can be seen that at the end of the protocol session, the principals A and B will end up with a new shared secret K, which will be used for secure communications between them. It can also be observed that the protocol is intended for both A and B to practically authenticate one another in the fourth and fifth messages by asking one another to encrypt a message using the session key K.

However, several flaws have been found in this protocol, most notably a potential replay attack and a lack of message origin identification. A couple of researchers have pointed out that it was possible to replay the third message since there is no component suggesting that the message, specifically the key K, is freshly generated. The second vulnerability is in the fifth message. As mentioned, there is no way for B to know whether or not the message is really from A, which could lead to a message spoofing attack. As a result, an improvement has been made to obtain what is known as an *enhanced Needham–Schroeder protocol*, which works as follows:

$$A \rightarrow B : A$$

$$B \rightarrow A : \left\{ A, N_{B1} \right\}_{K_{BS}}$$

$$A \rightarrow S : A, B, N_A, \left\{ A, N_{B1} \right\}_{K_{BS}}$$

$$S \rightarrow A : \left\{ N_A, B, K, \left\{ K, N_{B1}, A \right\}_{K_{BS}} \right\}_{K_{AS}}$$

$$A \rightarrow B : \left\{ K, N_{B1}, A \right\}_{K_{BS}}$$

$$B \rightarrow A : \left\{ N_B \right\}_K$$

$$A \rightarrow B : \left\{ N_B - 1 \right\}_K$$

It is evident from the enhanced protocol that the replay attack can be solved by the principal B generating their own nonce N_{B1}, which is also present in the fifth message. This way B knows that the component N_{B1} is new or fresh. Hence, if there is a replay, B should be able to detect it and ignore the message altogether. The enhanced version of the Needham–Schroeder protocol is now believed to be secure, provided that the cryptographic implementation is properly and securely done.

Even though the original Needham–Schroeder authentication protocol has several vulnerabilities, it is still a big influence on many existing authentication and session key establishment protocols today. At the very least, the Needham–Schroeder protocol was the first to implement a three-party protocol that consisted of authentication and key establishment with the help of a trusted third party. Many protocols today, such as Kerberos that will be discussed later in the chapter, have applied the idea as their foundation and built upon it to make them more secure.

Needham–Schroeder Public Key Protocol

Needham and Schroeder not only designed an authentication protocol that applied symmetric cryptography, they also designed one of, if not, the first authentication protocols that used asymmetric cryptography. The Needham–Schroeder Public Key protocol, again, is considered as the beginning of an idea of using public key cryptosystems in authentication protocols.

The Needham-Schroeder authentication protocol has an objective of having two entities, A and B, authenticate one another. Hence, mutual authentication is aimed to be accomplished after a protocol run. The protocol works as follows:

$$A \rightarrow B : \left\{ A, N_A \right\}_{+K_B}$$

$$B \rightarrow A : \left\{ N_A, N_B \right\}_{+K_A}$$

$$A \rightarrow B : \left\{ N_B \right\}_{+K_B}$$

where N_i is the nonce value belonging to an entity i,

$+K_i$ is the public key of the entity i, and

$\left\{ M \right\}_{+K_i}$ is when the message M is being encrypted with a public key $+K_i$.

The protocol begins with the entity A sending their identity A along with the newly generated nonce N_A, all of which are encrypted with the public key of the entity B. When B receives the message, they decrypt it using their private key, which is only known by the entity themselves. B then sends the component N_A back to A together with the freshly generated nonce N_B. All are encrypted with the public key of entity A. Finally, A receives the message and decrypts it with their private key. The entity A then checks whether the received N_A matches with the one they had sent earlier. If so, A sends the nonce N_B which is encrypted with B's public key back to the entity B. Having received the message, B decrypts the message to ensure that the received component is actually the nonce that they had sent earlier.

At the end of this protocol run, A is certain that the other entity is B if and only if the nonce N_A matches with the one in the first message. This is because B is the only one holding the private key that can be used to decrypt the message. Similarly, B is sure that the other entity is A if and only if the nonce N_B in the third message matches with the one in the second message. Again, only A possesses the private key that can decrypt the second message.

Needham and Schroeder have, thereof, shown that it is also possible to use asymmetric cryptography as a part of a protocol that can mutually authenticate the two participating principals.

Although the public key protocol shows some promises of the way to integrate asymmetric cryptography into a mutual authentication mechanism, there is one interesting flaw that was discovered almost 20 years after its birth and should be mentioned here. The protocol is prone to an attack called a *man-in-the-middle attack* or *MitM attack*. This type of attack practically means that an attacker C comes into the middle of the conversation between A and B with an objective of impersonating the entity A so that B believes that they are conversing with A. The man-in-the-middle attack is illustrated in Figure 7-2.

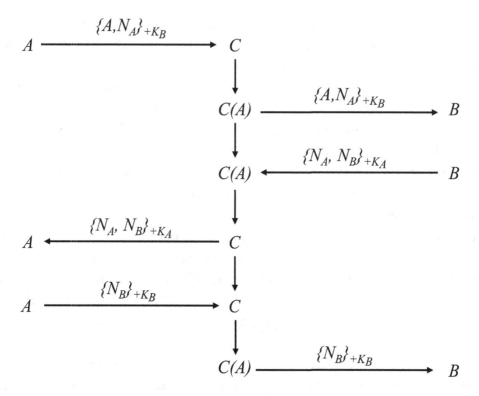

Figure 7-2. *Man-in-the-Middle Attack on the Needham–Schroeder*
Public Key Protocol

The problem actually occurs because there are no components specifying the identity of the message originator in the messages two and three of the Needham–Schroeder Public Key protocol. Therefore, one way to reduce the risk is by adding the identity components B and A in the second and third messages of the protocol, respectively. The resultant protocol thus becomes

$$A \rightarrow B : \left\{A, N_A\right\}_{+K_B}$$

$$B \rightarrow A : \left\{ B, N_A, N_B\right\}_{+K_A}$$

$$A \rightarrow B : \left\{ A, N_B\right\}_{+K_B}$$

Based on the preceding classic authentication protocols, it has been possible for researchers and protocol designers to deduce protocols that would be applicable to real-world usage. The following sections take a look at a couple of authentication protocols whose aims are to confirm the identities of protocol principals as well as to establish a new session key so that a more secure communication channel can be created. The two authentication protocols are known as *secure socket layer* and *Kerberos*, which work based on the use of asymmetric cryptography and symmetric cryptography, respectively. Although the technologies behind them are different, they do have similar objectives, as mentioned. The description of how each scheme functions is presented in the subsequent sections.

Secure Socket Layer (SSL)

The first real-world authentication protocol to be discussed is known as *secure socket layer* or *SSL*. This protocol is used as or is a basis of other protocols used for securing most Internet transactions. SSL originally dealt mainly with web browsing. However, nowadays, it has become a major part of many transactions on the Internet, which include those of mobile applications. If we map this with the computer network's OSI model, we will see that SSL is responsible for securing the HTTP in the application layer and the TCP protocol in the transport layer. Hence, SSL's subsequent version is called *Transport Layer Security* or *TLS*. Although the name has been changed from SSL to TLS, the aim of authenticating data transfer or transactions between entities still remains. The only major difference in the context of security is that TLS works with newer cryptographic algorithms including AES and key-based cryptographic hash functions.

Secure socket layer is an element used for safeguarding transactions between users and websites or between users' device and the server of the application they are using. One of the protocol's main purposes is to prevent transaction messages or packets from being eavesdropped. SSL is a protocol used to establish a secure channel between two points on the Internet, so that data can be encapsulated and hidden from attackers. However, prior to the action of securing communication channel taking place, one process that must be done is, of course, authentication which is an integral part of the protocol and will be explained later in the section.

In the case of websites, web addresses usually begin with HTTP, which stands for hypertext transfer protocol. Unfortunately, communication using this protocol is not secure and is prone to eavesdropping. This is, therefore, not recommended for transmitting such data as personal information, personal bank records, or credit card number. A solution to this problem is to use HTTPS or *secure* HTTP. By typing HTTPS instead of just HTTP at the beginning of a web address, SSL is effectively implemented.

It has been established that security of data in transit over the Internet is necessary. Some even see it as a must, these days. SSL, as already mentioned, is a protocol adopted for protecting data on the Internet. In addition to data privacy, SSL has the following objectives:

- Secure socket layer or SSL supports authentication between client and server. SSL applies asymmetric cryptography, specifically digital certificates and public key encryption, to authenticate communicating parties to each other.

- Secure socket layer provides a mechanism for ensuring data integrity. That is, during an SSL session, any data that has been tampered with will not be gone unnoticed.

- Secure socket layer provides data privacy as its main objective. Data transmitted between client and server will be protected from eavesdropping and will be readable only by the intended recipient.

SSL is better explained with an example. Suppose a user wants to buy a book from an online bookshop. Before providing their credit card information, the user must be sure that they are really dealing with a legitimate bookshop. That means the bookshop must prove to the user that it really is legitimate. After the user is satisfied that they are dealing with a trusted bookshop, private information can then be provided. In most cases, the user would want to have confidentiality and integrity. The user wants confidentiality because their credit card information needs to be kept secret. Integrity of data is also required because the exchanged information must be correct. For example, if the user orders one book, the number of books should remain one throughout the transactions. SSL is, therefore, a suitable solution.

SSL begins with a *handshake* phase. This handshake protocol is used to initiate an SSL session between a client and a server. During the handshake, various components, such as keys, digital certificates, and algorithms, are exchanged and negotiated so that a secure communication channel can be established. Entity authentication is also carried out here, in this phase. An overview of the SSL handshake protocol is shown as follows:

$$Client \rightarrow Server : SSLRequest, CipherList, N_{Client}$$

$$Server \rightarrow Client : Certificate_{Server}, Cipher, N_{Server}$$

$$Client \rightarrow Server : \{S\}_{+K_{Server}} , H\left(msg, CLNT, K\right)$$

$$Server \rightarrow Client : H\left(msg, SRVR, K\right)$$

$$Client \rightarrow Server : Data\ Protected\ with\ Session\ Key, K$$

where S is the "pre-master secret,"

K is the session key and is computed from $H(S, N_{Client}, N_{Server})$,

$+K_{Server}$ is the server's public key,

$Certificate_{Server}$ is the digital certificate belonging to the server,

$H()$ is a cryptographic hash function,

msg is representing all previous messages,

$CLNT$ is the ID of the client, and

$SRVR$ is the ID of the server.

The protocol can be explained as follows:

1. The client informs the server that they would like to establish an SSL connection. The message contains a list of ciphers supported by the client, a nonce, and other communication parameters, such as speed, that the server needs to communicate with the client.

2. The server responds with the cipher selected from the received list, its own nonce, and other parameters that the client needs to communicate with the server using SSL. One important component that the server sends here is its own digital certificate, $Certificate_{Server}$.

3. After receiving the packet, the client processes it by, first, validating the certificate. This is accomplished by verifying the certificate authority or the CA's signature on the certificate. If the signature verification is a success, it means that the certificate can be trusted, and the client obtains the server's public key. (Reader is referred back to Chapter 2 for the detailed process of digital certificate verification.)

4. In order to produce the third packet, the client randomly generates a pre-master secret, S, and encrypts it with the server's public key. The ciphertext is then sent to the server. At this stage, the client is also able to compute a secret session key, K, from the three components which are S, the client's nonce from the first packet, and the server's nonce from the second packet, namely, N_{Client} and N_{Server}, respectively.

5. After receiving the packet, the server decrypts the ciphertext to obtain S. At this stage, the server is also able to compute the same secret key, K, from the same three components, namely, the decrypted pre-master secret S, the client's nonce N_{Client} from the first packet, and the server's nonce N_{Server} from the second packet.

6. At this point, the client and server both possess the same symmetric session key, K, which is a symmetric key used to encrypt and decrypt information exchanged during this SSL session.

Note   We can see that a cryptographic hash function $H()$ is used in the third and fourth messages of the protocol. The main objective of it is to ensure data integrity of those messages. Specifically, the session key K is present as a component in $H()$. This allows for both the client and server to check whether or not the other entity is really possessing the exact same session key K.

At the end of the process described earlier, the client should have authenticated the server. The question is: where is the actual authentication process? Some may think that the certificate sent to the client by the server is where the authentication takes place. However, sending the certificate, even if it is valid, does not prove that the sender is really the server. In fact, the client is certain that the other party is the server because the pre-master secret component S is encrypted with the server's public key, and the only entity that can decrypt it is the server. The client knows that the server has decrypted S successfully because during the information exchange phase, both the client and server can encrypt and decrypt data successfully, in addition to the data integrity checking done by the cryptographic hash function $H()$. Hence, they both possess the same symmetric session key K, generated from the same pre-master secret S.

It can be observed that the preceding process is one-way authentication, since only the client authenticates the server. The server has not authenticated the client at all. SSL provides an option for doing authentication in the opposite direction, too. If the server requests client authentication, the client sends the server their certificate. The server randomly generates another pre-master secret and encrypts it with the client's public key. Similar to when the server is authenticated, if the client can decrypt the ciphertext, the server is certain that this is the client. Having said that, the request for client authentication is not usually done this way. Other means of authentication such as using a password is a more commonly adopted method.

As explained, at this point, the SSL handshake or the authentication process is complete. The client and the server can now use the newly established session key to encrypt and decrypt data as well as to validate message integrity using a category of cryptographic hash function known as message authentication code. Hence, a secure communication channel between the server and the client is generated in addition to a successful authentication procedure.

Secure socket layer provides us with enhanced security over the Internet. However, it does come with an overhead. Recently, there have been a lot of talks about the sluggishness of SSL. One factor behind this is the use of certificates. SSL uses certificates so that a client can obtain the server's public key, and vice versa, in the case of mutual authentication. In more detail, after a digital certificate is issued by a certificate authority (CA), it is possible that it is compromised and needs to be revoked. This is why a certificate revocation list (CRL), which is a database containing invalid and compromised certificates, needs to be present. This means that when an SSL handshake is carried out, the CRL has to be queried in order to ensure that the certificate is valid. The problem is the CRL servers are not usually geographically distributed or tuned for performance. This implies that some time will be added to the typical page load time.

On the whole, SSL has given better protection of data, albeit with a little overhead. Moreover, SSL is an authentication protocol based on the use of public key cryptography and digital certificates. The next section introduces another authentication protocol, but this time, it will be different since it is designed and implemented based on symmetric cryptography.

Kerberos

In Greek mtyhology, Kerberos is a three-headed dog that guarded the entrance to Hades. In the context of security, Kerberos was designed at the Massachusetts Institute of Technology or MIT as a solution to the insecurity of computer networks. *Kerberos* is an authentication system that uses symmetric key cryptography. It allows entities to communicate and to prove their identity to one another in a secure manner.

At MIT, a Kerberos consortium was actually founded. Its main objective is "to establish Kerberos as the universal authentication platform for the world's computer networks." Nowadays, Kerberos has become a major foundation of desktops, server operating systems, core networking infrastructure, and much more. One of the main uses of Kerberos is to provide a *single sign-on* (SSO) environment. It also has the potential to integrate password-less authentication mechanisms to form a more convenient security solution. Moreover, it has been suggested that Kerberos has grown to become the most widely deployed system for authentication and authorization in modern computer networks.

Prior to explaining how Kerberos works, a typical scenario needs to be set. Suppose on a network, there are many individuals such as Alice, Bob, and Charlie. There are also resources, systems, and applications that can be accessed by the users. They include an email system, a web application, and a database server.

For any users to access and use those systems, typically they are required to log in. For example, for Alice to access her email, she needs to authenticate herself with the email system. Similarly, if she wants to access the web application, she will be asked to authenticate herself again, and so on. This means that on this network, the email system, the web application, and the database server, each has its own authentication system. The users will have to carry out authentication each time they want an access to a system. This results in inconvenience and, more importantly, potential issues with password reuse and weak passwords. This typical scenario is displayed in Figure 7-3.

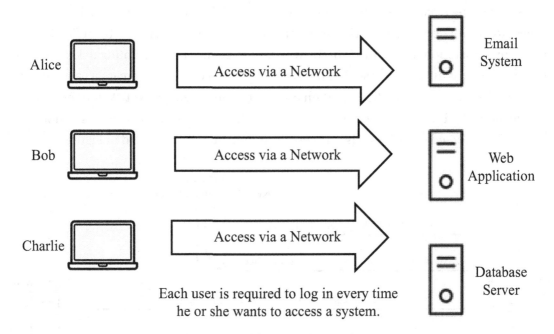

Figure 7-3. *A Typical Scenario on an Organization's Network*

Kerberos, as mentioned, functions based on the application of symmetric cryptography. Its main characteristics include the fact that it requires N keys for N individuals on a network and that the Kerberos authentication system relies on a trusted third party (TTP). Kerberos' TTP is known as a *key distribution center* or a *KDC*. The key distribution center's main job is to provide symmetric session keys and "tickets" for users to access the resources on a network. The key distribution center also shares a symmetric key with each individual, such as K_A with Alice, K_B with Bob, K_C with Charlie, and so on. The KDC also holds a master key of its own called K_{KDC}.

When using Kerberos, users accomplish two things. They are authentication for identity verification and session key establishment for secure communication. In order to achieve those two objectives, the key distribution center and the concept of Kerberos "tickets" are needed.

With reference to Figure 7-3, each individual is required to present a valid ticket to the system they are accessing before being granted the permission to access. In Kerberos, a ticket contains cryptographic key and other information required to access network resources. However, for any individuals to obtain those access tickets, another type of ticket has to be attained. That ticket is known as a *ticket granting ticket* or a *TGT*. That is, a ticket granting ticket is used to exchange for access tickets that are then used to allow access to network resources. For example, if Alice wants to access the web application on her network, as shown in Figure 7-3, she will have to get her ticket granting ticket verified by the key distribution center so that the key distribution center can create a valid access ticket and issue it to Alice. Alice will then present the obtained access ticket to the web application which will check its validity. If it is valid, Alice is granted an access. If not, Alice will be denied an access. The process described here is illustrated in Figure 7-4.

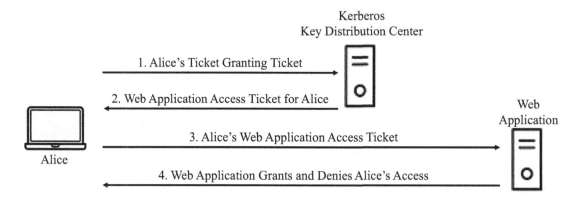

Figure 7-4. *A Typical Process of Using a Ticket to Access a Network Resource*

In more detail, each ticket granting ticket contains a session key, a user ID of the user to whom the TGT is issued, and an expiration time. One clever feature of Kerberos is that the ticket granting ticket is encrypted using K_{KDC} and can only be read by the KDC.

We now know that Kerberos is used for authentication and session key establishment. The protocol consists of various components including a key distribution center, a ticket granting ticket for each user, and access tickets for accessing network resources and systems. Let us now look at how Kerberos actually works, starting with the client login process and then Kerberos ticket exchange process.

Client Login

Before a user can access any resources on a network, they will have to complete the login process. The login process is a simple process that requires a user to log into their computer, which will communicate with the key distribution center (KDC). Kerberos will carry out its functions (which will be explained later). In the end, the key distribution center will hand a ticket granting ticket to the user. This client login process is shown in Figure 7-5.

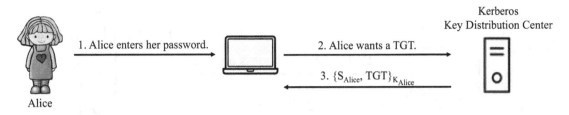

Figure 7-5. *Kerberos Client Login Process*

The Kerberos client login in Figure 7-5 begins with Alice entering her username and password into her computer. The computer derives the key K_{Alice} from Alice's password as $K_{Alice} = H(Alice's\ Password)$. It needs to be clarified that the key distribution center is not only responsible for distributing keys to users, it also acts as an authentication server, which means its other task is to authenticate users on the network. It, therefore, implies that K_{Alice} is the key shared between Alice and the key distribution center.

Alice's computer will use K_{Alice} to obtain a ticket granting ticket (TGT) for Alice from the key distribution center. The KDC receives the TGT request and generates a new session key S_{Alice} and a TGT for Alice. The KDC encrypts S_{Alice} and TGT with the key K_{Alice} before sending the packet to Alice's computer.

The next step is for the computer to decrypt the received packet with K_{Alice} to obtain the session key S_{Alice} and the TGT. The key K_{Alice} can now be forgotten. Note that the $TGT = \{Alice, S_{Alice}\}_{K_{KDC}}$, which means that it can only be read by the KDC since the key K_{KDC} is only known by the key distribution center itself. Alice can now use this TGT to exchange for access tickets for accessing network resources later on.

Kerberos Ticket Exchange

After Alice has completed the Kerberos client login process and obtained the TGT, Alice can now start thinking about accessing network resources. Suppose Alice would like to access a service such as a web application in Figure 7-3. If Alice's network utilizes Kerberos, Alice cannot just start accessing the required service straight away. There is a process of ticket exchange to be done beforehand. The ticket exchange process is illustrated in Figure 7-6.

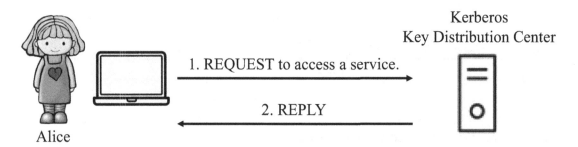

Figure 7-6. *Kerberos Ticket Exchange Process*

From Figure 7-6, a few components need to be defined. The first is the REQUEST, which is defined as $REQUEST = (TGT, Authenticator)$, where $Authenticator = \{Alice, Timestamp\}_{S_{Alice}}$. The next component is the REPLY, which is sent from the key distribution center to Alice's computer. The REPLY message is defined as $REPLY = \{ServiceID, K_{AS}, TicketToService\}_{S_{Alice}}$, where K_{AS} is the symmetric key shared between Alice and the service she is trying to access. Moreover, within the REPLY message, $TicketToService = \{Alice, K_{AS}\}_{K_{Service}}$.

Alice, more specifically Alice's computer, presents Alice's ticket granting ticket to the key distribution center, along with another piece of information called *authenticator*. The authenticator is composed of the user ID and timestamp, which is used to prevent replay attacks. The authenticator is encrypted using the client's session key, S_{Alice} in this particular example. After the key distribution center verifies the authenticator, it responds with a "ticket to service" or an access ticket. Alice can then use the received ticket to access the required service.

It needs to be clarified that an access ticket is issued for an access to one particular service only. If a user wants to access another service on the network, a new access ticket will have to be issued by the key distribution center by following the same process illustrated in Figure 7-6.

Let us take a look at the REPLY packet in a little bit more detail. The REPLY message sent from the KDC to Alice's computer contains three components: the name of the service "*ServiceID*", the key K_{AS}, and the "ticket to service" or *TicketToService*. The components are all encrypted with the session key S_{Alice} shared between Alice and the KDC. What does the REPLY message really say? It tells Alice's computer that the *TicketToService* is the ticket used to access that particular service, to communicate with the service, and the key K_{AS} must be used to secure the communications between Alice and the service.

The next step is for Alice's computer to hand the *TicketToService* to the required service so that the service can grant Alice an access and Alice and the service can begin their secure communication. The *TicketToService* is composed of two components: Alice's identity and the key K_{AS}. The two components are encrypted with the key, $K_{Service}$. Note that the $K_{Service}$ belongs to the service and this key is shared only between the service and the key distribution center. When the service receives the ticket from Alice, it decrypts the packet and sees that the key K_{AS} is to be used for communication with Alice. At this point, Alice and the service are now holding the key, K_{AS}, and, therefore, can securely communicate with one another.

It has been explained that Kerberos is a very useful protocol for accomplishing user authentication and secure communications between client and network services or resources. However, there are a couple of limitations to the protocol that should be stated. They are as follows: The first obvious drawback to Kerberos is a single point of failure. It can be seen that the key distribution center or KDC plays an important role in Kerberos. The KDC is involved from the client login process to the ticket generation process. If the KDC is compromised or down, these processes cannot be carried out; hence, Kerberos stops working. One simple solution to this problem is to use multiple Kerberos servers.

The second limitation of Kerberos is time restriction. Kerberos requires that the times of the hosts involved are synchronized or at least loosely synchronized. This synchronization is needed because Kerberos tickets have an authenticator, which contains a timestamp. If the clock on the client's side is not synchronized with the KDC, the timestamp checking process will fail and no further processes will be done.

It was mentioned earlier that one of the main uses of Kerberos was in a single sign-on environment. *Single sign on* or *SSO* is an authentication scheme that allows an individual to log into one service or application and that individual appears to be authenticated and signed into other services on the same network automatically. The word "appear" was used in the previous sentence because to the user, the process of authentication to other applications and services is practically nonexistent. However, what goes on in the background that allows the user to access those services and applications is actually Kerberos.

With reference to Figure 7-3 and with Kerberos being deployed, Alice carries out the Kerberos client login process to obtain a ticket granting ticket. When Alice wants to access her email, the ticket exchange is processed in the background so that Alice receives a ticket to access her email without having to log into the service. Alice then wants to use the web application on the same network, and the Kerberos ticket exchange is accomplished in the background, which means Alice is able to enter the web application without having to physically log in. This is how Kerberos is used for the single sign-on implementation.

It is evident from the previous sections that with clear objectives, it is feasible and possible to design an authentication protocol that can accomplish them. Unfortunately, it is not easy to have authentication schemes that do not have weaknesses. It, therefore, seems like a good place to take what has been learned from the classic and real-world authentication protocols and explain how authentication protocols should be thought of and designed. This is so that protocols with fewer vulnerabilities can be formed, while the required goals can still be achieved.

Designing Authentication Protocols

The three classic protocols explained in the earlier sections apply symmetric cryptography and asymmetric cryptography. They have all made a big impact in cryptographic and authentication protocol design, which has eventually led to the two real-world protocols in security socket layer (SSL) and Kerberos. However, as seen, the protocols explained previously, especially the classic ones, contain vulnerabilities. Potential attacks on these authentication schemes include replay attacks and man-in-the-middle attacks. Fortunately, there are mechanisms available to combat them. They include the use of a nonce value and a challenge-and-response method, as already explained in the beginning of the chapter. This section, based on what we have learned from those protocols, will provide an explanation of how we should look at authentication protocols and what we should consider when designing them so that we end up with a more secure scheme as a result.

It can be observed from all the protocols explained in the chapter that two main processes are involved within each protocol run. The first is authentication and the second is the establishment of a new session key. These mechanisms are evident in the Andrew Secure RPC, Needham–Schroeder, secure socket layer, and Kerberos protocols. Let us, therefore, talk a little bit about them here.

In early literature, all protocols concerned with setting up a new session key were commonly referred to as authentication protocols. However, many researchers and security practitioners did not think that this was satisfactory. It has since been suggested that the two mechanisms should be clearly distinguished between them. In other words, protocols that provide the process of identity confirmation or verification are to be called *entity authentication protocols*, while protocols that involve the process of setting up a new key are to be known as *key establishment protocols*.

We have already learned that the goal of authentication protocols is to confirm the identity of an entity. That is, an authentication mechanism is carried out in order to ensure that the entity is really who the entity claims to be. A key establishment protocol is something that we have not really formally come across before. Fortunately, we have seen that it is an important part of many of the existing protocols. Its goal is different from that of authentication in that key establishment protocols must generate a fresh session key, which is known only to the protocol participants and possibly some trusted third parties. What it means is that a key establishment protocol is aimed to set up a new key every time a protocol is executed in such a way that the key is fresh and unknown to unauthorized entities.

Even though authentication and key establishment are two very different processes, many researchers, including Whitfield Diffie and Martin Hellman, who are considered the gurus of the field, suggest that both mechanisms should be considered jointly, rather than separately. The claim has been supported by Mihir Bellare and Phillip Rogaway, another two cryptography experts, who have said that

> *"an entity authentication is rarely useful in the absence of an associated key distribution (establishment), while key distribution (establishment), all by itself, is not only useful, but it is not appreciably more so when an entity authentication occurs alongside."*

Let us consider what those claims mean for a moment. Basically, when an authentication process is done without key establishment, the entities involved in the process are certain of the other party's identity. The problem is without a newly established session key, there is a question of how these entities will be able to securely communicate with one another. Conversely, if a key establishment process is carried out without authentication, it will mean that the protocol principals will have no idea who they are communicating with. In other words, it is possible that a key is established with an unknown entity, which could also be an attacker. This would, therefore, be against the aim of a key establishment protocol which states that the key must only be known by authorized entities. However, in this non-authentication case, we have no idea who is participating in the protocol session. This is why it is common to have both authentication and key establishment mechanisms in a protocol run, usually in that order, so that the protocol entities are first certain of the identities of other entities prior to setting up a fresh session key. Hence, today's protocols are known as authentication and key establishment protocols.

Due to the fact that it appears possible to design an authentication and key establishment protocol with vulnerabilities, especially with potential replay and man-in-the-middle attacks as well as lack of message confidentiality and integrity, it is essential to have principles that can be followed so that the risk of exposing protocol weaknesses can be reduced. We think it would be better to categorize these principles into two separate groups, which are specific principles and generic principles. No matter what group they belong to, it is recommended that when designing a protocol, these principles should at least be considered.

Specific Principles

When designing an authentication and key establishment protocol, there are several questions to be answered. Suppose A and B are the two entities participating in the protocol. How can A be sure that the other entity is really B? How do both A and B know that the established session key is secure? How does A know that B also possesses the same newly established session key at the end of the protocol run? These are the questions that require the following principles to be acted upon:

- Message Authenticity – This principle states that an entity A must be able to believe that an entity B is really the one who has just sent a message. In other words, for every message sent, the recipient must be able to identify and recognize who the sender is.

- Entity Authentication – Following from the previous principle, the second goal is for A to believe that B has recently replied to a specific challenge. That is, if B is able to reply to some challenge posted by A, A should be able to be certain to a certain degree that the other protocol participant is actually B.

- Secure Key Establishment – Once entity authentication is done, the process of setting up a new key is to be carried out. When a session key is established, A must be certain that the key K is good and secure enough to be used in communication with B. This principle suggests that it is important to have both A and B establish a new session key which is known and accessible to them only, not any other unauthorized parties.

- Key Freshness – Not only that the session key needs to be secure and hidden from unauthorized entities, *A* must ensure and believe that the session key *K* is freshly generated. In other words, the key is not an old key from any previous sessions.

- Key Confirmation – After *A* has established and distributed the session key, this principle states that the protocol must contain a mechanism for *A* to receive evidence that *B* also possesses the same key. This way, both entities will be sure that the key can really be used to set up a secure communication channel between them.

- Mutual Understanding of Shared Session Key – This is considered an add-on to the previous principle. It is important not to forget that when two entities are involved in the protocol, each of them must confirm with the other that the same newly established session key *K* is now in possession. In turn, each of them must also acknowledge and believe that the other party really holds the key, which is secure and good for further communication.

On the whole, the preceding six principles are there so that protocol designers can think of and come up with some mechanisms in such a way that all the principles (some may think of them as goals) can be accomplished. It is to be noted that we call them specific principles because the ideas are to be considered and applied to actual protocol messages. More generic principles are presented in the next section.

Generic Principles

Over the years, many authentication and key establishment protocols have been designed and implemented. Many have been in use in real-world situations. However, some are admittedly not very secure, as already seen in the classic protocols in the previous sections. This section, therefore, provides an attempt to present design principles for authentication and key establishment protocols. These principles have been gathered by security researchers, especially by Martin Abadi and Roger Needham, with an aim of having them as a basic guideline so that previously made mistakes can be avoided.

It has been evident that many authentication and key establishment protocols apply either symmetric or asymmetric cryptography. Hence, the very first thing that we would like to state is that protocol designers must choose provably secure encryption algorithms as part of their protocol. For example, AES should be considered rather than DES for symmetric encryption. For asymmetric cryptography, RSA is still claimed to be secure with Elliptic Curve Cryptography (ECC) being a possible alternative. As for cryptographic hash functions, MD5 and SHA-1 should probably be avoided since collisions can potentially be found. The SHA-2 family such as SHA-256 or SHA-512 or even the upcoming SHA-3 should be considered instead. These are just examples for more secure cryptographic algorithms that should be applied in authentication and key establishment protocols. What we will do next is to get into the generic design principles to help avoid previously published blunders.

Principle 1: Importance of message meaning

Every message of the protocol should say what it means. In other words, the meaning or the interpretation of each message should be from the components of the message. Assumptions should not have to be made by any entities. Protocol entities should be able to understand what each message means by the message itself. Moreover, it should be possible to express or explain each protocol message in plain written or spoken language.

For example, a server S may want to transmit a message to an entity A which is intended to be interpreted as "the server S sends to an entity A a secret key K, which is to be used for communications with another entity B." This first principle recommends that every element that is necessary for this interpretation must be included in the message. This is so that the recipient, in this case A, can understand the intention without having to wait for any other messages.

In addition, it has been said that the trust in the message really depends on the elements within itself as well as previously received components. Therefore, every message must contain correct and complete components so that it is adequate to communicate the true intention of the sender.

Principle 2: Clear condition for protocol messages

The condition for a protocol message to be acted upon must be clearly specified so that any future protocol inspection can decide whether or not this particular condition is acceptable.

This second principle follows on from Principle 1. For a protocol message to be acted upon, purely understanding the meaning of the message is not enough. Any condition necessary for the correct protocol function must also hold. It is essential for protocol designers to express that a protocol message will only have an impact upon the protocol if this condition is true.

For example, in an authentication and key establishment protocol, one condition is intended by a protocol designer that a secret key K to be used in communication by entities A and B must be generated by a server S. Therefore, if there are messages in the protocol which suggest that K is generated by any other entities other than S, then these messages will not have any impact or influence on the protocol. This is because the specified condition has not been correctly followed.

Principle 3: Identification of protocol principals

If the name of an entity or the identity of the protocol principal is essential to the meaning of the protocol message or the authentication and key establishment on the whole, it is important to explicitly specify that identity in the protocol message.

In authentication and key establishment protocols, it is necessary to explicitly state the identity or identities of protocol participant or participants involved in a protocol run. In many cases, not specifying the identities can lead to potential attacks on the protocol, especially the man-in-the-middle attack and impersonation attack. This can simply be illustrated as follows.

Suppose that principals Alice A and Bob B are involved in an authentication protocol with Alice and Bob trying to authenticate one another. This is done by proving to one another that they possess the same secret key K_{AB}, which is the symmetric key shared between Alice and Bob. First, Alice sends a message to Bob saying that she is Alice, along with her nonce value $Nonce_A$. When Bob receives the message, he encrypts the component $Nonce_A$ with the key K_{AB} shared between Alice and Bob. The ciphertext is transmitted to Alice together with Bob's nonce value $Nonce_B$. Once Alice receives the message, she first decrypts the ciphertext to examine whether or not the resultant plaintext matches with $Nonce_A$ she has generated and sent earlier. If they match, Alice knows that Bob shares the same key as hers. She then encrypts the component $Nonce_B$ with the key she holds and sends the ciphertext to Bob. Finally, Bob decrypts the message to see whether or not the resultant plaintext matches with his $Nonce_B$. If so, Bob knows that Alice possesses the same key as his. This mutual authentication process can be expressed as follows:

$$Alice \rightarrow Bob : I'm\ Alice, Nonce_A$$

$$Bob \rightarrow Alice : Nonce_B, \{Nonce_A\}_{K_{AB}}$$

$$Alice \rightarrow Bob : \{Nonce_B\}_{K_{AB}}$$

where $Nonce_i$ is the nonce value of an entity i,

K_{AB} is the symmetric key shared between Alice and Bob, and

$\{M\}_{K_{AB}}$ is when a message M is being encrypted with the key K_{AB}.

It can be seen in the protocol that no identities of any of the protocol principals are specified in any of the messages. The problem with this is that the preceding protocol is vulnerable to an impersonation attack which can be explained in the following way.

Suppose there is an attacker called Charlie C who wants to impersonate Alice A. The attack begins with the first two messages that are the same as a normal protocol run, but this time, the first message is initiated by Charlie who begins his process of pretending to be Alice. When Charlie receives the second message from Bob B, of course, it is not possible for Charlie to encrypt $Nonce_B$ because he does not possess the key K_{AB}. What Charlie can do here is start a new authentication session with Bob. During the new session, Charlie sends $Nonce_B$ to Bob, who will follow the protocol by encrypting it and sending the ciphertext back to Charlie. Charlie, having received the ciphertext of $Nonce_B$, goes back to the first session and sends the ciphertext back to Bob. Bob will believe that Charlie possesses the same key as his and, therefore, will think that he is really communicating with Alice. As a result, Charlie has successfully impersonated Alice. Charlie's attack can be expressed in the following manner:

Message 1: $Charlie \rightarrow Bob : I'm\ Alice,\ Nonce_A$

Message 2: $Bob \rightarrow Charlie : Nonce_B, \{Nonce_A\}_{K_{AB}}$

Charlie begins a new session.

Message 3: $Charlie \rightarrow Bob : I'm\ Alice,\ Nonce_B$

Message 4: $Bob \rightarrow Charlie : Nonce_{B'}, \{Nonce_B\}_{K_{AB}}$

Charlie goes back to the old session.

Message 5: $Charlie \rightarrow Bob : \{Nonce_B\}_{K_{AB}}$

where $Nonce_i$ is the nonce value of an entity i,

K_{AB} is the symmetric key shared between Alice and Bob, and

$\{M\}_{K_{AB}}$ is when a message M is being encrypted with the key K_{AB}.

The impersonation attack done in the way Charlie does in the preceding protocol works because there are no identities of the protocol principals in the protocol messages. That means that an easy way to solve the problem and thus to prevent such impersonation attack is to include the identity of the sender in the message as follows:

$$Alice \rightarrow Bob : I'm\ Alice, Nonce_A$$

$$Bob \rightarrow Alice : Nonce_B, \left\{ ^"Bob^", Nonce_A \right\}_{K_{AB}}$$

$$Alice \rightarrow Bob : \left\{ ^"Alice^", Nonce_B \right\}_{K_{AB}}$$

where $Nonce_i$ is the nonce value of an entity i,

K_{AB} is the symmetric key shared between Alice and Bob, and

$\left\{ M \right\}_{K_{AB}}$ is when a message M is being encrypted with the key K_{AB}.

After stating the identity of the message sender, it is now not possible for Charlie to carry out the same impersonation attack on the protocol. This is evident that Charlie cannot use the ciphertext he receives from Bob in Message 4 (in the attack) and uses it to reply to Bob, because Bob will see his own identity in the message and knows that Charlie is not the one who encrypts the message. Hence, Charlie's impersonation attack is unsuccessful.

Principle 4: Needs for encryption

It needs to be precisely clear why encryption is being used in the authentication and key establishment protocol. This is because encryption is not synonymous with security and not a computationally cheap process. An improper use of encryption could lead to a vulnerability and unnecessary computation.

There are many objectives to encryption. Protocol designers must clearly express their reasons why encryption is done and what it is used for. Examples of encryption uses include:

- Encryption is used to preserve confidentiality of information. In this case, the message recipient must possess the correct key in order to decrypt the message.

- Encryption is used to show authenticity of the message. In this case, the message does not necessarily need to be a secret. However, the sender encrypts it to show that the message is really from a trusted entity. If symmetric cryptography is used, the sender simply encrypts it with the key they are holding. If asymmetric cryptography is used, the sender's private key is used in the form of digital signature.

- Encryption is used to produce random numbers. Some authentication and key establishment protocols, specifically the ones that apply a challenge-and-response mechanism, require the generation of random numbers or nonce values. Encryption can be used as a method to produce such numbers.

As already stated previously, because there are several objectives that encryption can be used to achieve, protocol designers must be clear to what encryption is used for. Some even suggest that an inappropriate use of encryption could actually lead to protocol errors. Furthermore, improper implementation of encryption algorithms could lead to protocol vulnerabilities waiting to be exploited by adversaries.

Principle 5: Inconclusiveness of message content knowledge

When a protocol entity digitally signs an encrypted message containing data, the recipient should not conclude that the sender knows the content of the message.

This can be explained with a simple example. Suppose that Alice A transmits a message M encrypted with Bob's public key along with her signature to Bob B. Bob is the only one who can decrypt the message since the decryption process requires the use of Bob's private key. The signature part can also be verified by Bob using the public key of Alice. The message that Alice sends to Bob can be written as

$$Alice \rightarrow Bob : \{M\}_{+K_{Bob}}, \{H(M)\}_{-K_{Alice}}$$

where $\{M\}_{+K_i}$ is when a message M is encrypted with the public key of an entity i, $H(M)$ is the hash value of a message M, and $\{H(M)\}_{-K_i}$ is the digital signature of an entity i on a message M.

In this case, Bob should not automatically believe that Alice knows what M actually is. For example, if M is some secret message or even a password, Bob cannot be certain that Alice knows it. As for the hash value of the message $H(M)$, it is always possible that Alice may have received it from someone else. It is even worse when Alice sends the following message:

$$Alice \rightarrow Bob : \{M\}_{+K_{Bob}}, \left\{ H\left(\{M\}_{+K_{Bob}} \right) \right\}_{-K_{Alice}}$$

where $\{M\}_{+K_i}$ is when a message M is encrypted with the public key of an entity i, $H(M)$ is the hash value of a message M, and

$\{H(M)\}_{-K_i}$ is the digital signature of an entity i on a message M.

It can be seen that all Alice does is that she takes the encrypted message $\{M\}_{+K_{Bob}}$, hashes it, and then signs it with her private key. In this example, Alice could have intercepted $\{M\}_{+K_{Bob}}$, signed it, and transmitted the message with her signature to Bob. It is, therefore, not wise for Bob to immediately be certain that Alice knows the content of the message.

One way to solve this issue is perhaps for the sender to sign the message with their private key before encrypting it for confidentiality.

Principle 6: Freshness of protocol messages

The entire or a part of a message transmitted between protocol principals must be fresh.

This principle ensures the freshness of protocol messages, which is important because freshness can help prevent a form of attack known as a replay attack. An example of a replay attack can be referred back to Figure 7-1. It can be simply described as the retransmission of previously used messages. Of course, one way to reduce the risk of being attacked by a replay is the use of cryptographic nonce. A cryptographic nonce or a nonce can be used to guarantee the freshness of each protocol message, usually also through a challenge-and-response mechanism. However, one thing to be considered is the protection of the nonce. This is especially the case if a predictable form of cryptographic nonce is used. It is, therefore, recommended that the nonce is protected so that an adversary cannot simulate the challenge as well as the response.

Cryptographic nonce is not the only method that can be used to prove the freshness of protocol messages. Another method is the application of *timestamps*. Many protocol designers prefer timestamps because they think that it is easier to use the time than to produce a random number for a nonce. However, a couple of things need to be considered when using timestamps. Firstly, the clocks on the sender and the recipient's machines have to be synchronized so that when the message is received, the time of the message generation can be correctly inspected. This is by and large the case for Kerberos whose mechanism depends so much on timestamps. Secondly, if the synchronization of the clocks on the machines involved in the protocol cannot be perfectly done, the difference of the time should not be larger than the allowable age of the message. Otherwise, a replay attack will be possible if an adversary retransmits a message within the time interval. Hence, if the allowable age of the message and the time difference between the clocks are too large, it becomes more likely that a replay attack will be a success.

Before ending the section and chapter, there is one other point that we would like to emphasize. That is, the secrecy of some information in protocols is essential to their functioning. This is mainly true with cryptographic keys used for encrypting and decrypting purposes. Protocol designers need to be aware that losing such information could easily lead to the loss of confidentiality, integrity, and authenticity of protocol messages.

On the whole, what has been learned from many existing authentication and key establishment protocols can be extracted to become the six basic principles that we can follow. They are not absolute in any means. They simply provide suggestions for protocol designers to consider so that the same mistakes as the vulnerable classic protocols are not made in future authentication and key establishment protocols.

Summary

Many authentication protocols have been designed, implemented, and applied in real-world situations. Their importance will only increase in the future. We, therefore, think that there is a need for us to learn from other existing protocols so that more secure protocols can be designed.

The chapter begins with an explanation of what an authentication protocol is and how it is related to the process of session key establishment. We have given several examples of what we consider classic authentication and key establishment protocols in Andrew Secure RPC Protocol, Needham–Schroeder protocol, and Needham–Schroeder Public Key protocol. All of them have become major influences for today's authentication protocols. Furthermore, secure socket layer and Kerberos, the two most commonly used authentication and key establishment protocols today, have also been explained in this chapter.

The mistakes and vulnerabilities that were made in the classic protocols and the way that secure socket layer and Kerberos work are then turned into protocol design principles. These principles can be considered as a basic guideline for authentication and key establishment protocol designers so that fewer vulnerabilities will be present and more resilient authentication and key establishment protocols can be proposed in the future.

Bibliography

Abadi, M., & Needham, R. (1994). Prudent Engineering Practice for Cryptographic Protocols. *Proceedings of 1994 IEEE Computer Society Symposium on Research in Security and Privacy* (pp. 122–136). IEEE.

Boonkrong, S. (2010). Some Remarks on Andrew Secure RPC. *Proceedings of the 10th International Conference on Innovative Internet Community Systems (I2CS)*. Bangkok: Gesellschaft fur Informatik.

Boonkrong, S. (2011, June). Designing Cryptographic Protocols (in Thai). *Journal of Information Technology, 7*(1), 52–57.

Boonkrong, S. (2014). A More Secure and Efficient Andrew Secure RPC Protocol. *Security and Communication Networks, 7*(11), 2063–2077.

Boyd, C., Mathuria, A., & Stebila, D. (2003). *Protocols for Authentication and Key Establishment.* Springer.

Clark, J., & Jacob, J. (1995). On the Security of Recent Protocols. *Information Processing Letters, 56*(3), 151–155.

Gong, L., Needham, R. M., & Yahalom, R. (1990). Reasoning about Belief in Cryptographic Protocols. *Proceedings of the IEEE Symposium on Security and Privacy* (pp. 234–248). IEEE.

Hickman, K. E. (1994). *The SSL Protocol.* Netscape Communications Corp. IEFT.

Lampson, B., Abadi, M., Burrows, M., & Wobber, E. (1992). Authentication in Distributed Systems: Theory and Practice. *ACM Transactions on Computer Systems, 10*(4), 265–310.

Linn, J. (1996). RFC1964: *The Kerberos Version 5 GSS-API Mechanism.* USA: IETF.

Oppliger, R. (2009). *SSL and TLS: Theory and Practice.* USA: Artech House, Inc.

Satyanarayanan, M. (1989). Integrating Security in a Large Distributed System. *ACM Transactions on Computer Systems, 7*(3), 247–280.

Steiner, J. G., Neuman, C., & Schiller, J. I. (1988). Kerberos: An Authentication Service for Open Network Systems. *Proceedings of USENIX Conference,* (pp. 191–202).

CHAPTER 8

Current and Future Trends

It is not the intent of this book to provide a detailed implementation of authentication functions. Nevertheless, the previous chapters provide the understanding of fundamental technologies behind authentication mechanisms. Also recall that authentication is a process that is used to confirm one's identity and consists of three main methods, namely, something you know, something you have, and something you are.

In this final chapter, we give an overview of some of the current and future trends of authentication technologies. This is so that it can be seen how the already explained foundation and technologies of authentication can become an integral part of real-world situations. Moreover, we will provide a sketch of future directions of how the basis of authentication technologies can be extended to provide state-of-the-art approaches for user authentication.

On the whole, this chapter contains three major parts. The first describes some examples of what the world is doing regarding the current state and practice of user authentication. The second and third parts will be dedicated to the future trends of authentication technologies known as continuous authentication and cancellable authentication, respectively. Additionally, relevant information will be supplied to the reader who desires future authentication applications and research directions.

The ID4D Initiative

We have already discussed the reasons for needing to have authentication. The main reasons are, of course, to prevent such cyber attacks as impersonation and information theft. However, to put things into perspective, it is important to look at the need for authentication technologies for social reasons, in addition to technical reasons.

© Sirapat Boonkrong 2021
S. Boonkrong, *Authentication and Access Control*, https://doi.org/10.1007/978-1-4842-6570-3_8

The *ID4D* or *Identification for Development* is an initiative that operates across the World Bank Group with an aim to help promote the importance and the use of digital identification systems. In other words, the goal of ID4D is for all people to be able to access services, both private and especially public, via the use of digital identification. It is interesting to learn that the ID4D Initiative directly supports the United Nations' *Sustainable Development Goals (SDGs)* number 16.9, which states that by the year 2030, everyone should be provided with legal identity including free birth registration. What digital identification will do is that it will assist in reducing inequalities as well as increasing health and financial coverage. In fact, digital identification will play a contributory role for other SDGs, too. This includes access to finance via know-your-customer (KYC) mechanism (Goal 1 Target 1.4), access to basic health services via unique ID for health insurance (Goal 3 Target 3.8), access to basic education via school registration (Goal 4), and labor mobility (Goal 10 Target 10.7).

In order to put things into perspective, the ID4D's research in 2018 showed that approximately one billion people all over the world still lacked an official proof of identity, many of which lived in Africa and South Asia, with almost ninety million were from East Asia, Pacific, Europe, and Central Asia. The good news is that a lot of work to solve this identity gap has already begun with many having adopted such technologies as biometrics, smart cards, and authentication infrastructure.

Identity Life Cycle

One of the problems we face today is to have a digital identification and authentication method that is interoperable across the globe since there are varieties of actors, interests, technologies, and priorities. What ID4D has done to reduce the size of the problem is to create an understanding of the basic process of digital identification by providing the concept of *identity life cycle* which is illustrated in Figure 8-1.

The identity life cycle consists of five stages which are registration, issuance, identity authentication, authorization, and identity management. They can be explained as follows:

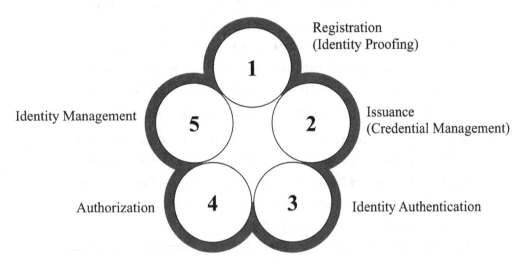

Figure 8-1. Identity Life Cycle

- Registration – The registration or identity proofing process is considered a very important initial stage which includes the processes of enrollment and identity validation. The enrollment process involves capturing and recording data of a person including biographical data such as name, date of birth, gender, and biometric data such as fingerprints. Nowadays, many more attributes are also being collected. The validation process during the registration stage is to ensure that the registered identity really exists, that is, the person is still alive and the data is not a duplicate of anyone else.

- Issuance – The issuance or credential management process is when the authority or credential provider issues a variety of credentials to the identity owner. The credentials may include an e-passport, a smart card, or an electronic ID card. One thing that has to be considered when issuing these credentials is interoperability. Some such as an e-passport will have to be interoperable across countries and continents.

- Identity Authentication – Once a person has been given credentials from the previous stage, they must be able to confirm the identity before accessing the required services. The way to achieve this is nothing other than the methods already explained in the previous chapters of this book, namely, something you know, something you have, something you are, or even the combination of them. For example, a citizen could use their electronic ID card to access tax payment services. They could also use the biometric data for the know-your-customer mechanism when opening a new bank account.

- Authorization – The authorization process defines the access rights of an individual. These access rights are usually independent of the identity provider but dependent on the organization providing the service to the individual. For example, a financial institution exercises the access restrictions for its customer. However, the national authority that issues citizen ID cards is not the one designing such restrictions.

- Identity Management – The identity management or identity maintenance process is the ongoing process designed for the retrieving, updating, and revoking of identities. This stage also includes the writing of policies for which personal attributes are to be deleted and added for each identity. The identity management stage ensures that the credentials are accessible and up to date. More importantly, this stage will help maintain the privacy and security of personal data.

Although it is the aim of ID4D, which also means the aim of the authorities, to collect and create digital identification, it is the responsibility of users to make sure that their identity attributes such as address, professions, and even biometric data are updated. Moreover, as mentioned in the identity management phase, the authority must ensure that invalid identities are revoked to prevent identity fraud. This is especially the case of the death of an individual. With the introduction of the life cycle of identity for governments, organizations, and practitioners to understand to agree upon, it is natural to look at the next step which is the assurance levels of authentication.

Assurance Levels of Authentication

We have mentioned the importance of interoperability (in the issuance phase of the identity life cycle) for the authentication methods. A standard or a framework is, therefore, necessary. The National Institute of Standards and Technology (NIST) has provided such framework which specifies the levels of credibility for each type of authentication factors (NIST calls them "authenticators") so that an authentication factor or mechanism can be used appropriately for the services. Many countries have adopted this *NIST Special Publication 800-63B* so that the authentication process is in compliance with an international standard, which then leads to interoperability across countries.

There are three assurance levels specified by the NIST for authentication. This section explains what each authentication assurance level (AAL) is and what authentication factors can be used to meet the requirement for each assurance level.

Authentication Assurance Level 1 (AAL1)

AAL1 provides some assurance that the claimant is really the person already registered with a system or a service provider. Some practices state that AAL1 provides medium level of authentication assurance. AAL1 requires that the user being authenticated must at least provide a single authentication factor. However, if higher security is needed, multi-factor authentication can also be done.

For AAL1, the authentication factors that are acceptable include (1) a memorized secret, which is something you know; (2) a hardware authentication token, which is something you have; (3) a software authentication token, which is something you are; and (4) any other authentication factors that are accepted in authentication assurance levels 2 and 3.

Even though this is the first level of authentication assurance, it is required that the communication channel between the user and service provider is protected or cryptographically secure in order to preserve the confidentiality of authentication credentials and to prevent such attack as eavesdropping and a man-in-the-middle attack. In addition, a re-authentication process must occur at least once every 30 days. In other words, the user of service is required to be authenticated by the provider at least once per 30 days, especially for an extended session. When the time limit is reached, it is recommended that the session is terminated and the user is logged out and is asked to carry out authentication again.

It is interesting to see that biometric data is not mentioned here at all. This is because based on NIST Special Publication 800-63B, biometric data on its own is not recognized as an authentication factor. This means that it will have to be used with at least one other authentication factor to be accepted, which leads us to the authentication assurance level 2.

Authentication Assurance Level 2 (AAL2)

AAL2 provides a system or a service provider with a higher confidence that the user being authenticated is really who they claim to be. This is done with a proof that the user can provide two distinct authentication factors. This means that any one factor of authentication on its own will not be accepted by any services requiring the authentication assurance level 2.

Since AAL2 only considers two-factor or multi-factor authentication, usually a combination of any two authentication factors will be acceptable. These authentication factors can include a memorized secret or the something-you-know factor together with a something-you-have factor in a one-time password device, a hardware authentication token, or a software authentication token. Moreover, as mentioned previously, biometrics which serves as the something-you-are factor can also be used in conjunction with the something-you-know factor in order to satisfy the AAL2's requirements.

It needs to be understood in the cases of authentication in mobile applications that when a user unlocks their smart phone with a fingerprint scan or face recognition feature, this will not be counted as one something-you-are factor by the mobile applications. This is because the mobile applications, in this particular scenario, or the identity verifiers do not have any control of how the smart phone authenticates the user.

Similar to AAL1, AAL2 also requires that the communication channel between two entities, namely, the user and identity verifier, is secure in order to reduce the risks of a man-in-the-middle attack and a replay attack of the authentication information. Furthermore, a secure communication channel can help preserve the confidentiality of user credentials used for authentication.

The re-authentication process of AAL2 is stricter than that of AAL1. That is, AAL2 requires that a user is to be re-authenticated at least once per 12 hours. In addition, if there is a period of inactivity lasting 30 minutes or longer, the session will be terminated and the user must carry out authentication again to continue with the session.

Authentication Assurance Level 3 (AAL3)

AAL3 is the highest level of authentication assurance, according to NIST. The level provides the highest confidence level that the user being authenticated is really the person who has registered with the service provider and is really the person they claim to be. The authentication in this level is done based on the proof that the person being authenticated possesses a cryptographic key through a cryptographic protocol. The claimant must also show that they possess two or more other authentication factors to be successfully authenticated by the service provider or the system.

One of the things that is stated as a possible way to carry out authentication in AAL3 is the use of multi-factor cryptographic device. A *multi-factor cryptographic device* is a piece of hardware that can perform cryptographic operations using cryptographic keys. The device is activated through a second factor of authentication. This means that authentication is done by the user who must first prove that they own the device. The device, already containing one or more cryptographic keys, can then perform an authentication function with the service provider or authenticator using the key or keys available. Hence, the possession of cryptographic key or keys is proved as required by AAL3.

Multi-factor cryptographic device usually comes in the form of hardware. However, it is now known that *multi-factor cryptographic software* is also available. Multi-factor cryptographic software works a little differently from the hardware version in that cryptographic keys are stored on a hard disk, rather than on a device specially designed for authentication purposes. When AAL3 authentication is required, the user being authenticated will need to access those keys via the use of second factor authentication such as a password or a fingerprint. Once the cryptographic keys are accessible, they can then be used to continue with the authentication process with the system or service provider.

Multi-factor cryptographic device and multi-factor cryptographic software are just examples of authentication factors that can be used to accomplish AAL3 authentication. It is actually stated that they can be used on their own. However, it is recommended that other factors of authentication should be applied in addition in order to increase the level of confidence. For example, a hardware authentication token can be used with a multi-factor cryptographic device. Software authentication token and a password can also be used with a multi-factor cryptographic device when carrying out AAL3 authentication.

Again, it is required that the communication channel between the person being authenticated or a supplicant and the authenticating system is secure. This is to prevent both eavesdropping of authentication credentials and a man-in-the-middle attack. Moreover, the re-authentication process is to be done once per 12 hours during an extended activity and regardless of what the user's activity is.

NIST Special Publication 800-63B, as already seen, provides us with the concept of authentication assurance levels. This guideline has already been studied and applied by many countries, which include the US Homeland Security, the United Kingdom's Government Digital Service (GDS), and Thailand's ETDA Recommendation on ICT Standard for Electronic Transactions. Furthermore, the NIST publication has been held as the foundation of many financial institutions' identity management services, too. Having said that, at the time of writing, many countries have admitted that the authentication assurance level 3 is still difficult to achieve due to the unavailability of multi-factor cryptographic devices.

We have now seen from the previous sections what the current status of authentication is and what technologies or authentication methods are required to achieve different levels of authentication assurance. We will now take a look at the emerging trends of authentication technologies in the subsequent sections so that we can be prepared for what to come in the near future.

Continuous Authentication

Authentication is, of course, concerned with confirming the identity of an individual. Usually, it is used for the purpose of protecting personal information and computer systems from unauthorized access. Moreover, there are times when it is important for the system to know who the person using the system actually is during the session, even though they may have already successfully passed the authentication process at the start of the session (or the point of entry). For example, in the era of online education, students or learners are required to study and take examinations via an online platform. The questions that have been in and bothered the mind of educators are: How do we know that it is the actual students studying the lessons and taking the examinations? How do we know that the students have not asked anyone else to sit at their computer or use their mobile device and take the exams for them? All these uncertainties still remain even though the students have already logged into the online education platform at the point of entry.

One way to solve this problem is known as continuous authentication. *Continuous authentication* is a process of verifying a user's identity on an ongoing and real-time basis. In other words, successful authentication is not only required at the point of entry or the beginning of a session, but the user also needs to be able to provide valid credentials as they carry out the tasks on a computer or a mobile device. These valid credentials could range from a password, a PIN code to biometric information. In order to gain some understanding of this emerging technology, this section provides an overview of continuous authentication together with the challenges that it might face.

Conventional Approach

A common, but not considered state-of-the-art, example of continuous authentication is when a user uses a mobile banking application to carry out financial transactions. When the application starts, the user is asked for a password or a PIN code. This is authentication at the *point of entry*. Suppose the same user would like to transfer their money to another account during this same session. Before the money is actually transferred, the application prompts them to *re-authenticate*, usually by reentering the password or the PIN code. This is one form of continuous authentication. We can see that while the user is trying to get a task done, fund transfer in this case, the application does not just let them click the transfer button. The user is required to provide the valid credentials again before the task can be completed. This particular example of continuous authentication is considered *static* since the user needs to provide their credentials each time the system or application asks in order to be verified.

Having said that, most systems or applications that have adopted continuous authentication apply either something you know or something you are, specifically physiological biometrics, as a factor of authentication. In spite of their simplicity and ease of use, both something-you-know and something-you-are approaches come with a shortcoming in the context of continuous authentication. The drawback of these methods is that the users of the continuous authentication systems face the inconvenience of frequently being asked to reenter their credentials, which means they have to stop doing their task. This may eventually put them off from wanting to use the systems altogether.

As a result, continuous authentication has been gaining interest in the security community, especially with the availability of higher computational and storage resources on both ordinary computers and mobile devices than what they used to have in the past. This is to bring a newer approach to authentication technologies.

Emerging Approaches

One of the problems of the conventional continuous authentication approach is that users are usually interrupted by the system asking them to reenter authentication credentials such as a password, a PIN code, or physiological biometric information. There is, therefore, a need to overcome this difficulty in order to at least increase the usability of the continuous authentication process. In truth, for continuous authentication, researchers have been stepping away from the something you know authentication factor due to the risks of shoulder surfing and many other issues such as password dictionary and password reuse. What has gained more interest by researchers is the application of physiological biometric factor of authentication.

As already discussed in Chapter 5, physiological biometrics can provide high efficiency, accuracy, and user acceptance. This is its advantage when used in a one-factor authentication mechanism at the point of entry. Unfortunately, in the context of continuous authentication, users still have to interact with the biometric system. This means that they are still aware of the actual re-authentication process that is going on, including the biometric capturing process and biometric verification process. This, therefore, implies that both something-you-know and physiological biometric factors fall short of what is actually required by a continuous authentication mechanism. These requirements and expectations are that a continuous authentication should be *transparent, implicit, nonintrusive, non-observable*, and *adaptive* to the users of the system. To put it simply, when continuous authentication is done, users should not be aware that the process is taking place. The users should be able to continue with their task without feeling interrupted. Consequently, *behavioral biometrics* have now become the technology of choice that has the potential to meet the stated requirements and expectations.

Note   Just a reminder, behavioral biometric-based authentication includes the use of such information as walking patterns (or gait), typing patterns (or keystroke dynamics), and handwritten signature (or motion).

Behavioral biometric-based authentication is a process that applies users' behavioral patterns for the purpose of identification and verification. The framework for a system requiring continuous authentication based on behavioral biometric information is illustrated in Figure 8-2.

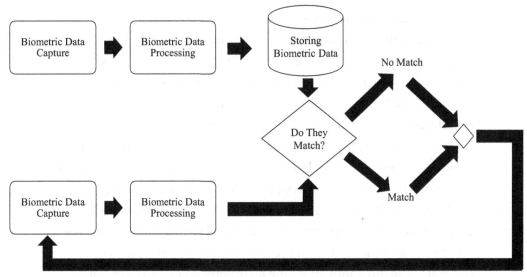

Data Re-Capturing for Continuous Authentication

Figure 8-2. *Framework of Behavioral Biometric-Based Continuous Authentication*

The general framework of behavioral biometric-based continuous authentication in Figure 8-2 is an enhancement of how conventional biometric authentication works. It can be seen that there are three main processes in Figure 8-2. They are enrollment, authentication, and re-authentication. They can be explained as follows:

- Enrollment – There are two approaches to the enrollment for continuous authentication. The first is known as the template-based enrollment. The second is known as the model-based enrollment. For the *template-based enrollment*, behavioral biometric data such as a user's walking pattern or a user's keystroke dynamics is collected to establish a behavioral template for that particular user. Once the template is established, it will be used to verify the user. The verification is a success or a failure depends on whether or not the level of similarity between the authenticating data and the template equals or exceeds the specified biometric threshold value. For the *model-based enrollment*, behavioral biometric data is also collected, but this time, the data is used for training a machine learning model. The verification process is done by the model deciding whether or not the authenticating biometric data belongs to the legitimate user.

- Authentication and Re-authentication – For a continuous authentication system, authentication is done at the start (or at the point of entry) and throughout the session. The *point of entry authentication* is processed in the same way as any ordinary biometric authentication system. That is, the system checks whether or not the entered or collected biometric credentials match the stored template with the level higher than the prespecified threshold. (Reader can refer back to Chapter 5 for a more detailed explanation of how biometric authentication works.) The *re-authentication* process works in a similar way, but the process is carried out periodically until the user is no longer using the system. During re-authentication, the system also tries to match the user's behavioral data with the template. The threshold matching technique is applied in the same way as the point-of-entry authentication. One thing, however, that needs to be considered for the re-authentication process is the *frequency* of verification. The frequency of verification is important because the sufficient amount of time needs to be allowed of behavioral biometric data acquisition, data processing, as well as user verification. Moreover, the computational power and battery consumption are the other two factors to be taken into account when designing and implementing continuous authentication.

We have now seen the basic process of how continuous authentication works. It has to be said that the scheme has not been widely adopted yet. One of the reasons is the lack of standards and guidelines for implementing it. However, there have been researches, such as those by Mohammed Abuhamad and Vishal Patel and their respective research teams amongst others, that have looked into various behavioral biometric methods that can be applicable to continuous authentication.

Keystroke Dynamics

Keystroke dynamics is one of the methods that can be used to distinguish users from one another. It is also known simply as *typing patterns*. The keystroke-based authentication works on both a personal computer and a smart phone under an assumption that different individuals possess distinctive typing behaviors. When an authentication process based on keystroke dynamics is conducted, the following features are usually considered, although not all are used simultaneously.

The first is *key down frequency*, which measures the frequency of the key down events. The second is *key up* or *key release frequency*, which measures the frequency of the key up events. From the first two features, the third and fourth criteria can be calculated, namely, dwell time and flight time, respectively. *Dwell time* is basically the time between key down and key up, while *flight time* is the time between key down and the next key down and between key up and the next key up. Sometimes the dwell time and flight time are called the latency and hold time. The fifth feature is the *error rate*, which can be measured by looking at the number of times that the backspace key is pressed during the typing session. These five features can be determined on both an ordinary keyboard and a smart phone.

Recently, two more keystroke dynamics features have been added specifically for smart phones. They include the *finger's pressure* while pressing or touching the screen and the *press area* which is the size of the user's fingers.

It has been known that keystroke-based authentication can provide the accuracy that ranges between 83% and 99%. However, the technique comes with a couple of issues. Firstly, the changes in the user's behaviors can result in unsuccessful authentication. For example, capturing a typing pattern while a user is sitting might be different from when a user is walking. Even the emotion of a user can affect their typing pattern. For example, when a user is happy, they might have a different keystroke pattern from when they are angry. The second challenge with keystroke dynamics is when a user types in different languages. This situation is said to have some effect on the typing style, too.

Although keystroke dynamics appears to be a major candidate for being a factor of continuous authentication, further research is still required to overcome the challenges.

Gaze Patterns

The keystroke dynamics is a method that can be applied on both a personal computer and a smart phone. However, gaze patterns or eye movement patterns, considered a subset of motion-based authentication, have mostly been designed specifically for continuous authentication on smart phones (and on a computer with a web camera).

Let us talk a little bit about motion-based authentication before discussing gaze patterns. Most smart phones today are equipped with such sensors as accelerometers and gyroscopes. Collectively, they are known as motion sensors. Many researchers have attempted to design motion-based continuous authentication using those sensors. The first use of motion sensors for continuous authentication is called *air-written signature*. This is when a user holds their smart phone and pretends to write their signature in the air. This, of course, fails because continuous authentication requires that the process is transparent and non-interrupting. This also leads to the failure in using waving gestures in continuous authentication.

Most smart phones fortunately also come with a built-in front camera. Therefore, one possibility for continuous authentication is the detection and verification of *eye movements* or *gaze patterns*. The gaze pattern technology began with trying to identify a user based on their eye movement in response to visual stimuli. This method was proved to be able to detect an impersonator with an accuracy of around 91%. The problem with this early technique is that it is not suitable for continuous authentication since the user is interrupted with visual stimuli. Today's eye movement-based authentication works in a similar way but without the need of visual stimuli. The gaze patterns are recognized by tracking the user's eye movement while using their smart phone in order to carry out identity verification.

One advantage of tracking the eye movement using the front camera of the smart phone is that there is no need for any disturbance on the user's side. The system simply tracks the movement of the user's eyes and tries to identify whether or not this is the legitimate user. However, one small issue of using this method for continuous authentication is its accuracy of approximately 88% which is lower than the keystroke dynamics and the original gaze pattern recognition technique. Moreover, for the gaze pattern to be recognized, it is recommended that the duration for capturing the eye movement should be at least ten seconds, which may affect the frequency of continuous authentication.

Walking Patterns

The recognition of an individual's walking patterns is another method that has been designed to specifically work with smart phones or wearable devices. It has also gained a lot of interest in recent years. *Walking pattern recognition* or more widely known as *gait recognition* is a process of identifying an individual from the way they walk by using motion sensors on their smart device.

In fact, there is another method for gait recognition, but that requires computer vision techniques which is unsuitable for continuous authentication. It is almost deemed unusable for continuous authentication because cameras need to be set up and walking images need to be captured prior to the processing of data. All of these are actually against the requirements of continuous authentication which asks for transparency and nonintrusiveness. This is why motion sensors on smart devices are considered more appropriate.

Walking pattern recognition works in four steps. The first is *data acquisition* which is when the device records a user's walking activities. The second is *data pre-processing*, sometimes known as *data cleansing*, which is when noise reduction is carried out. The third is *walking pattern detection* which is when walking features are extracted for identity verification. The walking features that are often used include walking speeds and walking stride parameters. Finally, the fourth step is the *analysis* step which is when the authentication system decides whether or not this is the gait pattern of the legitimate user.

A strong point of using gait recognition in continuous authentication is that it can be transparent to users. This is because the users do not have to be interrupted by the re-authentication process. They are unaware of all the steps from the capture of walking data to the authentication decision. This is the case as long as the users are on the move. The obvious problem with this method is that it is only suitable for some specific applications. In other words, if the users do not walk, this continuous authentication method will not work at all. More importantly, the accuracy of walking pattern recognition is still an issue, especially when compared with other methods. For gait-based authentication, the average accuracy in detecting legitimate users is around 80%. Some have been reported to have accuracy as low as 53%. This implies that for the walking patterns to be considered appropriate for continuous authentication, further study and research are still required.

Other Interesting Methods

The three techniques in typing patterns, gaze patterns, and walking patterns are the upcoming schemes that have been studied and improved so that they can be used as a part of continuous authentication. They are not the only ones being considered, however. There are a couple of other methods that have been examined although further investigation is still needed in order to increase the possibility of using them for continuous authentication. These methods are:

- Location Familiarity – This continuous authentication method works by sensing Bluetooth or Wi-Fi signals transmitted by nearby objects in order to identify the level of authenticity of a user. Location familiarity works based on an assumption that users tend to work on their tasks or use their applications within a similar environment. The location familiarity scheme is said to fulfill the main requirements of continuous authentication, especially the transparent and non-observable factors. This is because when the re-authentication process occurs, the user's device just senses the surrounding signals without the user being aware of what is happening. Unfortunately, the precision of detecting legitimate users is still on the low side with the average of being able to detect safe environments around 85% and being able to detect unsafe environments around 30%.

- Power Consumption – This approach is when a system attempts to verify a user based on how much power is consumed on a particular device. It has been studied that the power consumption is highly correlated to the usage pattern on the device. Although the ability to verify a user by the power consumption pattern recognition achieved the equal error rate of around 6.5%, the results do not appear stable because the power consumption depends on many other uncontrollable factors such as the way an application is implemented and functions.

Continuous authentication is an emerging and evolving field of cybersecurity and will become an integral part of future applications. Even though there are techniques that appear to be suitable for such scheme, there is still a need for further study, research, and investigation so that continuous authentication is more usable, more accurate, and more secure.

Cancellable Authentication

Continuous authentication is not the only future trend of authentication. Another upcoming technique that is related to authentication, specifically biometric authentication, is known as cancellable authentication.

Biometric authentication is, of course, when we use our physical characteristics such as fingerprints, the iris, and faces or our behavioral characteristics such as typing patterns and walking patterns to identify each individual. This is because it is believed that both the physical and behavioral characteristics are unique to an individual.

Let us remind ourselves briefly how a typical biometric authentication system works. During the registration or enrollment phase, a person's biometric data is captured and stored as a template in a database. When an authentication process is carried out, the person's biometric data is captured and compared with the biometric template. If they match to a certain level (or a specified threshold), then that person is successfully authenticated by the system. Otherwise, the authentication fails.

Issues with Biometrics

Biometrics, although has increased its popularity due to its strength in the fact that users do not have to memorize any secrets and the ability to distinguish users, still raises several concerns regarding security and privacy. Some of them have already been mentioned in Chapter 5, but we would like to reemphasize as well as add some other concerns here. They can be described as follows.

Firstly, *biometrics is not secret*. The something-you-know authentication method relies on secrecy. That is, passwords are only known to the person who owns them. However, biometric information such as the face, handwritten signature, and even fingerprints can easily be captured and recorded, a lot of times without the knowledge of the user. The problem is that it becomes possible for an unauthorized person to at least attempt to impersonate the legitimate user.

The second security concern is that *biometrics cannot be revoked or cancelled*. Biometric information is forever associated with an individual. Biometric information is captured and stored as a template in the registration phase. If an adversary somehow gains access to that database, it will mean that they will get hold of the biometric information. The problem is that unlike passwords which can easily be changed, it is infeasible to change a person's biometric information such as their face or fingerprints. *This* particular problem of biometrics is actually one of the reasons cancellable authentication has received a lot of interest in recent years.

Thirdly, *biometrics can lead to the problem of cross-matching*. For the something-you-know authentication method, it is recommended that different passwords are used for different systems. This is to prevent an attack called credential stuffing, which is explained in Chapter 3. However, with the something-you-are authentication method, it is not easy to have different biometric data for all the systems. A fingerprint is used across many systems and applications, for example. This implies that if an attacker gets hold of a person's biometric information, it is possible for them to attempt to use that information in a biometric authentication process in other applications, too. This is known as *cross-matching*. This problem has raised many concerns, which actually leads to the development of cancellable authentication as well.

It is evident that cross-matching and inability to revoke biometrics are two major issues that need to be resolved. This leads to the new thinking of the characteristics of authentication systems.

Characteristics of Biometric Authentication Systems

Due to the problems of revocability and cross-matching, there is a need to think about the characteristics that biometric authentication systems should possess. Several researchers have proposed some ideas which can be summarized as follows.

The first characteristic is that the authentication system should be able to confirm a person's identity with high confidence. The system should also have the ability to prevent a person from denying that they have attempted to carry out authentication. This is *non-repudiation*.

The second characteristic is the *revocability* or cancellation of a user's biometric template. This means that if the database of biometric templates is compromised, it should be able to revoke the compromised templates. Furthermore, it should be possible to issue new templates, too. Nowadays, it has even been suggested that the authentication system should reject the person or entity that attempts to carry out authentication using the data that is linked with the old template. This is another form of revocation.

The third characteristic is concerned with the *diversity* of biometric templates. We have mentioned that one of the problems of biometrics is that the same data or the same template is used across many applications. Therefore, in order to prevent cross-matching, it should be possible for the templates to be varied for the same user using different applications even though the same biometric information is to be used for authentication.

In order to meet these requirements, a new approach to authentication is necessary. This is where cancellable authentication comes in.

Biometric Template Protection

We have seen that the major issues with biometric authentication occur when biometric information, specifically biometric templates, is breached. In order to overcome the problems, researchers have studied and developed biometric template protection schemes, which can be divided into two categories. They are known as biometric cryptosystems and cancellable biometrics.

Biometric Cryptosystems

There are two different groups to *biometric cryptosystems*. The first is not really related to biometric template protection. It is, however, a scheme which generates cryptographic keys from biometric information. This type of biometric cryptosystems has been designed to solve the problem of people forgetting their cryptographic keys or even passwords which are usually used to access, encrypt, or decrypt data. In other words, biometric information since it is unique to each individual has the potential to generate unique cryptographic keys.

The second type of biometric cryptosystems is more closely related to the protection of biometric templates. During the enrollment stage, a biometric cryptosystem of this type simply encrypts the biometric templates before storing them in a database. During authentication, the biometric cryptosystem decrypts the associated template before the comparison between the template and authenticating data takes place. It can be seen that this method is similar to when passwords are encrypted before being stored in the database. This means that a similar problem is also present. The problem with this biometric cryptosystem method is key management. That is, we need to answer two questions. First, how many keys are needed for the encryption of biometric templates?

Will it be one key for all users or one key for each user? Second, how will the encryption keys be stored securely? It is not easy to find a solution to these questions. This is why cancellable biometrics have gained more interests these days.

Cancellable Biometrics

The idea of cancellable biometrics and cancellable authentication was introduced with cancellable fingerprints being the first to be worked on. Cancellable biometrics have been designed with an objective that a biometric authentication mechanism should still work securely even though biometric templates are compromised.

In *cancellable biometrics* or *cancellable authentication*, the original biometric data that is captured during registration is transformed or distorted intentionally before being stored in a database. The cancellable biometrics can be categorized into two main techniques. They are biometric salting and non-invertible transformation.

Biometric Salting

The *biometric salting* method works by combining a user's chosen data such as their password, random text, or a random number with the user's biometric data. The result of the combination of the two components is the distorted biometric template. The distortion function can simply be any arbitrary function $f()$ which takes both the user's data and their biometric data. This can be expressed as

$$BiometricTemplate_i = f\left(ArbData_i \| BioData_i\right)$$

where $BiometricTemplate_i$ is the biometric template of user i;

$ArbData_i$ is the arbitrary data of user i which can be a password or a random string of characters or numbers;

$BioData_i$ is the biometric data of user i which can be a fingerprint, a face, or an iris; and

$\|$ is the concatenation operation (or combination operation).

In the registration or enrollment phase, the resultant biometric template is stored in the database. In the authentication phase, the user presents their biometric data such as a fingerprint as well as their arbitrary data to the system. The authenticating biometric data will then be distorted in the same way as in the enrollment stage.

The resultant value is then compared with the biometric template. Of course, since this is still a biometric authentication method, it is very difficult to get an exact match. Therefore, a biometric threshold is still required. The enrollment and authentication processes of biometric salting are depicted in Figure 8-3.

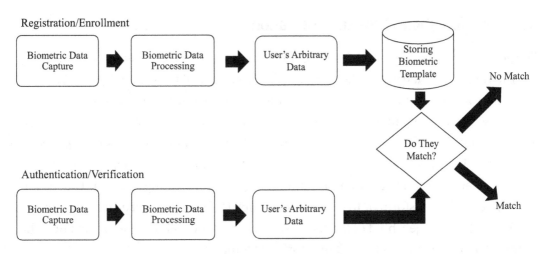

Figure 8-3. *Biometric Salting Registration and Authentication*

An advantage of biometric salting is that only the distorted version of biometric templates is stored in the database. Even if an attacker is able to access the database, the original biometric information of the users is still not compromised. What it means is that the users will only have to change their arbitrary data so that new distorted biometric templates are produced, stored, and used in the later sessions. Hence, the name *cancellable*.

However, there is a serious problem with the biometric salting method that depends on the user's chosen arbitrary data. Suppose the user's data is lost, stolen, or compromised, the whole of biometric salting authentication approach becomes vulnerable. In order to reduce the risk, there has been a research that proposed the use of random noise instead of the user's own data for the distortion of biometric template. The main issue with adding noise is the fact that the noise will have to be stored somewhere that it can be retrieved during the authentication stage. This still makes it vulnerable because if an attacker gets hold of the noise values, the system is also compromised.

Even though there appear to be weaknesses to the biometric salting approach, it is believed that by intentionally distorting the user's biometric data, the risk of the original biometric data being permanently lost has been reduced. Having said that, there is still room for future research to produce a more resilient biometric salting method.

Non-invertible Biometric Transformation

The goal of cancellable biometric authentication is to protect the original biometric information or biometric templates by avoiding a storage of the original templates. This way, even if an attack is able to access the biometric template database, it should be impossible for them to produce the original biometric credentials. We have learned that the biometric salting method relies on the security of the user's arbitrary data for its security. The principal problem with the salting method is the difficulty of keeping the user's data secret. There is actually another issue to the salting method. That is, the function used to transform or to distort the biometric template is *invertible*. This means that if an adversary gets hold of the user's secret data, they will be able to transform the distorted biometric template back to its original template.

The non-invertible biometric transformation has, therefore, been designed to reduce the magnitude of the problem. In *non-invertible transformation*, a one-way function is applied on the original biometric data in such a way that the components or parameters of the biometric data are transformed. A new distorted biometric template is obtained as a result.

The first realization of the potential use of non-invertible function on biometric data, specifically fingerprints, was reported by Nalini K. Ratha and his team in 2007. It was suggested that there were three main methods to achieve the non-invertible biometric templates. They were the Cartesian transformation, the Polar transformation, and the Surface Folding transformation.

We will not get into the mathematical detail of all of the three methods. However, the way they work can be simply explained as follows. It should first be noted that all three methods are based on non-invertible many-to-one functions. In the *Cartesian transformation*, biometric data is put into a rectangular grid whose cells contain one single piece of data. The Cartesian transformation shifts the value in each cell to a new position, still in relation with other values in other cells, by using a non-invertible function. Since a many-to-one function is applied, it is possible that many of the original cell positions will map into the same position in the new cell. The *Polar transformation* works in a similar way in that the points and values are also shifted to new positions, but in Polar transformation, a circular area is used instead of a rectangular grid. In the *Surface Folding transformation,* the same principles are applied. That is, the location and direction of the biometric data are changed, again, by a non-invertible many-to-one function. However, a more complex transformation based on Gaussian is the foundation of this method.

We think it is better to illustrate the ideas of all three methods of non-invertible biometric transformation by displaying their examples in Figure 8-4. These examples are adopted from the research by Nalini K. Ratha and his team. It can be seen that the original values of the biometric data (middle diagram of each transformation) are transformed into new values, new positions, or even a new shape (rightmost diagram of each transformation).

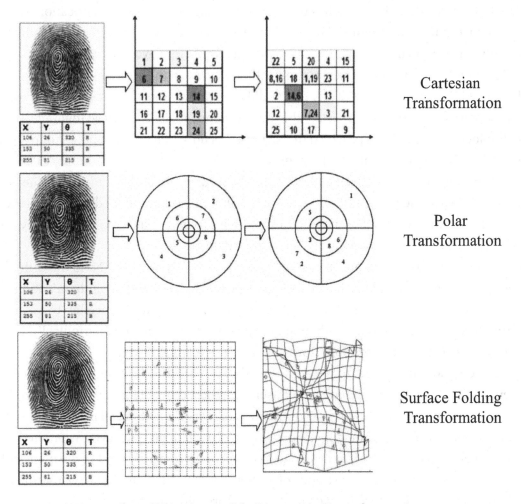

Figure 8-4. *Examples of Non-invertible Biometric Transformation*

An advantage of the non-invertible transformation scheme is that a one-way many-to-one mapping function is applied. This makes it infeasible for an attacker to revert the biometric templates back to its original form if they get hold of the transformed templates. However, one main disadvantage of this method is that its performance in terms of speed and more importantly accuracy is drastically decreased. Both of these factors really do play an important role in authentication on the whole.

Summary

Authentication, although a technology used in many hi-tech systems, is also a mechanism that can lead to basic services for a lot of people. The Identification for Development or ID4D Initiative has put identity management and authentication as the real needs in many regions of the world today. The reason is that without adequate identity verification technologies, it is almost impossible for anyone to access basic services such as education, finance, and healthcare. Due to these existing problems, the United Nations has realized and ensured that authentication becomes one integral component in their proposed sustainable development goals. We believe that the technologies and methods provided throughout this book will be a stepping-stone toward the solution in identity management.

Moreover, different levels of authentication assurance are also introduced in the chapter. The three levels of authentication assurance are recommended by the National Institute of Standards and Technology, or NIST. For international compatibility, they have now been adopted by many agencies around the world.

This chapter does not only discuss the needs realized by both ID4D and the United Nations and the NIST standard. It also looks at several future trends of authentication technologies. These trends include continuous authentication and cancellable authentication. In continuous authentication, users are authenticated periodically throughout their working session. However, further work is still needed to ensure transparency and non-interruptive mechanisms. The cancellable authentication has been designed to preserve the privacy of users since it is difficult for any unauthorized users to find out the real and original authenticating templates. Several methods are now available for transforming the original data into a distorted one. However, as pointed out in this chapter, a lot of work is still needed to improve both security and performance of such schemes. These upcoming trends of authentication, therefore, still have room for improvement, which in turn provide research opportunities in the future.

Bibliography

Abuhamad, M., Abusnaina, A., Nyang, D., & Mohaisen, D. (2020, May). Sensor-based Continuous Authentication of Smartphones' Users Using Behavioral Biometrics: A Contemporary Survey. *(Submitted to) IEEE Internet of Things Journal - arXiv:2001.08578v2 [cs.CR]*.

Badhib, A., Cherif, A., & Alshehri, S. (2019). A Survey of Continuous Authentication Techniques for the Internet of Things. *KSII Transactions of Internet and Information Systems*, 134–153.

Choudhury, B., Then, P., Issac, B., Raman, V., & Haldar, M. K. (2018). A Survey on Biometrics and Cancelable Biometrics Systems. *International Journal of Image and Graphics, 18*(1).

Dong, X., Jin, Z., Teoh, A. B., Tistarelli, M., & Wong, K. (2020, April). On the Security Risk of Cancelable Biometrics. *(Submitted to) Pattern Recognition - arXiv:1910.07770v3 [cs.CV]*.

Electronic Transactions Development Agency (ETDA). (2018). *ETDA Recommendation on ICT Standard for Electronic Transactions*. Bangkok, Thailand: Electronic Transactions Development Agency (ETDA).

Grassi, P. A., Fenton, J. L., Newton, E. M., Perlner, R. A., Regenscheid, A. R., Burr, W. E., . . . Theofanos, M. F. (2017). *NIST Special Publication 800-63B: Digital Identity Guidelines - Authentication and Lifecycle Management*. Standard, National Institute of Standards and Technology (NIST). doi:https://doi.org/10.6028/NIST.SP.800-63b

Identification for Development (ID4D). (2018, October). *ID4D Data: Global Identification Challenge by Numbers*. Retrieved from Identification for Development (ID4D): https://id4d.worldbank.org/global-dataset

Identification for Development (ID4D). (2018). *Technology Landscape for Digital Identification*. World Bank.

Identification for Development (ID4D). (2019). *Practitioner's Guide (for Digital Identification)*. World Bank.

Mamatha, R. (2018). A Review of Cancelable Biometric Authentication Methods. *Journal of Biometrics & Biostatistics, 9*(2), 1–6.

Patel, V. M., Chellappa, R., Chandra, D., & Barbello, B. (2016). Continuous User Authentication on Mobile Devices: Recent progress and remaining challenges. *IEEE Signal Processing Magazine, 33*(4), 49–61.

Ratha, N. K., Chikkerur, S., Connell, J. H., & Bolle, R. M. (2017, April). Generating Cancelable Fingerprint Templates. *IEEE Transactions on Pattern Analysis and Machine Intelligence, 29*(4), 561–572.

Shin, S., & Seto, Y. (2017). Study of Cancelable Biometrics in Security Improvement of Biometric Authentication System. *Proceedings of 14th Computer Information Systems and Industrial Management (CISM),* (pp. 547–558). Warsaw, Poland.

Stylios, I. C., Thanou, O., Androulidakis, I., & Zaitseva, E. (2016). A Review of Continuous Authentication Using Behavioral Biometrics. *Proceedings of the SouthEast European Design Automation, Computer Engineering, Computer Networks and Social Media Conference* (pp. 72–79). Kastoria, Greece: ACM.

Index

A

Access control mechanism, 45, 46

Accounting, 46

AddRoundKey() function, 11, 12

Advanced Encryption
   Standard (AES), 10–12

Air-written signature, 210

Ambient sound factor, 150

Andrew secure RPC protocol, 166, 167

Android pattern lock, 101–103

Asymmetric cryptography, 184
   concept, 15
   encryption and decryption, 15
   private key, 15
   public key, 15
   RSA, 16–18
   security, 14
   trap door one-way function, 14

Asynchronous token authentication
   process, 51, 137

Attack, 59

Authentication, 4, 26
   access control, 46
   definition, 45
   entity authentication, process, 46
   factors
      somebody-you-know, 57–59
      something-you-are, 52, 53
      something you know, 49, 50
      something-you-process, 54, 55

somewhere-you-are, 56, 57
synchronous/asynchronous
   tokens, 50–52
parties, 47
process, 47, 48
threats
   credential stuffing, 63, 64
   default password, 60
   eavesdropping, 60
   man-in-the-middle (MitM)
      attacks, 62
   password guessing, 62, 63
   replay attack, 61
   social engineering, 64–68

Authentication assurance
   level 1 (AAL1), 201, 202

Authentication assurance
   level 2 (AAL2), 202

Authentication assurance
   level 3 (AAL3), 203, 204

Authentication performance
   metrics, 119, 120

Authentication phase, 114

Authentication protocols, 163–166
   entity, 185
   generic principles, 187–194
   specific principles, 186, 187

Authentication tokens, 50, 137

Authenticator, 47

Authorization, 46

Availability, 4

223